Uncontrollable Women

Uncontrollable Women

Radicals, Reformers and
Revolutionaries

Nan Sloane

I.B. TAURIS

LONDON • NEW YORK • OXFORD • NEW DELHI • SYDNEY

I.B. TAURIS
Bloomsbury Publishing Plc
50 Bedford Square, London, WC1B 3DP, UK
1385 Broadway, New York, NY 10018, USA
29 Earlsfort Terrace, Dublin 2, Ireland

BLOOMSBURY, I.B. TAURIS and the I.B. Tauris logo are trademarks of
Bloomsbury Publishing Plc

First published in Great Britain 2022
Paperback edition published 2024

Cover design by Adriana Brioso
Cover illustration by Rachael Stott

A catalogue record for this book is available from the British Library.

A catalog record for this book is available from the Library of Congress.

ISBN: HB: 978-1-8386-0663-3
       PB: 978-1-3504-5978-6
       ePDF: 978-1-8386-0714-2
       eBook: 978-1-8386-0713-5

Typeset by RefineCatch Limited, Bungay, Suffolk
Printed and bound in Great Britain

To find out more about our authors and books visit www.bloomsbury.com
and sign up for our newsletters.

'. . . an uncontroulable woman, whose tongue no human effort could check.'

Wheeler's Manchester Chronicle, 21 August 1819

Contents

Illustrations

Foreword

Ayesha Hazarika

Apart from Mary Wollstonecraft, you won't have heard of most of the women in this book, because women don't often make it into the history books, particularly when it comes to politics.

Political history in Britain, as everywhere else, is usually seen as the epic tales of men squaring up to each other with their big ideas and fighting about power, who should have it, and what should be done with it. That's the sort of history most of us learn at school, whether it's in the form of battles and kings, or Vikings and the Second World War.

Of course, we have made some progress, but it's pretty thin gruel. We have reached the dizzy heights where there is some recognition of Florence Nightingale; we know the suffragettes were a big deal; and a few people have even heard of Mary Seacole.

Women courageously wanting the vote or women bravely caring for others, but on the whole not much in between.

Nan writes about a very different kind of woman. 'Uncontrollable Women: Radicals, Reformers and Revolutionaries' tells the stories of some of the first women to publicly get involved with politics as activists, campaigners, agitators, writers and thinkers.

As an outspoken political commentator, these are women after my own heart. They put their heads above the parapet, had strong views and weren't afraid to be criticized and abused for their opinions. Many of them were silenced, which is why we don't know about them, but they led vivid, brave lives.

Like Susannah Wright born in Nottingham in 1792. A woman driven by a profound belief in her right to make up her own mind about everything, including religion. She ended up becoming a heroine for the cause of free discussion and was sent to prison for her beliefs. She spoke eloquently and defiantly in court prompting this reaction from the

New Times, which loathed radical women (an early *Daily Mail*) – 'It is manifest that these female brutes came prepared, not only to applaud what the She-Champion of Impiety had already done; but to hear her load with fresh insults the law of her country and the law of her GOD.'

As somebody who writes and talks about politics for a living, I didn't know about these incredible women doing the same thing 200 years ago. Our dramatic narrative of history is still mostly shaped by the Jane Austen remake or Bridgerton for a bit of 'modernity' – all bonnets, balls and frenzied husband hunting. But guess what? Women in those times were also writing about revolution, democracy, war, civil rights and much more besides. Others were fighting for parliamentary reform, or freedom of the press, or the separation of church and state. Some of them paid a heavy price, but carried on regardless. And yet we've barely heard of any of them.

It's important to note that other people are excluded besides women, and the kind of history we generally hear about also lacks working-class people, is often London-centric and usually excludes people of colour. The further back you go, the more marked these omissions are. Which is why this book is so important. Nan shines a light on some truly amazing women who lived in genuinely revolutionary times and refused to accept the status quo.

The range of issues these women were involved with is impressive. Some were early feminists, but many were not, and very few thought it even remotely possible that women would one day have the vote, stand for election or lead countries. But they fought the battles of the day, and in the face of repressive and sometimes oppressive governments, they were strong and resolute. Few of them were wealthy or privileged, and even when they were, they chose to step outside the protections society offered in order to make their point. Their lives are interesting and important, but also inspirational.

Needless to say, in an age when women were supposed to be silent in the political, public space, the ones who spoke up were subjected to a deluge of abuse. There was no Twitter (so it wasn't all bad), but the journalists and commentators of the day received public hatred and vitriol for their views. Almost all the chapters in this book have specimens of the abuse political women received. And the further down the social scale the women were, the worse it was. Women such as Jane Austen, who famously never wrote (overtly, at any rate) about politics, were tolerated, but women like Anna Laetitia Barbauld, who wrote with spirit and insight about discrimination, democracy and the immorality of war, could expect to be attacked. Working-class women were vilified even when they were dead. Those women killed at Peterloo, for instance, were smeared in deeply misogynistic terms, accused of being drunkards and prostitutes.

These women deserve to be written about, known and celebrated. And our understanding of the history of women's politics and history more widely is poorer because they are absent from it. We seem to have the notion that women only became political when they began to campaign for the vote, but as this book shows, that is wrong. Women have always been political, because politics has always had a direct influence on women's lives.

Sometimes we can hear these women's stories in their own words, and sometimes we have to rely on the reports of others, but always we can hear the echoes of our own world. These women laid the foundations of the political freedoms we now enjoy. That we know so little about them is not only a shame, but also unjust. This book brings to life the legacy left by the radical women missing from history and restores them to their rightful place. In doing so it raises questions that are still with us – from women's wages, health and poverty, to power, representation and the criminal justice system.

Nan has written a powerful, illuminating book that will educate and inspire. But most importantly, she has introduced us to these hidden feminist figures from 200 years ago. We stand on their shoulders and it is only right that we honour them.

Acknowledgements

This book was written during the COVID-19 lockdown, and would therefore not have been possible without the continued support and encouragement of my husband, Christopher, who had to share the experience with me. I am also grateful to my children, family and friends for their unstinting – if sometimes bemused – tolerance and occasional (constructive) criticism. Thank you!

After *The Women in the Room* was published, I was amazed and inspired by the interest there was in the history of political women, and I am grateful to everyone who has allowed me over the years to lecture them at length about women they've never heard of. Their interest, positivity and enthusiasm have helped to keep me going.

I am also grateful to Olivia Dellow and Tomasz Hoskins, my editors at I.B. Tauris, who allowed me to overrun deadlines, as I struggled with research that had to be done with little or no physical access to libraries and archives, as well as to Adriana Brioso for the design, and Rachael Stott for the excellent cover illustration. I am also indebted to Sophie Campbell, Merv Honeywood and everyone who worked on editing and proofreading. This book could not be what it is without you. Thank you.

Notes on text

When quoting texts I have used the original punctuation and spelling, except where it was necessary to adjust it to clarify meaning.

Pre-decimal currency is denoted in pounds, shillings and pence (£ s d), in which one pound sterling (£1 or 1l) = twenty shillings (20s or 20/-) and one shilling = twelve pence (12d).

Introduction

On the evening of Monday, 16 August 1819 a woman was arrested outside Mr Tate's grocer's shop on Oldham Road in Manchester. It had been a long and terrifying day and in the warm summer evening tempers were still running high. Mr Tate had got hold of a flag belonging to the Female Reformers of Manchester, which had been taken as a trophy from St Peter's Field, and it was now hanging in an upstairs window. A crowd of women and youths had gathered to protest and throw stones, and soldiers were trying to disperse them. The woman who was arrested was furiously angry and did not care who knew it. Perhaps she had friends who had been killed or injured by the troops' charge into the crowd of unarmed demonstrators that afternoon. Perhaps she herself had narrowly missed being trampled under the feet of the horses or crushed by the falling masonry of collapsing walls as people tried to escape. She may have been part of the group of workers who were attacked by mounted soldiers as they left a nearby mill that evening. She had probably had a drink or two, but she may also simply have been driven by pent-up rage and despair, and the fear of being shot by trigger-happy soldiers. Whatever her reasons, she was so furious that she was described as:

> 'an uncontroulable (sic) woman, whose tongue no human effort could check. . . . this conduct shewed the shocking virulence which has been excited in the minds of Women in this quarter, by the artifices of, and want of principle in the courses pursued by, Radical Reformers.'[1]

As is so often the case, we have no way of identifying this woman for certain. She appears for a split second and then vanishes, frozen in a moment which, for us, represents the whole of her life. We know nothing about her except that, on that distant August evening 200 years ago she was filled with a loud and ungovernable rage.

This is a book about radical, reformist and revolutionary women between the outbreak of the French Revolution in 1789 and the passing of the Great Reform Act in 1832. Very few of them are well-known today; some were unknown even in their own day. All of them contributed something to the world we now inhabit. At a time when women were supposed to leave politics to men, they spoke, wrote, marched, organized, asked questions, challenged power structures, sometimes went to prison and even died. History has not usually been kind to them, and they have frequently been pushed into asides or footnotes, dismissed as secondary, or spoken over, for, or through, by men and sometimes other women. In this book, they take centre stage in both their own stories and those of others, and in doing so bring different voices to the more familiar accounts of the period.

Ever since Sheila Rowbotham published her seminal *Hidden from History*, historians and others have been trying to uncover the lives and achievements of our foremothers. This is a positive act, but it is possibly worth also recalling that women were not always concealed or discarded by accident. To mix the metaphor, they were consigned to the dustbin of history because of positive decisions by both women and men to put them there. Moreover, the 'popular' history of women tends to be restricted to royalty, the suffrage movement and Florence Nightingale, with a few nods to philanthropists, such as Elizabeth Fry. Women such as Susannah Wright, a working-class heroine who was persecuted by the state and emerged triumphant, are unknown. Although she is one of the people to whom we owe our right to criticize both the state and its religion in public, Susannah is unknown to the descendants of the people who supported her with both their hearts and the pennies they donated to her relief fund. Even by some academics she is dismissed as a side-show, or as the mouthpiece of her friend, Richard Carlile. Yet, this was a woman who refused to keep quiet and could calmly tell the Chief Justice of England when he interrupted her that: 'You, sir, are paid to hear me.'[2]

Some of the reasons why these women are obscure certainly have a great deal to do with patriarchal, monarchical, 'great-man' versions of history, but some are also related to the prism through which we so often view women's political history. This is now focused so heavily on the fight for the vote that other kinds of political engagement are seen as having less value, and it is tempting to think that women had no political presence at all before the 1860s. Moreover, there is a tendency – at least in popular history – to value women's activism only when it was about women's rights, leading to the rather questionable habit of describing every female activist as feminist regardless of whether or not she actually was. By the same token, women whose views were clearly not feminist in the modern sense are discarded, ridiculed or treated as 'quaint'. But women fought for all kinds of freedoms – Anna Laetitia Barbauld for an end to religious discrimination, Mary Fildes for parliamentary reform and Susannah Wright for the separation of church and state, to name but three. None of them argued for women's suffrage, but they did contribute to the development of modern ideas about democracy and the state, as well as to the politics of their day. Naturally, as possession of the vote came to define men as part of a democracy, women applied the same measure to themselves, too. However, long before that happened to any great degree, women were intensely political, supporting a wide range of causes and campaigns, and speaking for themselves as well as for others. All of the women in this book should be judged on the basis of what they did during their own lives, not the lives and opinions we might wish for them. The franchise is only one part of our political freedoms; the right to vote without freedom of expression, for instance, is not, in reality, a right that can be exercised properly at all.

The public political space of the eve of the French Revolution was entirely a male affair. Women could not hold any kind of public office, had almost no legal or political rights and were thought to be immoral if they ventured out of the private realm, but nevertheless a small number persisted in doing so. Although the Victorian ideal of the 'angel in the house' had not yet taken up its stranglehold on women's lives, members of 'the fair sex' were still expected to adhere to the rules laid down for them by religion, society and the law. Married women were the property of their husbands, who had complete control over every aspect of their lives. Wifely obedience was a religious as well as a social duty. Women had no independent existence in law, and no legal power over their own finances, children or bodies. Nor was divorce possible, or, at least, it was available only to very wealthy men who could get an Act through Parliament. Couples could separate, however, coming to either formal or informal agreements about how that was to be managed. Men had a legal duty to support their wives and families, but the social and financial consequences of living apart from their husbands could be catastrophic for women, who frequently lost access to their children and were ostracized by 'respectable' society. Single women and, to a lesser extent, widows, had more independence, and might at least be able to control their own money, but even then there were challenges. For no woman was the kind of independence and freedom of action enjoyed by even the poorest of men possible, and, rather startlingly and inexplicably to modern sensibilities, nor would most women ever have thought it either right or desirable that it should be.

As always, however, and whatever the difficulties, the reality of most people's day-to-day life was much more nuanced than either the legal position or debates about the relationship between the sexes would suggest. Many couples worked out for themselves how their lives would be organized, and many marriages were obviously happy and settled. People grumbled, but actual rebellion was the exception rather than the rule. Girls who had been trained from birth for a life of dependence and obedience were unlikely to challenge a system that seemed so utterly normal, not to mention instituted by divine decree. But, on a personal level, marriages were often open to a degree of negotiation, and were frequently presented as a partnership in which both sides brought something unique and complementary to the arrangement. Men were supposed to protect women from the rough and tumble of the world, whilst women – even working-class women – were expected to retain a modest ignorance of it. Breaches of this arrangement were to be frowned upon. In 1819, for instance, one journalist writing about women involved in the campaign for parliamentary reform demanded: 'But what can be said of the feelings or morals of the fathers, and husbands, and brothers, who have permitted or encouraged this violation of that sacred female privacy, of which they are the appointed guardians?'[3] Men's standing and reputation were, as so often, bound up in the actions of women, for whom they were held responsible. Partnerships were certainly both possible and common, but they were hardly ever equal.

Since the power was all on one side, domestic and sexual violence was rife, and many women suffered abuse as a matter of routine. As Mary Smith bitterly observed when she petitioned Parliament for the vote in 1832, for many married women 'the husbands, as the courts of law abundantly testify, so far from being protectors, are the only persons against whom their wives have occasion to sue for protection'.[4] For a handful of women, the grim experience of a bad marriage prompted them to think more widely about power, who held it and how it was used; the philosopher Anna Doyle Wheeler endured years of marital misery before becoming a pioneering socialist and feminist thinker. But for the vast majority there was no escape and no refuge, and it is therefore hardly surprising if most wives simply found it easier to accept things as they were.

Women's interests were seen as being in every sense inseparable from men's. Women – particularly married women – had no need of independent voices when there were men to speak for them. The philosopher James Mill observed in 1821 that children did not need to be directly represented in a democracy since their parents would look after them, adding that: 'In this light, also, women may be regarded, the interest of almost all of whom is involved either in that of their fathers or in that of their husbands.'[5] Women were likewise supposed to avoid unpleasant political subjects, particularly if they were controversial. Criticizing the author Helen Maria Williams for writing about the French Revolution, a reviewer in the *Gentleman's Magazine* remarked that: 'Miss Williams must excuse us if we say she debased her sex, her heart, her feelings, her talents, in recording such a tissue of horror and villainy, . . . whose result we defy her to shew us has yet been productive of one single good . . .'[6]

Despite the weight of respectable opinion, however, there were always women willing to ask questions. In the Preface to her 1792 book *Desmond*, for example, the novelist Charlotte Smith laid out the double bind in which women found themselves:

'. . . women, it is said, have no business with politics. – Why not? – Have they no interest in the scenes that are acting around them, in which they have fathers, brothers, husbands, sons, or friends engaged! Even in the commonest course of female education, they are expected to acquire some knowledge of history; and yet, if they are to have no opinion of what <u>is</u> passing, it avails little that they should be informed of what <u>has passed</u>, in a world where they are subjected to such mental degradation; where they are censured as affecting masculine knowledge if they happen to have any understanding; or despised as insignificant triflers if they have none.'[7]

The turn of the nineteenth century was a period when new egalitarian ideas struggled against old ones about the God-given rights of elites. Unfortunately, however, this did not prevent many radical women holding some highly unpalatable views. Most white women, even those who fought slavery, had opinions on race that were at best questionable and at worst deeply offensive. Religious prejudice was widespread, and Catholics and Protestant dissenters were routinely denied civil and political rights. Many middle-class women, even when they meant well, and even when, like Mary Wollstonecraft, they are now feminist icons, had views about the working class that were both narrow-minded and patronizing. A depressingly large number of women actively subscribed to the misogyny of the age or at least deeply disliked or distrusted their own sex. Most women uncritically accepted moral and sexual codes that are now repellent. Fed by religious proscription, extreme homophobia was endemic, and sodomy was a capital offence. People who were heroic in some respects were anything but in others and casually held opinions that are repugnant regardless of the times.

It is not enough to excuse all this simply by saying that societies and cultures were different. They were, but bigotry and injustice are the same whenever they are encountered, and there were always some people who knew that. 'Either no member of the human race has any true rights', said the French aristocrat and revolutionary Nicolas de Condorcet in 1790, 'or else they all have the same ones; and anyone who votes against the rights of another, whatever his religion, colour, or sex, automatically forfeits his own'.[8] At the time this was not a popular view, not even in the new and supposedly egalitarian United States of America. Despite this, people such as Condorcet, Anna Doyle Wheeler and others were able to think their way through to what society might look like if everyone was able to enjoy their true rights. As Anna Laetitia Barbauld pointed out more than once, there was always a choice to be made, and ignorance was neither a defence nor necessarily genuine.

The notions and assumptions that people had about class were largely rooted in a rather romanticized and less industrial past. Given that at the time many people struggled with the concept of an urban and industrialized working class as a political entity, it is hardly surprising if there was as yet very little economic class consciousness.[9] However, there was a strong social sense of class that relied heavily on education and accomplishments, as well as wealth and birth. Working-class people were often ridiculed, particularly for their accents. In 1819, the London press took great delight in poking fun at the dialects of members of the northern female reform societies, and when Bolton-born Eliza Sharples gave public lectures in London in 1832 she was derided by *The Times* for her Lancashire vowels. There was a huge amount of snobbery, and much fear and resentment between rich and poor. But there was also a degree of social mobility, particularly in the Midlands and the North, where the middle and working classes were still emerging from the primeval industrial soup and had yet to define their boundaries with later, and more inflexible, degrees of precision.

As is usually the case, the majority of people largely accepted the conventional attitudes of the society into which they had been born. The British prided themselves on their liberties, their tolerance and their freedom of speech, but they were, in fact, largely intolerant of any dissent or deviation from standards that they themselves had set and, as we shall see, freedom of thought and of the press had to be fought for with grit and determination. For much of this period Britain had one of the most repressive governments in its history. This was supported even by people now thought of as heroes. William Wilberforce and the evangelical sect known as the Clapham Saints worked tirelessly to abolish the slave trade and (after some persuasion) slavery itself, but they also funded the Society for the Suppression of Vice, which secured the prosecution for blasphemy of (predominantly) working-class people selling political works, such as Tom Paine's *Rights of Man*. Working-class women rejected birth control on the grounds that it was part of a Malthusian plot to control the birth rate in the lower orders as well as because they suspected it would enable men to ruin and abandon them with even more impunity. Ideas that are fundamental to feminism now seemed much more uncertain 200 years ago. Thus, although some of the choices women made may appear odd, shocking or just plain wrong by modern standards, they were often courageous by those of their day. It is possible to admire bravery without particularly liking the people exhibiting it, and not everyone who fights injustice is necessarily commendable in every respect. Views about sex, race, class and many other things changed because they were challenged, however tentatively, by flawed women and men over the centuries.

Sadly, almost all of the female voices we can still hear from the turn of the nineteenth century are white, not because there were no women of colour, but because they left very little of themselves behind. Even when they did tell their own stories, they were obstructed from speaking directly either to their contemporaries or to us. The *History of Mary Prince*, the first autobiography of an enslaved black woman to be published in Britain, was dictated to a middle-class white woman. She, though well-meaning, manipulated the narrative to make it fit her purposes, smoothing it out to make it more acceptable as propaganda for the anti-slavery movement rather than an account of Mary Prince's life in her own voice. Much of what little personal agency Mary had been able to exercise, particularly if it made her seem anything other than a victim, was changed or left out altogether, thus reducing her to something approaching a stereotype. As it happens, we know a little more about her from other sources, including court cases, and despite everything her autobiography remains both a literary and a cultural landmark. But she is a lone voice, and there is much work still to be done to identify diversity in the various campaigns touched on in this book. We know, for instance, that there were black men involved in the fights for parliamentary reform and free speech, but of black women in those causes there is at present little trace. It is much to be hoped that new research will rectify this, and that future histories of radical women in this period will be able to include a wider range of characters and experiences.

Middle class white women activists are easier to find because they wrote letters, books and sometimes diaries. Many – though by no means all – female poets and authors left accounts of themselves and their lives that illuminate the times through which they lived. This is much less the case with white working-class women. They wrote very little, and almost everything they did write has long since been lost. Occasionally, however, something survives simply because an oppressive but meticulously bureaucratic government preserved it; the letters of radical women to their imprisoned husbands in 1817, for instance, exist because they were confiscated by the Home Office and are now to be found in the National Archives. It is reasonable to suppose that if the women wrote these letters they must have written others, but since nobody thought them worth keeping we do not have them. Very few working-class women had books published, and often their own voices are hard to hear since they were reported – and therefore mediated – by men. Jane Carlile was a white working-class woman whose life comes to us filtered through her husband. This leaves many gaps and inconsistencies, and sometimes makes it hard to sort the truth out from the lies. The (largely male) historians writing about Richard Carlile have almost all accepted his version of events, and thus Jane tends to feature as a defamed aside in someone else's story rather than a heroine in her own. It is in this latter capacity that we shall meet her in these pages.

As always with a book of this kind, choices have had to be made and there are many fascinating and remarkable women who have had to be left out. This is not to lessen or underestimate their achievements, and there is much more work that could be done on the women of this period and their contributions to the development of democracy. There are also many women who were omitted simply because there is so little information available about them; it would be very interesting, for instance, to know more about Ethelinda Wilson from Hull who was present at Peterloo in 1819, attended reformist meetings in London carrying a loaded pistol, advocated direct action and had an affair with another reformer that caused his wife to inform to the Home Office on him,[10] but sadly this is more or less all the information we have about her. There are many more Ethelindas (though few who carried loaded firearms), and future research may be able to uncover them. Until then, however, we are able to meet them only in passing.

Many – though by no means all – women activists came to radical politics through the men to whom they were related, and this is sometimes used to dismiss their contribution. But, at the time, such relationships were understood as a strength, and the family-based nature of society meant that it would have been next to impossible for politically engaged women to publicly oppose their husbands or fathers. Even for the relatively few people who met the many and varied qualifications for voting, a vote was seen as a family possession and, indeed, nurturing the family's political interests was one way in which elite women (who do not feature much in this book) were able to exert political influence. Moreover, in a world in which very few women identified their interests as separate from men's, it was inevitable that they would support the same causes. This is not a weakness, nor should their instincts to protect their families be seen in that light.

This is a book about women's political activism and voice at one of the most important and exhilarating times in British history. However, it is not a thorough history of the period, and some well-known episodes are therefore not covered in any detail; some, such as the Battle of Waterloo, are even conspicuous by their almost complete absence. This reflects the types of activities in which radical women were engaged rather than the relative importance of particular events. Equally, some individual women who are very well known feature hardly at all. This does not make them less interesting, and many have been much researched, written about and featured in television programmes. Princesses, queens, duchesses, actresses, authors and social reformers from these years all have their biographies, but although this book may touch on some of them it does not dwell on any. As a result, to readers with a knowledge of the period, the historical setting might look slightly askew, as indeed it is. On the other hand, it can also be argued that leaving the vast majority of women out of the history we know skews it in the opposite direction. Putting women, rather than men, centre stage in the story does leave some rather unexpected gaps, and inevitably to some extent results in history as a series of snapshots rather than a panorama, but this can be remedied (at least in part) by reading some of the other excellent histories available.

Widespread interest in public affairs and politics meant that the early nineteenth century was full of campaigns for progress in a wide variety of fields. Organizations were set up to fight for parliamentary reform, the abolition of slavery, the abolition of the Corn Laws, the abolition of the Poor Law, the limiting of the hours of work in factories, the protection of marriage, the abolition of marriage and much, much more. By no means all of these are included in this account, if only because not all of them were particularly radical. They were also not necessarily about the nature of the body politic itself, whereas the women featured in this book were all, to one extent or another, trying to influence the nature of democracy and change political structures. Thus, the campaigns for parliamentary reform, free speech and a free press are all well to the fore, but the campaign against slavery is much less present. This does not mean that the abolition campaign was unimportant. Radical women supported abolition, and many wrote or spoke about it. But it was not directly a part of the struggle to change the balance of power in British politics, and many of its leaders, including Wilberforce himself, supported repressive legislation directed against radicals and reformers. As always, the reality is more nuanced (and more interesting) than the mythology would lead us to believe.

Focusing on women and their experience leads to a different emphasis on how their lives are considered. For most married women in this period – and those who had heterosexual relationships outside marriage – pregnancy and childbirth were almost inevitable, and, then, as now, these were life-changing events. The care of babies and children, the worry about whether or not they would survive, and the all-too-frequent deaths shaped and informed women's daily lives in all classes, and to leave them out, or to gloss over them, is to fail to understand how those lives were lived. Thus it has been a conscious choice to name the children wherever possible, and to include them as part of the stories. Their parents' trials and sacrifices were also theirs, and must have affected their later lives. Both Jane Carlile and Susannah Wright fought their uneven battles with the law with very small babies in their arms. Women lost children to disease, accidents and violence, whilst others were deprived of them by hostile husbands. Childbirth itself carried a risk, and many women of childbearing age were pregnant at least once a year for two decades or more once they married. Miscarriage was common. For some, as for Mary Wollstonecraft, birth or its consequences could be fatal. Integrating this aspect of women's experiences into their political activism gives us a more rounded view of them and restores to them some of the fullness of their lives.

This book is divided into four parts. The first looks at three radical middle-class women who lived through and wrote about the revolutionary times of the 1790s. The second tells the stories of working-class women who fought for their communities in the reform movement between 1812 and 1819, whilst the third explores the lives of female free thinkers and 'infidels' in the early 1820s. The last part covers emerging ideas about socialism and women's political rights, and a short Epilogue examines what is usually referred to as the first petition for the vote from a woman. Each part has a short introduction covering the relevant background to the succeeding chapters. With one exception, the chapter titles are all taken from things said about women and their political activism at the time. Then, as now, women had to brave a barrage of hostility in order to get their voices heard, and, as we shall see, the misogynistic abuse of political women was not in any way the invention of twenty-first century social media.

The period between the French Revolution in 1789 and the passing of the Great Reform Act in 1832 was alive with radical and even revolutionary ideas and causes, and women played a part in all of them. This book looks at just a few, often the lesser known ones, and often those whose contributions have been most overlooked. But these women and many others played a part in developing political ideas and freedoms as we know them today, and some fought battles that still remain to be won or raised questions that are still unresolved. These are their stories.

PART ONE

Frantic 'Midst the Democratic Storm

In 1793, the caricaturist Thomas Rowlandson produced a cartoon comparing British and French liberty. Unsurprisingly, this played entirely to Britain's advantage. On the righthand side, in a blue roundel, he put Britannia with her union flag, her scales of justice and a copy of the Magna Carta. Behind her a ship in full sail rides on a calm sea. Beneath her are listed what were thought of as British virtues, including loyalty, justice, prosperity, industry, security and happiness. Opposite her, in a red roundel, he drew a grim Medusa-like hag standing with her foot on the chest of a decapitated corpse. In one hand she carries a trident onto which is speared a head and two hearts shaped like Caps of Liberty. In the other she brandishes a sword. Behind her, a second corpse swings from a lamp post, and beneath her are listed French evils – atheism, anarchy, murder, madness, treachery and equality amongst them. 'Which' demands the caption at the foot of the page 'is best?'.

For decades – if not centuries – this was how patriotic British people thought, not only about the French, but also about themselves. It was not just that to be foreign, or to support revolution, was a positive evil, but that to be British, and to support British values, was a positive good. The French revolutionary version of Liberty was seen as a hideous perversion of an ancient British virtue. Hence the appearance of a true Cap of Liberty in the British roundel and distorted human hearts in the French. The Cap was an important symbol, the origins of which went back to the Roman habit of presenting freed slaves with a conical felt hat. In the popular mind it was connected with the liberty of the lower orders from oppression and tyranny, and in the 1770s it had been used by American colonists in just this way.[1] However, after the French Revolution many British people came to think of it as drenched in blood. Fearsome women sitting at the foot of the guillotine were supposed to have been knitting them. For the conservative Briton, false liberty was bloody, ugly and French, and true liberty was calm, beautiful and British.

The fall of the Bastille on 14 July 1789 remains to this day one of the most iconic events of European history, and almost everyone who witnessed or heard about it at the time knew instantly that it had a significance well beyond the physical event. The forbidding fortress, which had stood in the centre of Paris since medieval times, was an emblem of repression and royal power, and although in recent years there had been much talk of demolishing it and replacing it with some kind of urban open space, it remained a visible reminder of tyranny. At the point of its fall it was almost empty and about to be closed, but it was still a powerful reminder of the tyrannical power of absolute monarchy, and its destruction was quintessentially symbolic of the fall of the old order. In Britain, it was widely understood as exactly that, and led to a great upsurge of hope amongst Whigs (the parliamentary opposition), radicals and both the emerging middle classes and the artisans and labourers in towns and villages across the country. The poet Wordsworth famously wrote that it was 'bliss to be alive', and he was by no means alone in this opinion. The revolution in America a decade earlier had already produced an outpouring of democratic and reformist thinking, and now France gave new impetus to both radical and more conservative political ideas.

In the early days of the Revolution, the political faction in Paris that seemed to hold out most hope for the future of France were the Girondins. Subsequent events meant that they came to be seen as the moderate wing of the Revolution, and their heroes and heroines as martyrs to a constitutional path that might have been. In fact, almost from the beginning, the Girondins were precisely what alarmed conservative loyalists, such as the philosopher Edmund Burke and the moralist author Hannah More. In Girondin hands, French foreign policy meant actively and evangelically exporting the Revolution across Europe by any means necessary, including war. Yet, this was also a bourgeois faction of intellectuals and writers, and for many British radicals the Girondin political salons exuded a new kind of glamour and power that fascinated people more accustomed to dissenting chapels, endless opposition and modest dinners at one another's houses. They did not see the desire to spread the Revolution throughout Europe as threatening; it was, in fact, one of the Revolution's great strengths and internationalism seemed an attractive and invigorating idea.

For women, particularly, the ascendant Girondins offered unexplored vistas of liberation and possibility. Women's rights were being discussed in ways that were new because of the real possibility of doing something about them. In 1792, France became the first country in Europe to legalize divorce on demand on an equal basis for men and women.[2] For those who saw women's imprisonment in marriage as one of the principal obstacles to their freedom this seemed a tremendous advance. But, for the majority of British people, it was merely an indication of the wickedness the Revolution brought in its wake. Marriage was a protection for women against the dangers of the world; if husbands could divorce them at will they might be left destitute and even end up on the streets. New French laws enabling daughters to inherit property equally with sons, or providing unmarried mothers with a modicum of protection and support, merely fed the idea that women were being forced out of their natural dependence upon men. Whilst some radical women saw this as the opening of new freedoms, most people saw only looming moral chaos.

Despite this, however, revolutionary ideas spread like wildfire, and in 1792 a group of artisans led by a shoemaker called Thomas Hardy set up the London Corresponding Society (LCS) to provide a forum in which working-class men could read and discuss political issues as well as campaign for reform, which at this stage mainly meant annual parliaments and universal (manhood) suffrage. At its height, the LCS had tens of thousands of members, though the patchy nature of the records mean that it is impossible to be certain exactly what the membership was. However, it was very active, not only promoting debate, but also publishing books and pamphlets, some of which were attacked as either seditious or blasphemous or both. Although very few people at this time were atheists, many LCS members were deists, believing that, although God existed, he was a god of reason and the natural world rather than faith, miracles and organized churches. In

1793, when Christianity was officially abolished in France and replaced with atheism, Notre-Dame de Paris and other cathedrals were converted into Temples of Reason. A few months later, however, the Jacobin leader Robespierre decided that the philosopher Voltaire had been right about the human necessity to invent God, and Reason was replaced in turn with the deist cult of the Supreme Being. Faced with what they saw as these appalling blasphemies, the authorities across the Channel in Britain were not inclined to distinguish between revolutionary atheism and the deism of shoemakers and tailors.

The ascent to power of the Jacobin faction in France, followed by the onset of the Reign of Terror soon after the founding of the LCS, dashed the hopes of many people, especially the middle classes, and an unnerved British government turned to full-scale repression. In 1794 they famously, and unsuccessfully, prosecuted the LCS leaders for treason. In 1795, Parliament passed the Treason and Sedition Acts, which made it treasonable to 'compass, devise, &c. the death, restraint, &c. of his Majesty or his heirs, or to depose them, or to levy war to compel a change of measures', as well as to write, print, publish or speak anything that would bring the King, government or constitution into hatred or contempt. Public meetings were restricted to a maximum of fifty people and premises that charged for admission to political meetings (for instance, to defray the expenses of speakers or raise funds for clubs) had to be registered and licensed. These two Acts[3] had an immediate impact on both the LCS and other groups that had sprung up around the country. They were followed up by others, including the Combination Acts and the Unlawful Societies Act of 1799, which made it illegal to form trade unions, attempt to improve pay, or take or administer oaths of loyalty, secrecy or mutual support. In July of that year both the LCS and the more militant United Englishmen (as well as similarly named organizations in Ireland, Wales and Scotland) were specifically outlawed. A short-lived, if intense, period of radical agitation was over.

Although there is some evidence that there may have been a Society of Women meeting in the same public houses as LCS branches, and although there seems to have been some idea of establishing a club of female patriots,[4] women were never admitted to the LCS and the attitude of the radical men who joined it and others like it was divided, and often equivocal. The veteran reform campaigner Major John

Cartwright, for instance, thought that since women could not bear arms and defend their country they had no right to be represented in its politics.[5] The radical working-class thinker Thomas Spence, on the other hand, thought that since women paid taxes they ought to be able to vote, but that their delicate natures rendered them 'ineligible, to all public employments'.[6] Radical men could certainly be supportive, but often it was more because they wanted backing and help from women than because they had any profound belief in sexual equality. For working-class radicals, the position became increasingly complicated by the matter of whether or not women should be allowed to work in the same industries as men, a question that is taking centuries to resolve.

Despite all this, however, women of all classes had always engaged in political activity of one kind or another. Working-class women attended meetings, organized friendly societies, took part in strikes, read political newspapers and pamphlets, and sometimes rioted. They were deeply interested in the political ferment following the French Revolution, and there were probably many more little reading groups and debating societies than we know of now. Hundreds of middle-class women wrote and published works of all kinds – volumes of educational advice, household hints, instruction manuals, religious tracts, philosophical and political pamphlets, poetry, plays and novels all poured from women's pens. Most wrote across several genres and almost all wrote for children as well as adults. Some, such as Anna Laetitia Barbauld were thought of by their contemporaries primarily as educationalists, but in fact wrote a great deal else besides. Others such as Charlotte Smith were well-known novelists who have been more or less forgotten today, and, in an age of poetry, a great many were poets, at least at the beginning of their careers. Mary Hays wrote moral essays, novels and history. The famous actress Mary Robinson (who was known as Perdita and had a brief affair with the Prince Regent) wrote poetry, plays and feminist tracts. People wrote what they thought would sell, and the market was huge as the circulating libraries developed and more people had time for reading. Charlotte Smith supported herself and a large number of children on her writings, and many a woman kept just on the right side of poverty by writing potboilers to pay the rent.

Jane Austen famously published all her books anonymously, but this was a matter of choice rather than compulsion, and the idea that female authors in this period all shrank from publicity or were forced by convention to avoid it is a misconception. In fact, women often published over their own names; Charlotte Smith, for instance, appeared on the title pages of her books as 'Charlotte Smith of Bignor Park' since this implied a certain social status which, in a society fuelled by snobbery, helped her sales. Others did publish anonymously, but this was by no means a practice unique to women. Even Walter Scott, one of the most successful male authors of the early nineteenth century, published at least the first couple of editions of some of his novels anonymously. Anonymous publication had a number of benefits; apart from anything else, the revelation of the name of the author of a successful work could be a publicity event in itself. The determining factor was as likely to be the nature of the work as the preferences or commercial judgements of the author or publisher; Mary Wollstonecraft published her *Thoughts on the Education of Daughters* under her own name, but a few months later published the *Vindication of the Rights of Man* anonymously. Helen Maria Williams published the early parts of her eight-volume account of the French Revolution over her own name, but when, for reasons we will come to later, it became dangerous to do that she retreated into a rather pointless anonymity.

Women's books were reviewed regularly in both newspapers and magazines, and, whatever reviewers pretended, rarely received more favourable treatment simply on the grounds of the sex of the author. Very few people were opposed to literary women *per se,* and although women with intellectual or political pretensions might be called 'blue stockings' and ridiculed, women writing about religion, education or other 'suitable' topics were taken very seriously. Some women slid their more contentious observations into conventional works. Mary Wollstonecraft's savage remarks about the limited employment opportunities open to middle-class women, for instance, appear in an otherwise fairly traditional educational work. Women wrote to pay the rent as well as to express opinions in the public space, and women's books sold well, especially if they were a little controversial.

Not everybody was comfortable with this. Edmund Burke deplored 'all that clan of desperate, Wicked, and mischievously ingenious women who have brought, or are likely to bring, Ruin and shame upon all those that listen to them'.[7] The Reverend Richard Polwhele, a man with a firm belief in his own opinions and a fine sense of indignation over those who disagreed with him, wrote *The Unsex'd Females* (1789), a long poem protesting against radical women writers. Polwhele was a Cornish vicar, a local historian and a noted translator of ancient Greek authors. He also mistakenly believed himself to be a poet of some skill, and wrote and published verse throughout his life. His politics were fiercely pro-church, King and the Tory government of William Pitt. He loathed radicalism in any form, and in his poem he consciously pitted women he deemed politically acceptable against those who were not. Good women knew their place, behaved modestly and wrote about subjects appropriate to them. Bad women behaved with 'impious arrogance', were 'frantic 'midst the democratic storm', and breathed 'their loose desires below'. Polwhele's allocation of women writers to one or other of these groups was largely arbitrary, but three of those he attacked are of particular interest for their wider political views. Only one would now be considered a feminist; the other two were much more interested in the political events through which they were living. Helen Maria Williams was based in Paris for much of the French Revolution and reported from it to a fascinated British public. She was so famous in her day that she could be identified immediately by her first name alone – Polwhele called her 'Helen, fir[e]d by freedom', a description which, given her political opinions, would not have been unacceptable to her. 'Veteran' Anna Laetitia Barbauld, a poet and then a polemicist of some repute, spoke truth to the power of a repressive British political establishment at a time when to do so was becoming increasingly dangerous. But we begin with Mary Wollstonecraft 'whom no decorum checks' and who, for Polwhele, personified all that was worst and most wicked about the radical unsex'd females he so abhorred.

Chapter 1
The Furies of Hell

Early one morning in August 1787, a young woman arrived on the doorstep of a publisher and bookseller in London. Joseph Johnson lived above his shop in St Paul's Churchyard and Mary Wollstonecraft was one of his many authors. However, she was yet to have any great success, and had spent much of the previous decade working as a teacher and governess. She had now returned to London determined to support herself with her pen. Johnson was a man with a talent for encouraging others, and she thought that he would help her. Luckily for both of them, she was right.

Joseph Johnson was the publisher of a wide range of material, but he is best remembered as a radical bookseller, the publisher of both Mary Wollstonecraft and Thomas Paine amongst many others. He gave Mary a job reviewing books for his *Analytical Review* magazine, found her a little house in Southwark and lent her some money; she remained in debt to him for most of the rest of her life. At his house she met two of her romantic obsessions – the (married) painter Henry Fuseli, and the anarchist philosopher William Godwin, who eventually became her husband. But, more importantly, Johnson encouraged her to write, published what she wrote, and dealt deftly with her uncertainties and her sometimes prickly personality.

Mary Wollstonecraft and Joseph Johnson had first come across one another in 1786 through friends at Newington Green, a hotbed of radical and reformist activity. In 1787 he published her first book, *Thoughts on the Education of Daughters,* a work which drew in a fairly orthodox way on her experience of teaching the young. Girls were educated for marriage alone, or, as she put it: 'No employment of the mind is a sufficient excuse for neglecting domestic duties . . . A woman may fit herself to be the companion and friend of a man of sense, and yet know how to take care of his family.'[1] Sometimes she also went on to contemplate what might happen to a girl of moderate or no means who did not marry, and she was scathing about the possibilities. For these women, she said: 'Few are the modes of earning a subsistence, and those very humiliating.'[2] She listed possible occupations for women who found themselves in this position, all of which were just as dreary as Mary, who had tried almost all of them, made them sound. She did not include the role of author in her catalogue, nor did she, despite her interest in political matters, touch upon politics. Yet, it was her political writing that would soon make her famous.

Political matters were by and large subjects that even the most successful of 'lady authors' were supposed to avoid, or, at any rate, to write about only in certain ways. Both novels and poetry could be intensely political, and allowed women to express opinions without necessarily having to own them. Helen Maria Williams (of whom more later) was able to write about the American Revolution and colonialism so long as she did so in verse, but when she strayed into prose she felt the need to justify herself; '. . . my political creed', she said, 'is entirely an affair of the heart, for I have not been so absurd as to consult my head upon matters of which it is so incapable of judgement'.[3] Similarly, the conservative Laetitia-Matilda Hawkins, writing to rebut Helen Maria Williams's enthusiasm for the French Revolution, considered it necessary to deny any political intent. Political issues, she said in her *Letters on the Female Mind*:

'. . . are not those, my dear madam, which I mean to discuss with you, I would rather convince you that they are points neither you nor I can discuss with propriety or success, . . . and that till we either are fitted by education to investigate all the abstract science of jurisprudence, or till intuition shall be judged the only requisite for deciding the most important questions, we must be content with a minor species of fame.'[4]

This convention that women were not qualified for politics and needed to be trained or educated before they could participate or express an opinion, was widespread and so deeply ingrained that it still regularly surfaces in the twenty-first century. Mary's famous female conservative contemporary, the impeccably moral polemicist Hannah More, published tracts called *Village Politics* anonymously, and wrote to her friend Mrs Boscowen that 'I heartily hope I shall not be discovered; as it is the sort of writing repugnant to my nature . . .'[5]

Mary Wollstonecraft was definitely very interested in politics, and her contact with the dissenting and radical circle at Newington Green enabled her to develop and refine her thinking. In 1784 she and her sisters, Eliza and Everina, had set up a girls' school there, and as a result she met the venerable radical Dr Richard Price, and was introduced to his circle of reformists and intellectuals. Like other thinkers of his time he was something of a polymath, and had a keen interest in mathematics, population, the workings of insurance and risk, and the possibilities of social insurance schemes for working-class people. His prognostications were not always right – he thought, for instance, that the population of Britain was falling when in fact it was rising quite fast – but he was always open to new ideas and debates. He had friends and contacts in political circles in both Britain and the new United States, but he himself was debarred from political office because men who were not members of the Church of England were banned from public office by the Test and Corporation Acts, passed in 1660. Campaigning for the repeal of these Acts often drew people into an interest in wider political reform as well, and as a result, mainstream resistance to the repeal of the Acts was caused at least in part by a belief that Protestant dissenters and non-conformists were likely to hold radical and even revolutionary views.

Price had actively supported the American Revolution in 1776, and had even turned down an invitation to go to America to advise the new nation on its financial policy. By the time Mary Wollstonecraft met him he held something of the status of the Grand Old Man of radical politics, and he introduced her both to new and interesting people (women as well as men), and to new ideas. From this point on, Mary was a radical intellectually as well as instinctively. By the time the French Revolution burst upon the scene in 1789, she had given up the sad business of teaching, turned full time to writing and become an integral part of a circle that would provide some of the key figures of radical and revolutionary London in the 1790s.

The fall of the Bastille on 14 July 1789 electrified people of all political opinions. The Revolution had been underway for some months at this point, and radicals in Britain already had high hopes for it. Despite the bloodshed, there was great anticipation and excitement about what might be possible in a country widely seen as having one of the most backward and reactionary regimes in Europe. The appalling poverty and oppression to which the French lower classes had been subjected was – at least initially – accepted as both a reason and an excuse for the violence, and the assumption was that reasonable, middle-class men would steer the ship of state into safer and more progressive waters. People hoped and believed that a new age was at hand, and although reactionaries were appalled and alarmed they were not initially in a majority. A great many people thought that there would now be (relatively) peaceful change, and that although there was certainly risk, there was also the opportunity for the French to move to a constitutional monarchy along British lines. There was indeed considerable support for this in France, but it was the American example that ultimately came to the fore on the Paris streets. French troops had fought for the rebels in the War of Independence, and the Marquis de Lafayette – young, handsome, and known as the 'Hero of Two Worlds' – had distinguished himself as a brave and popular commander in the cause of liberty. Although he remained throughout his life a democratic constitutional monarchist, he and other returning fighters had brought back with them dangerous ideas about freedom and self-government that had found ready interest across all classes of French society. Following the fall of the Bastille, the National Assembly, now effectively governing France, put Lafayette in charge of the National Guard, but his influence was much wider than simply military and, in consultation with the American Ambassador, Thomas Jefferson, he co-drafted the *Declaration of the Rights of Man and the Citizen,* which he presented to the National Assembly and which, despite the King's resistance, was adopted by it at the end of August.[6]

In October a series of events happened that changed the direction of the Revolution and had a direct influence, both on public opinion in Britain and on Mary herself. The French financial crisis that had originally prompted the Revolution had not gone away, and as summer drew into autumn, food shortages intensified. The King's intransigence over reform, coupled with the fact that he spent all his time at Versailles rather than in Paris, did not help, and many people thought that he should be made to come back and live amongst his people. Demonstrations were largely dispersed before they became riots, but by 5 October an impatience was developing that was easily turned into action. A large crowd of market women raided the town hall for arms and food, carrying both away in sizeable quantities.[7] Then, forming up into a long column and dragging with them a couple of cannons, they marched the dozen miles to Versailles in pouring rain to ask the King for bread and to explain their plight to the National Assembly.

By the time they got there they numbered several thousand, having been joined by other women along the way. They invaded the National Assembly chamber and a small delegation was admitted to speak to the King. Within hours he had not only agreed to send food to Paris, but had also been forced to agree to ratify the *Declaration of the Rights of Man* and other August decrees. After that, both palace and marchers settled down for the night.

In the morning, things took a considerable turn for the worse. A section of the crowd got into the palace and hunted for the Queen, Marie Antoinette, whom they loathed and blamed for many of their ills. Two guards who resisted them were killed and beheaded. The angry mob then broke into the Queen's bedroom and she and her ladies had to flee barefoot in their shifts to the King's apartments. Eventually the King was persuaded that the Royal Family must move to Paris, and they were put into carriages to be taken back along the long, muddy road to the capital. Together with wagon loads of food, they were escorted into the city in triumph, surrounded by thousands of women carrying bread, arms and two gory heads on pikes. From this point on the Royal Family were prisoners in all but name.

Once back in Paris, the women of what came to be known as the 'October Days' were lauded as heroines of the Revolution, given medals to recognize their achievements and granted the title 'Mothers of the Nation'. However, every aspect of the women's actions soon became the subject of controversy. For some they were heroines who had both fed the city and returned the King to his people. For others, they were a thing out of place, women shedding their natural reticence and taking on the political and revolutionary roles of men. Many people who supported the outcomes of the march nevertheless deplored the unseemly means by which they had been achieved.

Very quickly the men of the Revolution took control of the narrative. One of the most detailed sources for accounts of events on the first day is that of Stanislaus-Marie Maillard, a veteran of the assault on the Bastille, who presented himself as the hero who led the women and managed to talk them out of some of their more violent excesses. He claimed that when they arrived at the National Assembly, he 'urged the women to be silent and to leave to him the task of communicating to the assembly their demands . . . to this they consented'.[8] The *Annual Register* in London had a stronger slant; they recorded that: 'When arrived at the gate of the national assembly, Maillard undertook to speak for them, that he might prevent them speaking for themselves.'[9] According to him it was only after his presence was removed that the women became savage. In Maillard's account – as in others – the women lose both individuality and voice. Although they were acclaimed by Paris they were also feared as an amorphous mass needing male direction in order to avoid disorganized and irrational violence. This aspect of events was to be immortalized by anti-revolutionary writers and came to form part of the reactionary mythology of Marie-Antoinette as a good and beautiful wife persecuted by a vile mob later described by the British politician Edmund Burke as the 'revolution harpies of France, sprung from night and hell, . . . foul and ravenous birds of prey . . .'[10]

Across the Channel, news of the October Days immediately divided public opinion. For some, they seemed unspeakably grim, particularly when it came to the Queen's flight, the virtual imprisonment of the Royal Family and, as *The Times* put it, the 'ungovernable licentiousness of the lower classes *(which)* cannot terminate in any kind of public advantage'.[11] Others, however, hailed it as progress towards a new world order; remarkably little blood had been shed in the circumstances and the French example now shone as a beacon for everyone else. A new world of opportunity was opening up.

On 4 November 1789, a month after the women's march to Versailles, a club called the Revolution Society held a special meeting at Old Jewry in London. The Society had been established the previous year to mark the centenary of the so-called Glorious Revolution. This was the series of events popularly seen (both then and now) as having established the British constitution which, to the Anglican Protestant mind at any rate, marked Britain out as superior to any other country in political terms.

The constitutional monarchy established in 1688 and developed during the eighteenth century was a marked contrast to the tyranny of France, and even the so-called benevolent despots of Europe were considered deeply inferior to the enlightened and progressive British system.

The Revolution Society's members were largely middle-class non-conformists who met monthly to discuss political reform; they were not, on the face of it, at all the kind of people from whom insurrections were made. Much of their thinking went well beyond simply wanting to tinker with the basis of representation in Parliament, however, and they were viewed with deep suspicion by the government. The idea that political power derived from the people, and that if that power was abused the exercisers of it could and should be resisted, was highly alarming to conservatives who believed that such opinions bordered on treason. The Society's meeting on 4 November – a date that marked the 101st anniversary of the Glorious Revolution – was well attended, if only because the main attraction, Mary's friend Richard Price, was expected to give a good speech. Now well into his sixties, Price had grown, if anything, more radical with age,[12] and although he framed his lecture in terms of British history, his meaning was unmistakeable.

The title of his address was *A Discourse on the Love of our Country,* but after some introductory remarks on the subject of patriotism he soon moved on to the meat of his argument. Using the example of the Glorious Revolution he asserted that the French were now exercising the same fundamental rights as the British a century previously, and that they ought therefore to be accorded the same support. He had taken a similar view of the American War of Independence in the 1770s, but now it had a new resonance. Laying out the grounds that had underpinned the events of 1688, he repeated the three main 'principles of the Revolution':

'First; The right to liberty of conscience in religious matters.
Secondly; The right to resist power when abused.
And, Thirdly; The right to chuse our own governors; to cashier them for misconduct; and to frame a government for our selves.

'On these three principles, and more especially the last, was the Revolution founded. Were it not true that liberty of conscience is a sacred right; that power abused justifies resistance; and that civil authority is a delegation from the people – Were not, I say, all this true; the Revolution would have been not an ASSERTION, but an INVASION of rights: not a REVOLUTION, but a REBELLION.'[13]

The Glorious Revolution, said Price, had been a wonderful thing, but it was incomplete. Liberty of conscience did not exist in England because the Test and Corporation Acts still prohibited non-conformist participation in public life or appointments, or at least required a level of compliance with the Church of England that most dissenters either could not or would not provide. But the most important aspect in which the Revolution was incomplete was representation. Representation was the 'basis of constitutional liberty' and where it did not exist, government was 'nothing but a usurpation'. When, said Price, 'the representation is fair and equal, and at the same time vested with such powers as our House of Commons possesses, a kingdom may be said to govern itself, and consequently to possess true liberty'. However:

'When the representation is partial, a kingdom possesses liberty only partially; and if extremely partial, it only gives a semblance of liberty; but if not only extremely partial, but corruptly chosen, and under corrupt influence after being chosen, it becomes a nuisance, and produces the worst of all forms of government – a government by corruption – a government carried on and supported by spreading venality and profligacy through a kingdom.'[14]

There had long been complaints about the state of political representation in Britain, and since the American Revolution there had been a number of unsuccessful attempts to redress it. Now, said Price, his hearers had no greater duty as 'men who love their country, and are grateful for the Revolution, than to unite our zeal in endeavouring to get it redressed'. Towards the end of his lecture he said that he felt himself fortunate to have lived long enough to experience the exciting events now unfolding and to see the French people '. . . indignant and resolute, spurning at slavery, and demanding liberty with an irresistible voice; their king led in triumph and an arbitrary monarch surrendering himself to his subjects'.[15]

He finished with a rather inflammatory rhetorical flourish:

'Tremble, all ye oppressors of the world! Take warning, all ye supporters of slavish governments, and slavish hierarchies! . . . You cannot now hold the world in darkness. Struggle no longer against increasing light and liberality. Restore to mankind their rights; and consent to the correction of abuses, before they and you are destroyed together.'[16]

Following this, the members of the Revolution Society passed a congratulatory address to the National Assembly in Paris,[17] and Price's speech was printed as a pamphlet, which enjoyed wide circulation. Since women were not admitted to membership of organizations such as the Revolution Society, Mary Wollstonecraft may not have heard him deliver his lecture in person, but she must certainly have read it very soon afterwards. However, she seems not at this stage to have been contemplating producing a directly political work herself, and it was not until Edmund Burke published his landmark book attacking the Revolution that she felt compelled to rush into print.

Edmund Burke had been a Whig MP since 1766 and in the 1770s had been a great defender of the American Revolution. He was a national figure, famous not just for his stance on the War of Independence, but also for his attempt to impeach Warren Hastings, the Governor-General of Bengal. He believed the Glorious Revolution had established a complete and perfect system and should not be meddled with, and although he did not oppose the French Revolution *per se*, he was thoroughly alarmed by the prospect of it being imported into Britain. When he read Richard Price's address he was incensed, both against the man and the ideas. His response, *Reflections on the Revolution in France,* was published in November 1790 and was an immediate sensation. It is still viewed as one of the foundation texts of British conservative traditionalism.

As soon as they read it, radical writers and thinkers leapt to oppose him, and one of the quickest off the mark was Mary Wollstonecraft, whose *Vindication of the Rights of Men* was published anonymously on 29 November, less than a month after the *Reflections*. It thus bears all the hallmarks of having been written at speed without much, if any, time for revision. But, what it may have lacked in structure, it more than made up for in immediacy, courage and attack. It is rather a jumble of ideas, not always very clearly thought through, but it is also infused throughout with a sense of outrage at Burke's class's apparent inability to understand the devastation their system caused. She was scathing about his reliance on ancient custom and practice, which she thought led him into ridiculous and even immoral corners. She even derided his famous defence of the American Revolution, which she pointed out was incompatible with his belief in the immutable nature of existing arrangements, since:

> 'the whole tenor of his plausible arguments settles slavery on an everlasting foundation. Allowing his servile reverence for antiquity, and prudent attention to self- interest, to have the force which he insists on, it ought never to be abolished; and, because our ignorant forefathers, not understanding the native dignity of man, sanctioned a traffic that outrages every suggestion of reason and religion, we are to submit to the inhuman custom, and term an atrocious insult to humanity the love of our country and a proper submission to those laws which secure our property.'[18]

Security of property, she noted was 'the definition of English liberty. And to this selfish principle every nobler one is sacrificed'. But, she also bitterly observed that it was 'only the property of the rich that is secure; the man who lives by the sweat of his brow has no asylum from oppression . . .'

Throughout the work, Mary's tone is much the same – furious, almost conversational in its directness, and shot through with exasperation. Burke's ideas about the sanctity of property and tradition drew her sustained fire, but so too did his ideas about women. Put simply, these were based on the notion that there were distinct male and female virtues, which became vices if displayed by the wrong sex. This concern about the apparent merging of the sexes was an obsession for opponents of the Revolution, who believed that it was 'masculinizing' women and depriving them of their natural attributes and functions. Once overlaid with Burke's own romanticized notions about Marie Antoinette, whom he had met nearly two decades previously, right and wrong became tangled up with class. The Queen, a damsel in distress fleeing half-naked through the gilded halls of Versailles, represented all that was beautiful and good about the female sex; the women of Paris, pursuing her with knives and axes, depicted what happened when women adopted masculine behaviour and meddled with things that did not concern them. Mary, however, was having none of it. Depicting the return to Paris on 6 October, Burke had described '. . . the royal captives . . . slowly moved along, amidst the horrid yells, and shrilling screams, and frantic dances, and infamous contumelies, and all the unutterable abominations of the furies of hell, in the abused shape of the vilest of women'. Mary, on the other hand, understood that these were women whose experience of life had been very different from his, but who still deserved some respect. 'Probably', she said to Burke:

'you mean women who gained a livelihood by selling vegetables or fish, who never had had any advantages of education; or their vices might have lost part of their abominable deformity, by losing part of their grossness. . . . the great and small vulgar claim our pity; they have almost insuperable obstacles to surmount in their progress towards true dignity of character . . .'[19]

Although Mary defended the poor women themselves against Burke's attacks, she did not necessarily defend their actions. She took the view that the market women and the Queen alike were suffering from a lack of education, and were thus denied the possibility of developing into rational beings. Poor women in France had hardly any education at all, and therefore, rather than being nurtured and refined, their characters were coarsened by deprivation and a brutalizing poverty. Women in the middle classes and the aristocracy, on the other hand, were trained from birth that, in her words, 'littleness and weakness are the very essence of beauty', and their livelihoods depended in large part on their ability to seem beautiful. It was hardly surprising, therefore, if they also turned out to be devious and manipulative; it was in their interests to appear to be the things they should be, and for many women that was inevitably going to mean concealing their true characters. Burke and, indeed, wider society, confined 'truth, fortitude, and humanity, within the rigid pale of manly morals', and argued that 'to be loved – woman's high end and great distinction! – [women] should learn to "lisp, to totter in their walk", and nick-name God's creatures'.[20]

However, although Mary thought that most women were essentially rather silly, she also maintained that they had been led into artificial and simpering manners by societal expectations and were kept in a state of permanent childishness by their legal and economic inferiority. Since she attributed this state almost wholly to a lack of suitable education, she applied the same remedy to queens as to bourgeois women and fishwives. Marie Antoinette, running for her life along the corridors of power, was as much in need of help as the market woman pursuing her; both were condemned by ignorance to folly, unbridled passions and the capacity for viciousness. Women of all classes were stunted by society, each displaying this in ways suitable to her situation, but all suffering from the same malaise.

Mary's view of the women of her time was thus often sympathetic, but hardly what would now be seen as 'sisterly'. However, she was filled with optimism for what women might be if they could just escape Burke's ideas about the differences between male and female virtue and capacity. She believed passionately that women could be fundamentally changed by education, and that this in turn would benefit society as a whole. However, for most radical men – and some women – female education was never a priority. Very few of the great Enlightenment thinkers and authors of the eighteenth century had seen the education of girls as anything other than a process of making them fit for the men under whose control they would live. The philosopher Jean-Jacques Rousseau, in particular, had been very clear about the need to educate boys for the world and girls for the home. Rousseau was the guiding spirit of many radicals and revolutionaries across Europe, and of all thinkers was most in tune with the revolutionary age he had not lived to see. Like many other people, Mary held him in very high regard, but in the matter of the value of both women and their education, she repudiated him absolutely.

At the end of the book. Mary proposed a solution to the problem of poverty that would certainly not have met with the approval of people such as Burke. 'Why', she demanded:

'cannot large estates be divided into small farms? these dwellings would indeed grace our land. Why are huge forests still allowed to stretch out with idle pomp and all the indolence of Eastern grandeur? Why do the brown wastes meet the traveller's view, when men want work? . . . Domination blasts all these prospects; virtue can only flourish amongst equals, and the man who submits to a fellow-creature, because it promotes his worldly interest, and he who relieves only because it is his duty to lay up a treasure in heaven, are much on a par, for both are radically degraded by the habits of their life.'[21]

The phrase 'virtue can only flourish amongst equals' is often quoted as though Mary wrote it about relations between the sexes; in fact it was part of her attack on the economic status quo and the vexed question of land usage, and was written in a work that was primarily about the rights of men. To attribute it to her views about women is to miss one of the most important features of Mary Wollstonecraft's thought; it was about the politics of society as a whole, which, in her view, included female rights, but was not solely restricted to them.

Ideas about issues such as land use were much discussed in the radical groups at Newington Green and London, and Mary's proposals were neither original nor unique to her. However, it was unusual for a woman to be so directly political without first either apologizing for her temerity or attempting to minimize her intelligence or understanding. It was even more startling for a young woman to challenge a man of Burke's age, status and intellectual weight. The sheer impertinence of a woman, a creature believed to be incapable of reason, saying directly to a man of Burke's standing and reputation: 'let us, Sir, reason together',[22] was striking. Indeed, despite the speed with which she had produced her riposte, this aspect of things does seem to have occurred to her. Joseph Johnson typeset and printed the pages as she wrote them each day, but at one point she told him that she didn't think she could finish it. Johnson, well used to dealing with nervy authors, told her that if that was really how she felt, he would immediately destroy what was already done. Mary went straight home and continued writing at the same breakneck speed.

The *Vindication of the Rights of Men* was an immediate success, and the second edition, brought out less than a month later, had Mary's name on the title page. Suddenly she was famous on both sides of the Channel, hailed by London radicals and French insurgents alike. Through the 150 pages of the *Vindication of the Rights of Men*, Mary Wollstonecraft burst angrily into male political territory to claim her place. Her next work, the *Vindication of the Rights of Woman,* would take many of those ideas into new directions again, but both *Vindications* had their roots in her rage with Edmund Burke.

In March 1791 the first part of Tom Paine's *Rights of Man* was published. Paine was a long-standing radical who had first made his name with the publication of *Common Sense* in 1775. This had provided some of the thought and propaganda underpinning the American Revolution, an event in which Paine had taken an active part. During the years since he had continued to develop a wide range of ideas about government, finance, religion and human progress. In 1787 he arrived in France and made contact with leading political figures both there and in Britain. By 1790 he was already writing a book about the French Revolution; once Burke's *Reflections* had come out it became a response to that. It was originally intended that Joseph Johnson should publish it in February, but Johnson was worried about being prosecuted, and the hunt for another publisher delayed its production by a month. Once out, it was an immediate and sensational success on a huge scale, selling thousands of copies and reaching, not just middle-class reformers and London political clubs, but ordinary men and women in the Midlands and the North. In April 1791, Paine returned to Paris and became deeply involved in the Revolution, particularly after the Royal Family's escape attempt was stopped at Varennes in June. In July he returned to London and wrote the second part of the *Rights of Man*, which was published in February 1792 and propelled his republican opinions into new and potentially seditious territory. Many people were convinced that he was trying to stir up revolution in Britain and (correctly) that prosecution was only a matter of time.

Meanwhile in France, women still entertained hopes that the Revolution would bring them new freedoms. Divorce on demand was made legal on an equal basis for both sexes, and daughters were allowed to inherit, but there was little further progress, and discussion of citizens' rights and a new citizenship law was ominously male. There were to be two kinds of citizen; the 'active', who paid tax above a certain level and would have full citizenship rights, and the 'passive', who would include servants and those who paid less tax; these would still be citizens but would not be able to vote. All women were to hold passive citizenship, meaning that their role was to be what it had always been; secondary, equated with servants and without its own political agency. The new revolutionary regime was also very interested in education, and in September 1791, Charles-Maurice de Talleyrand[23] produced an extensive report proposing a new national education system. However, this was only to be for boys; again, following Rousseau, the education of girls was to be restricted to the skills necessary for domesticity and subordination.

To Mary Wollstonecraft the revolutionary leaders seemed to be about to miss a huge opportunity, and she set about writing a companion piece to her *Vindication of the Rights of Men*. As before, she wrote in haste, revising little and not always connecting her thoughts together. But this time she produced a much weightier work, which still stands as a cry of infuriated exasperation as the chance to make men and women equal citizens slipped by.

Published in January 1792, a month before the second part of Paine's *Rights of Man,* Mary's book was dedicated to Talleyrand himself. Opening it she asked:

'. . . when men contend for their freedom, and to be allowed to judge for themselves respecting their own happiness, be it not inconsistent and unjust to subjugate women, even though you firmly believe that you are acting in the manner best calculated to promote their happiness? Who made man the exclusive judge, if woman partake with him of the gift of reason? . . . *[Tyrants]* are all eager to crush reason, yet always assert that they usurp its throne only to be useful. Do you not act a similar part when you force all women, by denying them civil and political rights, to remain immured in their families groping in the dark? for surely, sir, you will not assert that a duty can be binding which is not founded on reason?'[24]

What followed was a detailed argument against the inferior position to which women were being condemned by the revolutionary government. This covered a wide range of questions, sometimes revisiting and expanding upon ideas touched on in the *Vindication of the Rights of Men*, but at others entering new or seldom visited ground. Needless to say, her arguments fell on deaf ears. It is doubtful whether Talleyrand ever read her book, and when he visited London some months later and met her he was not impressed.

In London, the *Vindication of the Rights of Woman* was greeted with acclaim in some quarters and condemnation in others. The poet Anna Seward called it 'that wonderful book', and this was an opinion many shared. It was also avidly read by people who simply wanted to know what was in it, regardless of whether they were likely to agree with it or not. The author Anne MacVicar Grant wrote from Glasgow that: 'I have seen Mary Woolstonecroft's *(sic)* book, which is so run after here, that there is no keeping it long enough to read it leisurely. . . . It has produced no other conviction in my mind, but that of the author's possessing considerable abilities and greatly misapplying them.'[25] The conservative evangelist and author Hannah More, was also scathing and declined even to read such nonsense. 'I have been', she wrote to Horace Walpole:

> 'much pestered to read the *Rights of Woman*, but am invincibly resolved not to do it. . . . there is something fantastic and absurd in the very title. How many ways there are of being ridiculous! I am sure I have as much liberty as I can make a good use of . . . so many women are fond of government, I suppose, because they are not fit for it.'[26]

Radical men were more likely to agree with Rousseau and Talleyrand about women's education and political role than with Mary. Though often relatively progressive in some respects, many still tended to have rather conventional ideas when it came to women's roles in politics and society. The sight of the working-class women of Paris marching armed to Versailles horrified many of them almost as much as it did their reactionary opponents. Women might engage with radical movements, but they were not accorded leading places in them, and although a time might come when women would be the equal of men, that time was not yet.

Nowadays, Mary Wollstonecraft is primarily thought of as a feminist, but this is not how she thought of herself, nor is it how her contemporaries saw her. As an educationalist she was acceptable, but when she strayed into politics, people found it less comprehensible. The *Edinburgh Review*, for instance, was convinced that the author of the *Vindication of the Rights of Men* was a man, and was irritated to find that she was, in fact female; it would, it said, have affected how they reviewed it had they known. During her lifetime it was often Mary's politics rather than her other interests that infuriated people. In 1795, for instance, Horace Walpole signed off a letter to Hannah More with: 'Adieu, thou excellent woman! thou reverse of that hyena in petticoats, Mrs. Wollstonecraft, who to this day discharges her ink and gall on Marie Antoinette . . .'[27]

The publication of Paine's *Rights of Man* brought the government's rumbling anxiety to a head and the book was banned. Paine himself was charged with seditious treason but returned to France before he could be arrested. In December 1792 he was tried in London and convicted *in absentia.* His books went underground but remained seminal texts for reformers and radicals for decades to come. Mary's *Vindication of the Rights of Men* was later eclipsed by the much better-known *Rights of Woman*, which in turn has become more a feminist text than a political one. Thus, although her place in feminist history is assured, and merited, her political contribution is obscured. This pattern, of women being required to be either feminist, or political, but preferably not both, has been repeated many times during the ensuing centuries, and to some extent still influences expectations about female politicians.

1792 had been a difficult year for Mary in terms of her personal life, with her love for the painter Henry Fuseli going unrequited and her suggestion to his wife that they form a kind of ménage á trois rejected with outrage. In August she had been part of a group that had tried to go to Paris but been turned back. In December, she decided that she needed change and set off for France by herself. 'I shall not now halt at Dover I promise you', she wrote as she went, 'for as I go alone, neck or nothing is the word'.[28] Tucked safely into her bag she carried with her several letters of introduction, one of which was to the famous author Helen Maria Williams, one of the most remarkable women of the age.

Chapter 2
Wicked Little Democrats

Helen Maria Williams is nowadays more or less reduced to a footnote in Mary Wollstonecraft's story, but in her day she was one of the most famous and widely-read authors in Britain. As a writer embedded in revolutionary Paris, she created a vivid record of the experience of living through one of the most remarkable episodes in European history, and she did so with almost unrivalled first-hand knowledge. As an early foreign correspondent reporting from the heart of a major world event, she is a significant witness, one who knew many of the central characters and events of an extraordinary period and could write about them with authority. She herself understood the importance of being able to give an eye-witness account. 'I am a spectator of the representation', she said:

> 'I am placed near enough the scene to discern every look and every gesture of the actors, and every passion excited in the minds of the audience. I shall therefore endeavour to fill up the outline of that picture which France has presented to your contemplation . . .'[1]

Helen Maria had established her reputation as a poet in the early 1780s, and in 1790 published a very successful novel, *Julia*. Her verse had always had a political edge to it; her 1783 *Ode to the Peace* was about the American Revolution and her 1784 epic, *Peru,* was highly critical of colonialism. She actively supported the campaign for the abolition of the slave trade, and she was also well-connected in radical circles, including that at Newington Green. But her fame reached far beyond this. She corresponded with a wide range of poets and writers, including

Robert Burns, who described parts of her poem on the slave trade as doing 'honour to the greatest names that ever graced our profession'.[2] Helen Maria sometimes attracted (and still attracts) a certain amount of condescension from more obviously intellectual people; she was small, pretty and sociable with what Mary Wollstonecraft later called 'affected' manners. But she also had intelligence, principles and, as time would show, a dogged courage that took her through an unusually adventurous life. In London she held her own literary salon at which she and her mother welcomed guests to her elegant tea table. In the days before the French Revolution, political society was less polarized than it subsequently became, and Helen Maria had friends and acquaintances amongst Tories as well as Whigs and radicals. She was even admired by figures such as Samuel Johnson whose biographer, James Boswell, recorded that when Johnson met her he was effusive in his praise, quoting her own work back at her and paying her the compliment of calling her 'amiable'. Johnson's friend, the conservative hostess Hester Thrale Piozzi, often invited Helen Maria to stay at her home at Streatham Park, and the two women remained friendly for some time after Helen Maria's move to France in the 1790s.

When the Revolution began, Helen Maria Williams had just turned thirty and was living comfortably in London with her mother, also called Helen, and her two sisters, Persis and Cecilia. When the Bastille fell they shared the general excitement and like many others Helen Maria travelled to France as soon as possible to see for herself what was happening. She arrived in time for the celebrations marking the first anniversary of the fall of the Bastille, and wrote enthusiastically about the extensive festivities she witnessed. It was, she wrote:

'not a time in which the distinctions of country were remembered. It was the triumph of human kind; it was man asserting the noblest privilege of his nature; and it required but the common feelings of humanity to become in that moment a citizen of the world.'[3]

In September she was back in London and soon published the first volume of her *Letters from France*. This did very well, combining as it did travel, entertaining prose and first-hand descriptions of exciting and interesting events. At this stage she was writing without the advantage of hindsight and was therefore still hopeful. Later volumes (ultimately there were eight) would be less buoyant, and Helen Maria would be accused of inconsistency by her detractors. Given that, in 1790, she could hardly have anticipated the course her life would take, this is a little harsh. Certainly the events she saw and was involved in in later years were considerably darker than the celebrations of 1790, but despite all the betrayals, turns and tragedies the Revolution came to encompass, she retained throughout a belief in its fundamental principles, in the potential of humanity and in internationalism. In 1794 she asked:

> '. . . shall we, because the fanatics of liberty have committed some detestable crimes, conclude that liberty is an evil, and prefer the gloomy tranquillity of despotism? If the blessings of freedom have sometimes been abused, it is because they are not yet well understood. Those occasional evils which have happened in the infant state of liberty, are but the effects of despotism.'[4]

With her friend, the revolutionary Madame (Manon) Roland, she understood that many crimes had been committed in Liberty's name, but even when things were at their worst she never abandoned the idea of liberty itself.

In 1791, Helen Maria returned to England, but left for Paris again in September. The following summer she paid a fleeting visit to London to see her family and publish the second volume of her *Letters*. In August 1792, now accompanied by her mother and sister Cecilia, she returned to Paris. At this point she still intended to stay away for only a couple of years, but as time and events moved on it became more and more difficult to return to Britain. The choices she made tied her to France where, unknown to her in 1792, the rest of her life was to be spent.

On arrival in Paris, Helen Maria joined a small community of British revolutionaries and radicals that included a businessman called John Hurford Stone. Stone was married, but he and Helen Maria formed a relationship that endured until his death nearly thirty years later. Its exact nature remains open to speculation; Helen Maria always maintained that it was unimpeachable, but they lived in the same house (often together with Helen Maria's mother and sisters) for long periods, travelled together and are buried together in Père La Chaise Cemetery in Paris. Stone was himself a committed revolutionary and republican, and was the President of the British Club that met at White's Hotel in the Passage des Petits-Pères. The Club included many British, Irish and American expatriates and, unsurprisingly, it was frequently infiltrated by spies from both the British government and the French. Many members, including Stone and Helen Maria themselves, were suspected of spying for one side or the other, or at times even both. Stone almost certainly did dabble in espionage in one way or another, but in Helen Maria's case, although there are grounds for speculation, it is hard to be certain either way. As so often with radical societies, the British Club at Paris was prone to arguments, splits and sectarian differences, and the atmosphere of heightened tension and excitement in which many of its members lived no doubt contributed to the rumours they circulated about one another.

On Sunday, 18 November 1792, a few weeks before Mary Wollstonecraft's arrival in Paris, the British Club held a dinner to celebrate France's victories in the wars and to agree a congratulatory address to the French Convention. Although France was not yet at war with Britain, many people saw it as only a matter of time, and this was therefore an event which, whilst not actually treasonable, could certainly be seen as bordering on it from the perspective of the British government. It was attended by about 100 people, who were entertained by bands playing revolutionary airs. Helen Maria had written the verses for a song to be sung to the tune of the Marseillaise, and she and the novelist Charlotte Smith, who was not present but who was much admired in radical circles, were toasted together as 'lady defenders of the Revolution'. Unusually for such an event, Helen Maria was present and participated. In London, men and women still dined separately in public, and women were not generally allowed at political dinners, but in Paris things could be different. This difference was not universal, however. Helen Maria was excluded, for instance, from the dinners held by Madame Roland because Madame Roland did not believe that – apart from herself – women should express political opinions in public. This did not prevent Helen Maria from admiring Madame Roland very greatly, and writing of her after her death as 'one of those illustrious women whose superior attainments seem fitted to exalt her sex in the scale of being'.[5] Unlike Mary Wollstonecraft, Helen Maria Williams was a recorder and reporter rather than a philosopher; she was more interested in the way in which people lived (and, during the Revolution, died) than in theories and frameworks. Mary thought her way through problems, whereas Helen Maria was more likely to react instinctively. However, her instincts were sometimes more radical than many of the conclusions Mary reached, and she believed in liberty as a fundamental good without feeling the need to identify exactly what it was, or what it should become.

One of the biggest differences between Mary Wollstonecraft and Helen Maria Williams, however, was their view of women themselves. Mary Wollstonecraft focused so heavily on women's education because she thought that, although women had potential, they were not yet ready for the kind of responsibility that public life would confer on them. On the other hand, she was furious that the opportunity for a proper education was systemically denied to them for no other reason than their sex, and she saw with increasing clarity how they were discriminated against, belittled and oppressed, and that that oppression was structural rather than accidental. Helen Maria Williams saw women quite differently. She did not make any claims for them, and she was certainly not interested in women's rights in the way that Mary was, but she liked and respected women both as individuals and as a whole, and she understood the sense of sisterhood that arose amongst women at times of crisis. Her descriptions of women such as Manon Roland and Charlotte Corday, who famously murdered the revolutionary Marat in his bath, are full of admiration for them as political actors as well as as women. Mary thought that women – particularly working-class women – were not capable of thinking or acting alone politically, and she came to think that even the Women's March and the October Days must have been organized and manipulated by men. Her political vision was larger than Helen Maria's, and her identification of the challenges facing women in the public space much more structural and intellectual, but Helen Maria saw women as having political agency regardless of their status, and observed and celebrated their exercise of it. This is not to say that Mary Wollstonecraft could not be supportive of women generally, and did not believe that, properly educated and no longer subjugated to social and legal restrictions, they would be capable of great things. But in some ways she lacked a certain warmth and sisterhood, whilst, though a more sympathetic character, Helen Maria was not interested in analyzing women's position or the role of patriarchy in the Revolution's shabby treatment of women. Both had interesting and relevant things to say about women and politics; that one is now restricted in the popular mind to a role as a feminist icon, whilst the other is almost erased altogether, effectively denies us the full range of two informed and pertinent voices on a significant period of history.

Although women were generally barred from many political activities, hosting a salon remained a socially acceptable way in which they could discuss politics without jeopardizing their femininity. As it had been in London, Helen Maria's salon was a meeting place for all kinds of people, but now they were revolutionaries as well as writers and philosophers. The great Tom Paine, by then in his fifties, was prone to drinking too much when things went awry, but he was still thinking furiously and writing fearlessly. Paine was one of the foreign members of the Convention,[6] and appeared at both the British Club and Helen Maria's tea table. The Irish revolutionary Lord Edward Fitzgerald was a frequent guest, as was the rather austere radical philosopher William Godwin, whom Mary Wollstonecraft had first met in London and with whom she had not got on particularly well. But, Helen Maria's Sunday evening gatherings also attracted members of the Girondin faction, including their principal spokesmen, Jean Pierre Brissot and Pierre Vergniaud, as well as the egalitarian Nicolas de Condorcet, and Rouget de Lisle, who had composed the Marseillaise. A much more alarming visitor was Bertrand Barère, who had begun the Revolution half-inclined towards the Girondins, but soon became the eyes and ears of the extremist Jacobin leader Robespierre and the man who, on 5 September 1793 would urge the National Convention to 'make terror the order of the day!' Helen Maria described him as the man 'in whose power my life was placed, . . . now the lacquey of Robespierre, and the great inquisitor of the English at Paris'.[7] Barère brought danger right into Helen Maria's home, but despite this everyone who was anyone still arrived sooner or later at her tea table, and those who did not were desperate for an invitation. This made it particularly attractive to Mary Wollstonecraft, who soon made use of her letter of introduction when she arrived in Paris at the end of 1792. The meeting went well, although given that Helen Maria was a much more successful author than Mary, there is a distinct tinge of unwarranted superiority in Mary's comment in a letter to her sister Everina that:

'Miss Williams has behaved very civilly to me, and I shall visit her frequently, because I rather like her, and I meet French company at her house. Her manners are affected, yet her simple goodness of heart continually breaks through the varnish, so that one would be more inclined, at least I should, to love than admire her. Authorship is a heavy weight for female shoulders, especially in the sunshine of prosperity.'[8]

Conversation at Helen Maria's parties was wide-ranging and, like everything else, deeply political and overhung by an air of excitement, danger and possibility. The Paris of late 1792 was very different from that of the early days of the Revolution, and had already begun the dark turn that would take it into the Reign of Terror the following year. In September, more than 2,000 prisoners had been massacred by their gaolers and the mob. Men, women and children had been slaughtered, some with considerable cruelty, and many British radicals had begun to falter in their revolutionary enthusiasm. Some now drifted towards Burke's side of the question, but for others, the bloodletting was the unsurprising by-product of revolutionary necessity. 'Children of any growth', wrote Mary Wollstonecraft to a friend before she travelled to Paris, 'will do mischief when they meddle with edged tools'.[9] This complacency in the face of mass murder now seems almost inexplicable from a woman who usually thought carefully about things, but it was not uncommon at the time, when the early revolutionary excesses were often justified as being the natural consequence of decades of tyranny and oppression. Rather less surprising, perhaps, is Mary's equation of the French people with 'children of any growth'. Despite her radicalism, Mary was as likely as any other English person to see foreigners as inferior, and unlike Helen Maria Williams, she did not yet consider herself a citizen of the world. Many radicals never came to think of themselves as such.

In Mary's case, however, reality soon altered her insouciant tone. She arrived in Paris in late December 1792, and from the window of her lodging she saw Louis XVI being taken through eerily silent streets to his trial at the Convention. She confessed to Joseph Johnson that it was a strange and even frightening experience. 'I have been alone ever since', she wrote to him:

'and though my mind is calm, I cannot dismiss the lively images that have filled my imagination all the day. . . . I want to see something

alive; death in so many frightful shapes has taken hold of my fancy
. . . for the first time in my life I cannot put out the candle.'[10]

Louis XVI was guillotined on 21 January and within days Britain and
France were at war. Paris became increasingly dangerous for foreigners,
and particularly for the English. At the end of May 1793 the Girondins
fell, and orders were issued for their arrest. In June, Mary Wollstonecraft
moved to a little cottage at Neuilly, just outside the city, where she would
be safer. In July, Charlotte Corday murdered Marat and was guillotined
within days. The revolutionary war in the Netherlands was not going well
for the French, and the commander of the Army of the North was
recalled to Paris and executed in August. Helen Maria Williams knew
that, despite the fact that she, her mother and her sister were a family
of 'defenceless women in a land of strangers', they were at risk, but she
remained in Paris. Though she made light of the danger in her later
accounts of the period she must have known how grave it was. The
family discussed what they would do if – or rather when – the police
knocked on the door. Preparations were made and incriminating
documents destroyed, including those of Madame Roland, who had
been arrested as part of the Girondin purge, and who had passed some
of her papers to Helen Maria for safe keeping. Every evening Helen
Maria and her family went to bed expecting to be hauled off to a
revolutionary gaol during the night. By now it was almost impossible to
leave Paris, so that even if they could have found a way back to England
they would not have been able to make use of it. The Sunday receptions
ceased, and the waiting must have begun to seem endless.

The Jacobin faction was now in full control, and in September the
Convention passed the Law of Suspects, permitting the Committee of
Public Safety to arrest anyone they decided was a threat to the
Revolution. Robespierre was the leading member of the Committee and
disliked Helen Maria personally, at least in part because he thought she
was a spy. He also resented what she was publishing about the
Revolution in Britain, and in any case he deeply disapproved of women
who occupied public space and had public voices. On 16 October the
Convention finally ordered the detention of all foreigners, but by then
Helen Maria and her family had already been locked up. Soldiers
knocked on their door at 2.00 am on 9 October, and although they were
polite enough there was no mistaking the peril the household was in.

Each woman was allowed to take with her nothing except as much personal linen as she could carry in a large kerchief; everything else had to be left behind. Helen Maria remembered with pinpoint clarity for years afterwards the moments when, standing on the staircase with her bundle she watched the soldiers seal up the door of her apartment. Trembling with fear, but doing their best not to show it, the three women were taken to the police station to be processed and allocated to a prison. Here they found crowds of people who, like themselves, had been arrested during the night, and 'Every half hour a guard entered, conducting English prisoners, among whom were no women but ourselves'.[11] They waited apprehensively for hours until at last they were sent to the former Luxembourg Palace, now pressed into service as a prison to accommodate the overflow from all the others. The lower parts of the windows had been blocked out, and the rooms were dark and intimidating. Later, standing on a table, Helen Maria was able to peer out of the top windows and glimpse the Luxembourg Gardens in their autumnal glory. With a faintly bizarre twist, the rooms – now cells – had been named after notable Romans and revolutionary virtues; the one in which prisoners were held in solitary confinement had 'Liberty' written over the door.

As the days went on the palace began to fill up with all kinds of people, some of whom had very little idea of why they were there. Despite all the horrors around them, the captives soon found themselves settling into a relatively mundane routine. In each room, which contained increasing numbers of people as the days wore on, a little democracy was instituted. 'Every chamber' said Helen Maria, 'formed a society subject to certain regulations: a new president was chosen every day, or every week, who enforced its laws and maintained good order'.[12] Singing was prohibited after 11.00 pm, and the occupants of each cell had housekeeping tasks allotted to them. Helen Maria's mother found a tea kettle and kept the English prisoners supplied with hot drinks; even in the shadow of the guillotine, Helen Maria had a tea table over which to preside. Meanwhile, in the public rooms, 'fine gentlemen and fine ladies, who had held the highest rank at court' gathered together in the evenings just as though they were at home, even persisting in the use of titles when they must have known that 'the fatal pre-eminence of rank was the surest passport to the guillotine'. There were also, however, 'many persons who had too much good sense not to observe a different conduct, who had proved themselves real friends to liberty, had made important sacrifices in its cause, and who had been led to prison by revolutionary committees on pretences the most trivial, and sometimes from mistakes the most ludicrous'.[13]

To keep herself occupied, Helen Maria wrote poetry and worked on a translation of the popular novel *Paul et Virginie*. However, this deceptively dull-seeming routine was frequently punctuated by moments of sadness, uncertainty and intense fear. Anyone who was taken away for trial was almost certainly not going to return, since an accusation alone was effectively a death sentence. But the worst days were those upon which the Commander of the Armed Forces of Paris, a man called François Hanriot, burst into their room to bellow abuse at them. Hanriot was a man of whom there was ample cause to be afraid; he had had a leading role in both the September Massacres of the previous year and the purge of the Girondins in June. Helen Maria recorded that on his first visit he:

'entered on a sudden our apartment, brandishing his sword, and accompanied by twelve of his officers. . . . he looked not merely as if he longed to plunge his sabre in our bosoms, but to drink a libation of our blood. He poured forth a volley of oaths and imprecations, called out to know how many guillotines must be erected for the English, and did not leave our chamber till one person who was present had fainted with terror. In this manner he visited every apartment, spreading consternation and dismay; and these visits were repeated three or four times in a week. Whenever the trampling of his horse's feet was heard in the court-yard . . . we remained crouching in our cells . . . till the monster disappeared. . . . Brutality, as well as terror, was the order of the day . . .'[14]

After some weeks, the English women were moved out of the Luxembourg and into the Convent Les Anglaises. Here the physical conditions were worse – it was freezing cold and they had to sleep in a passageway – but in other respects there was some improvement. Helen Maria and her family were dissenters and the nuns English and Irish Catholics, but religious differences disappeared under the weight of their common predicament. However, the threat of violence could still erupt with terrifying suddenness. One of the police officers who visited to check up on them was incensed to see a stone cross upright in the garden and a bell still in the belfry, and by the next day the nuns had been commanded to take them down and to stop wearing religious dress. Helen Maria and the other Protestant women spent a long night helping the nuns to turn their habits into safe, secular gowns and their veils into modest bonnets.

After a time, the prisoners were allowed to walk in the garden and to speak to friends through the grille at the gate. One visitor was a man who subsequently married Helen Maria's sister, Cecilia. He tirelessly – and bravely – tried to get the Williams family released, eventually succeeding by going to the local municipality rather than the government. In late November they were freed and returned to their home, which they were relieved to find much as they had left it. But almost everything else was changed; Helen Maria had been in prison for less than two months in total, but those few weeks had been drenched in blood and many people who had been alive when the door of her house was sealed up at the beginning of October were dead by the time she returned at the end of November. Marie Antoinette had been executed on 16 October. Almost the entire Girondin leadership, including many who had been regular visitors to her salon, had been guillotined in the space of twenty-five minutes on 31 October. The political activities of women had been curtailed, punished and crushed. The female political clubs that had sprung up earlier in the year had been dissolved and their leaders briefly imprisoned. Nicolas de Condorcet who continued to write about equality, was in hiding. Olympe de Gouges, who had published a Declaration of the Rights of Women,[15] and who had been arrested in July, was accused of 'attempting to pervert the republic with her writings' and went courageously to her death at the beginning of November, as did Manon Roland to hers a few days later. Robespierre, who followed Rousseau in his view of women's role in society, was determined to enforce French women's subjugation. In this he was largely successful; what he left undone was later finished by Napoleon Bonaparte.[16]

Helen Maria's judgement now was that, whilst her family was probably safe from further arrest, she herself was not. She continued to write, but she passed an anxious few months and her later description of passing 'the winter at Paris, with the knife of the guillotine suspended over me by a frail thread'[17] probably does little to convey her state of mind. Christmas was spent convivially enough, but it cannot have been enjoyable. In the summer of 1794 it was decided that Paris was too dangerous for either Helen Maria or John Hurford Stone, and that they should leave France for a time. They went to Switzerland, where they remained until early 1795.

Meanwhile Mary Wollstonecraft had been having troubles of her own. Before the fall of the Girondins, Condorcet had asked her to write a paper for him on education, but when he went into hiding there seemed little point in finishing it. She was already planning to write a book about the history of the Revolution, but she was also deep into an affair with a man she may well have met at Helen Maria Williams's salon. Gilbert Imlay was an American adventurer, merchant and temporary diplomat who had left the United States to avoid debts and was now trying to make his fortune in Europe. He was in his late thirties, handsome, charming and with a less than savoury reputation. Despite (probably untrue) rumours that he had been Helen Maria's lover, Mary fell for him heavily. In the summer of 1793, as the Terror raged all around them, he visited her at her little house at Neuilly and by August she was pregnant. Americans were not included in the proscription of foreigners, and to avoid her being arrested as a British subject, Imlay registered Mary as his wife at the American Embassy. This gave her the protection of American papers, and she started to use his name. As the Reign of Terror bit during the summer and autumn, however, people began to disappear, and Mary was deeply distressed as one friend or acquaintance after another was guillotined. Even with her American documents she must have been fearful, particularly when Imlay was absent. Despite this, she visited detainees, including Helen Maria Williams, though the evidence of the tragedies unfolding horrified her and she was not always able to contain her disgust. In the biography he wrote of her after her death, William Godwin recounted that:

'. . . she happened one day to enter Paris on foot . . . when an execution, attended with some peculiar aggravations, had just taken place, and the blood of the guillotine appeared fresh upon the pavement. The emotions of her soul burst forth in indignant exclamations, while a prudent bystander warned her of her danger, and intreated her to hasten and hide her discontents.'[18]

Once Helen Maria had been released, Mary went to stay with her for Christmas. Helen Maria may or may not have been aware of Mary's pregnancy, but she must have known, if only by inference, that the relationship with Gilbert Imlay was in difficulty. Having registered Mary as his wife in September, he had gone to Le Harvre on business and showed little sign of returning. Mary was working on her book about the French Revolution, but was also increasingly uneasy. From Paris she went to Le Harvre in the spring to meet Imlay, and there gave birth to her daughter Fanny, in May 1794.

For a short while she was happy; the baby was thriving and Mary and Imlay talked, as they had done before, of moving to America. But Imlay had no intention of doing anything of the kind, and by the beginning of September he had left Mary and Fanny in Le Harvre and gone alone to London, telling her that he would send for them when he could. The baby contracted smallpox but survived, and since Imlay had not yet sent for them Mary took her back to Paris. Here things were desperate, with little food or fuel and a bitingly cold winter to endure. The streets were as dangerous as ever, and whilst the fall of Robespierre in July 1794 (or, in the revolutionary calendar, 9 Thermidor, Year II) had brought the worst of the Terror to an end, the future was still very uncertain. The book she had been writing, *A Historical and Moral View of the French Revolution*, was published at the end of the year, but still she had no money and had to endure the humiliation of asking Imlay's friends for help. Gradually it dawned on her that he might be abandoning her. Eventually he told her to come to London, where presumably (and correctly) he thought she would have a better chance of earning some money of her own. She went back to Le Harvre and got a passage to Brighton. Imlay had found a house in London for her, and for a short while even moved in with her, but he was cold and distant and soon moved out again. In May 1795, Mary made her first unsuccessful suicide attempt using laudanum. She spent the summer travelling in Scandinavia on business for Imlay (and wrote one of her best books about it), but made a second suicide bid in October by jumping off Putney Bridge. However, the following year things began to improve. She moved to a new house, and began an unexpected affair with William Godwin, who lived nearby. By the end of the year she was pregnant again, and she and Godwin married in March 1797. Her second daughter, Mary,[19] was born at the end of August, but the birth was followed by fatal complications, and Mary Wollstonecraft died on 10 September 1797.

She had always been a controversial figure, but now William Godwin did something so extraordinarily unwise that it is hard not to believe that his judgement was affected by grief. He wrote a biography of Mary, which he determined would be the unvarnished truth, and despite all advice to the contrary he included every episode of her life, which he must have known would shock and appal even some of her friends. It was written in haste and published at speed, and it destroyed her reputation more thoroughly than the work of any opponent could have done. If they had come from someone who disliked her, the stories Godwin told about Mary might have been counted as invention, but from her widower they had to be taken as true. Thus, her unrequited passion for the married artist Fuseli – criminal in some eyes even though unconsummated – her irregular relationship with Gilbert Imlay, her illegitimate child, her pretence of being married (she had called herself Mrs Imlay when she returned from France), her two suicide attempts – then criminal as well as religious offences – and the fact that she had been pregnant again when she and Godwin married, all made her a profoundly wicked figure in the eyes of many people. She became unmentionable in polite society and unreadable by anybody other than irredeemable radicals. Almost overnight, her reputation was buried in an avalanche of disapproval, and so thorough was the rejection that she was not unearthed from it even partially for decades.

Like Mary, Helen Maria Williams was viewed in Britain as a dangerous and immoral woman, a republican harridan whose relationship with John Hurford Stone was also adulterous and therefore criminal. Stone and his wife, Rachel, had been divorced under French revolutionary law in Paris in 1794, and rumours abounded that he and Helen Maria had been secretly married by a republican priest. Horace Walpole, never one to miss the opportunity to be offensive about anyone he disagreed with, referred to her as a 'scribbling trollope'.[20] By 1794, Helen Maria had become so notorious that Hester Thrale Piozzi, once one of her closest friends, had ceased to write to her altogether, calling her 'a proffess'd Jacobine resident at Paris' and 'a wicked little Democrate'.[21]

This was nothing, however, compared to the treatment of Helen Maria by the British press. The early volumes of her *Letters* had been greeted with praise and enthusiasm, which soon turned to condemnation as the Revolution and the war wore on. Her books were savaged by the critics, but her character was also attacked, her veracity was questioned, and both she and Mary Wollstonecraft had their reputations so tarnished that they were regarded in some quarters as no better than prostitutes; in the index to the *Anti-Jacobin Review* for 1801 the entry for Mary Wollstonecraft read 'See Helen Maria Williams, Godwin, prostitution'.[22] Even Samuel Johnson's biographer, James Boswell, resorted to downright lies to make the case against her. In 1793, referring to the massacre of 600 soldiers at the Tuilleries in Paris, where the Royal Family was then being held, he claimed that she had 'walked, without horror, over the ground at the Thuilleries *(sic)* when it was strewed with the naked bodies of the faithful Swiss Guards', and went on to suggest that Samuel Johnson himself had turned against her; 'From Dr Johnson she could now expect not endearment but repulsion.' This was despite the fact that Johnson had by this point been dead for more than a decade, and that Helen Maria had tried desperately to save the life of a soldier who died on her doorstep and been horrified by what she saw in the Tuileries Gardens when she unwisely ventured there.[23]

Other people thought that to write about the French Revolution at all was not only unwomanly, but also offensive in itself. The whole event had become so traumatic, so distasteful and so unpatriotic to the loyalist English mind that mere mention of it was enough to cause outrage. As we shall see, this attitude was to have implications for radical and reformist politics in the ensuing years, but it also affected writers and historians. Reviewing *Sketches of the State of Manners and Opinions in the French Republic*, published in 1801, the *British Critic* was scathing, beginning with the author's reputation.

'Among the most active labourers in the cause of France is Miss Helen Maria Williams, for that is the name by which she is content still to pass in this country , and it is indeed the only name which, by the law of England, she can claim.'[24]

After condemning 'her polluted pen' and attacking her veracity, the reviewer concluded with a final flourish of personal bile suggesting that Helen Maria and Stone had abandoned Stone's legal wife in Paris, making 'their escape into Switzerland during the tyranny of Robespierre, carrying with them the remains of the wife's fortune, and leaving the wife herself in a dungeon at Paris, destined for the scaffold, from which she was saved by the death of Robespierre'.[25] In fact, Rachel Stone had also gone to Switzerland, and by the time the *British Critic* was published may even have been in London, but this in no way inhibited loyalist and pro-government writers and publications from their attacks, which continued for most of the rest of Helen Maria's life. As a result, her last publication, *Souvenirs de la Revolution Française*, appeared in French only.

Despite the deluge of abuse to which she was subjected in Britain, however, Helen Maria was resilient, and resolutely refused to be intimidated by people who had sat safely at home whilst she had faced real danger. In the Preface to her *Sketches* she observed that she was:

'aware of the censure which has been thrown on writers of the female sex who have sometimes employed their pens on political subjects; nor am I ignorant that my name has been mentioned with abuse by journalists, calling themselves Anti-Jacobins. But however malignant may be the aim, these Anti-Jacobin darts fly harmless; those who have lived amidst scenes of a French Revolution, have learnt to parry or despise more formidable weapons.'[26]

She also retained the early hopes she had entertained; she hated terror, she wrote, but:

'however deeply I may lament the calamities and the crimes which have sullied the French Revolution, I shall not cease to hope, that it will yet ultimately terminate in the establishment of a perfect Government in the country where it originated, and the extension of liberty even in states still more despotic.'

By this time, Mary Wollstonecraft was dead, the radical and reformist movements in Britain had been forced into retreat, and much of British society had become insular, inward-looking and deeply xenophobic. Helen Maria knew that she was now a lonely voice, but still she was not silenced. She managed to incur the wrath of Napoleon Bonaparte and was briefly imprisoned by him, although unlike Robespierre he rather liked her personally. However, over the years she gradually sank into irremediable obscurity in Britain. In 1817 someone asked: 'What is she now? If she lives – and whether she lives or not, few know and nobody cares – she is a wanderer, an exile, unnoticed and unknown.'[27] In fact, she was still living in Paris, still holding her salons and still presiding over her tea table, very much alive though wiped from the record in England. She and John Hurford Stone became naturalized French citizens; Stone died in 1818 and Helen Maria at the age of sixty-eight nearly a decade later. She continued to the end to write about the causes that had driven her. In *Souvenirs de la Revolution Française*, which was published in the year of her death, she wrote about the experiences of her life, but was also interested in more recent struggles, and was passionately supportive of the campaign to free Greece from the Ottoman Empire. To the last, she believed in the redemptive possibilities of true liberty. 'I have always', she said, 'sincerely loved liberty' and, with an echo of her long-dead friend Condorcet's Enlightenment belief that progress was constant and would tend to perfection, she added that in her view 'the march of modern peoples heads towards liberty, and therefore towards happiness'. Looking back she concluded that:

'I could not have been an indifferent spectator of the events which accumulated before me. It is not true that I preached in turn, as some have said, the symbols of terror, the imperial eagle and the white flag . . . Far from humbly admitting guilt of such a fault, I dare, on the contrary, claim a share of merit from the friends of liberty, for having so long defended its cause.'[28]

Chapter 3
Such Mighty Rage

On 4 March 1790, the poet and essayist Anna Laetitia Barbauld sat down to write a pamphlet called *Address to the Opposers of the Repeal of the Corporation and Test Acts*. She was very angry and wrote fluently and at speed, so that within a matter of days it was finished and sent off to her publisher, Joseph Johnson. Despite its rapid production, the ideas it expressed were clear, coherent and still resonate. Under what seems a singularly unpromising title, Mrs Barbauld argued for the political and civil rights of minorities in a society that structurally denied them. It was, and remains, a masterly little piece of writing, less known now than it should be, but widely read and controversial in its day.

Like Helen Maria Williams and many other women writers, Anna Laetitia Barbauld had initially made her name through poetry, but she was best-known as the author of works on education as well as very popular children's books. When she took up her pen to write the *Address* she was forty-six years old, loved and respected, and undoubtedly one of the more celebrated literary women of her time. Before 1790 she had tackled political topics only obliquely, but now she was sufficiently infuriated to confront her subject head on. Although her name was not on the title page, Johnson made sure that it got out fairly quickly. One hostile reviewer, having damned the *Address* to the best of his ability on the assumption that it had been written by a man, was horrified to be told that it was, in fact, from 'a female pen! And in soft bosoms', he demanded, quoting Alexander Pope rather out of context, 'dwells such mighty rage?'.[1]

Anna Laetitia's rage was caused by the failure of the House of Commons to repeal the century-old Test and Corporation Acts. These prohibited non-conformist Protestants – known as dissenters – from holding any public office, entering Parliament, voting in elections or attending Oxford or Cambridge University. On the other hand, dissenters had to pay taxes to the state and, more controversially, tithes (a form of religious tax) to the Church of England. As the established church, the Church of England (or Anglican Church) had (and still has) a special and protected place in the British constitution; its members could hold any office and its bishops sat (and still sit) in the House of Lords. The only way in which a dissenter could overcome this discrimination was to take holy communion in an Anglican church, and this the vast majority refused to do. Dissenters therefore tended to go into occupations such as commerce, medicine or teaching. Quakers, Unitarians and Presbyterians all found themselves pushed to the margins of society, tolerated in a limited number of spheres but rigorously excluded from government or political influence. Roman Catholics, also excluded, were believed to owe their primary allegiance to a foreign power in the shape of the Pope, but dissenters were held responsible for the Civil War, the Puritan Commonwealth and the execution of Charles I, so that their history – and their possible propensity to repeat it – was still feared. Although during the eighteenth century some of the antipathy to them had softened, it had by no means evaporated, and their refusal to conform with the religious majority was perceived as perverse and untrustworthy. Many people were happy to send their children to be educated in one of the numerous excellent dissenter schools, but they were not willing to admit the people who ran and taught in those schools to any kind of political equality.

Anna Laetitia Barbauld was born in Leicestershire. When she was fourteen her father took a teaching post at the famous Warrington Academy in Lancashire,[2] where some of the best brains in the dissenting community were nurtured. Always keen to learn, Anna Laetitia had already acquired Latin and Greek, as well as more traditional subjects, and at Warrington she broadened her education further and developed a wide circle of friends. She began writing and publishing poetry in her early twenties, eventually making a name for herself with her first collection of verse in 1773. This was remarkably well-received, with the *Monthly Review* praising her 'justness of thought, and vigour of imagination, inferior only to the works of Milton and Shakespeare'.[3] The following year she married Rochemont Barbauld, a dissenting minister of French Huguenot descent who had been educated at Warrington. The couple moved to Suffolk where they ran a successful school for boys. Rather startlingly to twenty-first century sensibilities, upper middle class parents in the late eighteenth century often sent their sons to boarding school at an alarmingly early age; Anna Laetitia's establishment received them as young as four years old. Many of her pupils grew up to become high achievers, and retained fond memories of their early education. Later, the Barbaulds moved to London, where they came into contact with Richard Price and his group of radical reformers, but as the years went on Anna Laetitia wrote less and less, and by 1790, although her books were still in print and were very popular, she had published nothing for nine years. It was the failure of the Test and Corporation Acts repeal bill that brought her back to address her public again.

Over the years there had been several attempts to abolish the Acts, but none of these had been successful. In 1787 a bill was defeated by quite a wide margin, not helped by the fact that it was opposed by William Pitt, who by then had been in office for four years and was well on his way from his starting point as a reformer to his historical place as a reactionary. Soon after this, Richard Price preached a sermon on the subject of progress, both social and scientific, in which he looked forward to a world in which church and state would be separate, as they were in the United States of America. 'Alliances between church and state and slavish hierarchies', he said:

> 'are losing credit, long experience having taught their mischief. The nature of religious liberty is better understood than ever. . . . there is now conviction prevailing that all encroachments on the rights of conscience are pernicious and impious, that the proper office of the civil magistrate is to maintain peace, not to support truth. To defend the properties of men, not to take care of their souls. And to protect equally all honest citizens of all persuasions, not to set up one religious sect above another.'[4]

The tenor of this sermon was upbeat and hopeful, and indeed it did begin to seem as though the gap between those who were for and against repeal was narrowing. The whole topic took up much space in the newspapers and periodicals, and there was a flood of pamphlets, essays and texts supporting one side or the other. In May 1789 the dissenters' representative in Parliament, Henry Beaufoy, again introduced a repeal bill; again it was defeated, though this time by a much narrower margin. The prize seemed to be within reach.

However, the next attempt, in March 1790, turned out to be a disaster. In February, in a seemingly innocuous debate on the army budget, Edmund Burke had chosen to make a speech so inflammatory that Whigs and dissenters alike were stunned. Burke was at this point beginning to write his *Reflections on the Revolution*, which would be published later that year. France, he said, had now ceased to exist for all practical purposes. Outlining his view of the effect of the Revolution, he claimed that the French had 'laid the axe to the root of all property' and destroyed religion and good government. Changes to the army meant that France was no longer the historic military threat it had once been. Instead, the enemy was now within. It was, in fact, from 'persons in this country . . . who entertained theories of government, incompatible with the safety of the state, and who were, perhaps, ready to transfer a part, at least, of that anarchy which prevailed in France to this kingdom, for the purposes of effectuating their designs'.[5] A month later, in the debate on the repeal bill itself, Burke was even more explicit. He claimed that leading dissenters such as Richard Price and the scientist and educator Joseph Priestley 'were avowed enemies to the Church of England; that they acknowledged their intentions, and that thence our Establishment appeared to be in much more serious danger than the Church of France was in, a year or two ago'.[6] The bill was heavily defeated and Anna Laetitia's *Address* was one of the many consequences.

She began with a partially rhetorical question familiar to equalities campaigners: What are you afraid of? In the first paragraph she told her opponents that: 'We thank you for the compliment paid the dissenters, when you suppose that the moment they are eligible to places of power and profit, all such places will at once be filled with them.'[7] Are the Test Acts, she asked, like 'the dykes in Holland; and do we wait, like an impetuous sea, to rush in and overwhelm the land?'. On the contrary, all dissenters wanted was 'the removal of a stigma than the possession of a certain advantage', in other words to have the same right of access to public office and the universities as Anglicans. The threat was perceived by the oppressors rather than made by the oppressed.

Next, she thanked the opponents of repeal for stirring up people who had previously had no objection to dissenters but were now terrified of unknown dangers. 'How quick the alarm has been taken, and sounded from the church to the senate, and from the press to the people; while fears and forebodings were communicated like an electric shock!' She sarcastically observed that she had had no idea that the established church was so weak, so vulnerable to attack.

'What! fenced and guarded as she is with her exclusive privileges and rich emoluments, stately with her learned halls and endowed colleges, with all the attraction of her wealth, and the thunder of her censures . . . does she, resting in security under the broad buckler of the state, does she tremble at the naked and unarmed sectary? him, whose early connexions and phrase uncouth, and unpopular opinions, set him at distance from the means of advancement; him, who in the intercourses of neighbourhood and common life, like new settlers, finds it necessary to clear the ground before him, and is ever obliged to root up a prejudice before he can plant affection?'

Dissenters did not wish to destroy the Church of England, but only 'to be considered as children of the state, though we are not so of the church'. This did not seem to Anna Laetitia to be too much. 'But', she said:

'it is objected to us that we have sinned in the manner of making our request, we have brought it forward as a claim instead of asking it as a favour. We should have sued, and crept, and humbled our selves. Our preachers and our writers should not have dared to express the warm glow of honest sentiment, or even in a foreign country glance at the downfall of a haughty aristocracy. As we were suppliants, we should have behaved like suppliants, and then perhaps – No, gentlemen, we wish to have it understood that we do claim it as a right. It loses otherwise half its value.'

Like the idea that equality might be acceptable only if the people demanding it would grovel for it, Anna Laetitia found the word 'toleration' objectionable. 'What you call toleration', she said 'we call the exercise of a natural and inalienable right. We do not conceive it to be toleration, first to strip a man of all his dearest rights, and then to give him back a part; or even if it were the whole'. The next objection to pass under her eye was that what dissenters wanted was not religious liberty, but power. Dissenters wanted access to public office, but, she demanded, 'why should citizens not aspire to civil offices? Why should not the fair field of generous competition be freely opened to every one?'. Dissenters did not want to be constantly treated as different, but 'It is you, who by considering us as aliens, make us so. It is you who force us to make our dissent a prominent feature in our character'.

At this point Anna Laetitia switched to examining the motives of her opponents. Perhaps, she said, the objections were not moral or religious, but 'mathematical'. Perhaps Anglicans were afraid of the competition, and thought that if dissenters were allowed to apply for civil offices, good candidates would outnumber the mediocre. In that case, she said, again dripping sarcasm, 'we have been accusing you wrongfully. Your conduct is founded upon principles as sure and unvarying as mathematical truths; and all further discussion is needless. We drop the argument at once. Men have now and then been reasoned out of their prejudices, but it were a hopeless attempt to reason them out of their interest'.

The establishment had determined to view dissent as somehow shameful, but in Anna Laetitia's opinion, 'it is in our power to determine whether it shall be a disgraceful stigma or an honourable distinction'. She enumerated all the benefits of commerce, science, education and philosophy that dissenters brought, and noted that people would 'pay the involuntary homage due to genius, and boast of our names when, amongst foreign societies, you are inclined to do credit to your country'. Moreover, by excluding dissenters from office, Parliament had ensured that there would always be an honest extra-parliamentary opposition, since: 'We have no favours to blind us, no golden padlock on our tongues, and therefore it is probable enough, that, if cause is given, we shall cry aloud and spare not.' Far from being a threat, however, she thought that the dissenting community had in some ways become too comfortable with itself and had begun to melt 'into the bosom of the church under the warm influence of prosperity'. On the face of it, this melting might be considered a good thing, but, she warned Anglicans, dissenters brought with them inquiring and critical minds. If they were to be added to the many Anglicans who already 'in their hearts dissent from your professions of faith', the church would indeed be in danger from within. Dissenters had no actual desire to disestablish the Anglican church. In fact, the danger might arise from disaffected members of the church itself rather than those outside it.

She then turned to the reaction of dissenters themselves to the failure of the Bill. They were not downcast by their defeat, she said; in fact:

> 'You will excuse us if we do not appear with the air of men baffled and disappointed. Neither do we blush at our defeat; – we may blush, indeed, but it is for our country: but we lay hold on the consoling persuasion, that reason, truth and liberality must finally prevail. . . . You will grant us all we ask. The only question between us is, whether you will do it today; tomorrow you certainly will. You will even entreat us, if need were, to allow you to remove from your country the stigma of illiberality.'

Finally, she made an extended defence of the dissenting view of the French Revolution and the thinking around it. 'Whatever is loose must be shaken', she said,

> 'whatever is corrupted must be lopt away; whatever is not built on the broad basis of public utility must be thrown to the ground. Obscure murmurs gather, and swell into a tempest; the spirit of Inquiry, like a severe and searching wind, penetrates every part of the great body politic . . .'

Anna Laetitia understood that what was happening across the Channel was changing the world far beyond France in fundamental ways, and believed that it was foolish not to expect there to be repercussions in England.

> 'You see a mighty empire breaking from bondage, and exerting the energies of recovered freedom; and England—which was used to glory in being the assertor of liberty and refuge of the oppressed—England, who with generous and respectful sympathy, in times not far remote from our own memory, afforded an asylum to so many of the subjects of that very empire, when crushed beneath the iron rod of persecution; and, by so doing, circulated a livelier abhorrence of

tyranny within her own veins—England, who has long reproached her with being a slave, now censures her for daring to be free.'

England, said Anna Laetitia, referring to Burke's question about the existence of France, 'presumes to ask whether she yet exists', simply because the structures of the old tyrannies have fallen. However, '. . . all of her exists that is worthy to do so'; the dungeons, cloisters and nobility had gone and 'Millions of men exist there, who only now truly begin to exist, and hail with shouts of grateful acclamation the better birthday of their country'. At the point at which she was writing, in March 1790, the September Massacres and the Reign of Terror lay in the future, and radicals and dissenters still had reason to hope that the Revolution would be able to succeed. 'May you never', she said, addressing France directly in her closing text:

> 'lose sight of the great principle you have held forth, the natural equality of men. May you never forget that without public spirit there can be no liberty; that without virtue there may be a confederacy, but cannot be a community. . . . Triumph or despondency at the success or failure of our plans, would be treason to the large, expanded, comprehensive wish which embraces the general interests of humanity. . . . In this hope we look forward to the period when the name of Dissenter shall no more be heard of than that of Romanist or Episcopalian; when nothing shall be venerable but truth, and nothing valued but utility.'

This document is worth quoting at such length not just because it was written by a woman, or because of its immediacy and clarity, but because it reflects both its own times and those which came later. Many of the arguments and aspirations Anna Laetitia put forward were repeated again and again in different places and contexts in succeeding centuries. Many of them were not new when she made them, but she presented them in such a coherent manner, and with such force, that it is hard to resist the temptation to think that, had it been written about the position of women instead of dissenters, or had it been written by a man, it would be better remembered now.

The *Address* was well-received by those who agreed with it and reviled by those who did not. In particular, her defence of the Revolution came to seem more and more reprehensible in some quarters, and increasingly naïve in others. As time and events wore on, her own opinions also changed, although, like Helen Maria Williams, she never lost faith in the fundamental rightness of ideas of liberty and democracy. The *Address* launched her into a second literary career, and she continued to produce both prose and poetry supporting and explaining her views. In 1791, and despite much hope in abolitionist quarters, Parliament rejected a motion from William Wilberforce to halt the slave trade. Sadly, the majority against was significant, and fuelled by fear of being unable to compete with the French in the colonies should war come. Like many others, Anna Laetitia was bitterly disappointed and wrote a poetic *Epistle to William Wilberforce Esq. On the Rejection of the Bill for Abolishing the Slave Trade*. She understood, not only that the rejection was wrong, but that it was also shameful, both in the outcome and in the way in which the debate had been conducted in the House of Commons, when some MPs had sniggered at the story of a baby being tortured to death in front of its mother on a slave ship. Anna Laetitia sent a copy of her poem to the conservative abolitionist and author Hannah More, who liked it, but when Hannah in turn tried to persuade Horace Walpole to read it he declined on the grounds that he could not forgive 'the heart of a woman that is *party per pale [split down the middle]* blood and tenderness, that curses our clergy and feels for the negroes . . . [she] may cant rhymes of compassion but she is a hypocrite . . . *Your* compassion for the poor blacks is genuine, sincere from your soul, most amiable; hers a measure of faction'.[8]

In fact, the *Wilberforce* poem marks an early and, at the time, unusual, public statement of an idea that later became all too familiar, that a nation collectively could have all the ghastly details of evil explained to it and still intentionally choose that evil over good. Abolitionists had run a well-organized campaign of information aimed at both the public and parliamentarians, and no MP who voted against Wilberforce's motion could possibly have done so in ignorance of what he was voting to maintain. Anna Laetitia understood that this wilful acceptance of a manifest wrong would have consequences, and that it would, and should, be remembered as infamous by future generations both at home and around the world.

Early in 1793, Britain finally declared war on France. For most of the next twenty-two years, the two countries faced each other around the globe, dragging all of Europe into the dispute as well as the Caribbean, the Americas, the Ottoman Empire from Egypt to Morocco and the African slave trading ports. The colossal bloodshed and destruction of the conflict was not matched until the First World War a century later, and it is perhaps during these years that much of the mythology about gallant little Britain facing the world alone was born and codified. Initially, at least, there was much enthusiasm for the war, thought this was not shared by everybody, and many dissenters, in particular, were opposed to it from the start. Apart from the Quakers, most were not necessarily pacifists, but they did consider war to be a last resort, and they did not believe it right to shed British blood to restore a monarchy with which the French people themselves had decided to dispense. As was customary at times of national crisis, including wars, the King decreed a day of national fasting and prayer, to be observed by Anglicans and dissenters alike. A flurry of pamphlets and tracts followed. Again, Anna Laetitia took up her pen to attack the establishment, this time with less immediate rage but considerable courage. The government had already begun its repression of opposition and what Anna Laetitia was about to say came much closer to the edge of sedition than her *Address*. Nevertheless, she believed that she had a duty to speak, and *Sins of the Government, Sins of the Nation, or a Discourse for the Fast* was the result.

The climate in which Anna Laetitia wrote in 1793 was very different from that of 1790. The September Massacres had happened the previous year, and Louis XVI had been executed in January. Mary Wollstonecraft, whom Anna Laetitia knew if for no other reason than that in Joseph Johnson they shared a publisher, had just arrived in France, and Helen Maria Williams was still holding court in her Paris salon. In England, the initial wave of revolutionary enthusiasm had subsided, and a fierce reaction was beginning to set in. During four days of rioting in July 1791, 'Church and King' mobs in Birmingham had wreaked havoc, burning down the dissident scientist Joseph Priestley's house and laboratory and destroyed dissenting chapels and the homes of other leading non-conformist families. There was a strong suspicion that the riots had been instigated by local magistrates, and certainly a blind eye had been turned to them by the authorities. Priestley, a friend of Anna Laetitia's, was one of the great minds of his generation, but the intolerance and violence he was subjected to in Britain forced him eventually to emigrate to America.

Nor was the persecution restricted to famous people, such as Priestley. Anna Laetitia's brother, John, was a doctor in Yarmouth and found his practice vanishing before his eyes. People who had previously been friendly now practically ignored him, and there were moves to replace him as the town's physician. Even his children felt the weight of prejudice; his daughter Lucy later said that:

'It would scarcely be believed were I to recount the bitter persecution we poor children underwent . . . Children persecuted by children for words, for names, of the meaning of which none of them had the slightest conception. I have sat a whole evening while others were dancing, because nobody would dance with a Presbyterian. I have been pushed, hustled, even struck as I stood silent and helpless to the cry of Presbyterian.'[9]

Thus when she came to write *Sins of the Government, Sins of the Nation,* Anna Laetitia Barbauld was all too well aware of the dangers such outspokenness might present. The Birmingham mob's treatment of Priestley had enraged and saddened her, and she had already published a poem in his defence in which she criticized people who had stood by and not helped him and his family. But, in the increasingly fearful loyalist mind, dissenters were now irredeemably connected with revolution, and although Horace Walpole's detestation of anyone who even remotely sympathized with France may have been extreme, it was now much closer to government policy than it had been in 1790. *Sins of the Government* was less hopeful than the *Address* had been, and even more scathing of the British establishment. It also set out anti-war sentiments with clarity and persuasive force at a time when such opinions were contentious and militarism was commonplace.

She began by examining the differences between nations and individuals and how and when each should identify and repent of their sins. She considered the duties of the citizen in relation to his government; 'a good government', she said 'is the first of national duties', but required constant vigilance, since 'a people born under a good government will probably not die under one, if they conceive of it as of an indolent and passive happiness, to be left for its preservation to fortunate conjunctures, and the floating and variable chances of incalculable events; – our second duty is to keep it good'.[10]

She accepted that people should consider themselves subordinate to the law, but immediately made what was, for the time, a revolutionary assertion: 'To fix this subordination on its proper basis, it is only necessary to establish in our minds this plain principle, that the will of the minority should ever yield to that of the majority.' At this time no country, not even France or America, had universal suffrage, and even the best-run of countries was governed by privileged minorities. Anna Laetitia had visited the nature of democracy in her 1792 *Civic Sermons to the People*, where she had proposed the equally alarming idea that 'In bad Governments, such as Turkey, Government is a plot against the people, and therefore in all probability they will not obey it when once, they come to find out the plot', and although she had immediately added 'no one, I hope, will presume to say it is so in this kingdom',[11] her meaning was pretty clear. In *Sins of the Government* she pointed out that if the will of the majority was accepted 'the largest society may be held together with equal ease as the smallest, provided only some well-contrived and orderly method be established for ascertaining that will'. She did not explain what that method might be, but she was generally more interested in principles than process, and in any case that was for each country to work out for itself. She also saw that there were 'two descriptions of men who are in danger of forgetting this excellent rule; public functionaries and reformers'. The former she thought were 'very apt to confound the executive power with the governing will; they require, therefore, to be observed with a wholesome suspicion, and to be frequently reminded of the nature and limits of their office'. But she also saw that sometimes reformers were prone to assume that they knew best even if everybody else disagreed with them. 'Reformers', she said 'conceiving of themselves as of a more enlightened class than the bulk of mankind', were apt to 'contemn (the) swinish multitude' if the multitude did not fall in behind them, or see the world in the same way that they did. They wanted 'people to be happy their way; whereas every one must be happy his own way. Freedom is a good thing; but if a nation is not disposed to accept of it, it is not to be presented to them on the point of a bayonet'.

When it came to how nations should relate to other countries, she cautioned Britain against believing itself always to be better than every other, pointing out that: 'An exclusive admiration of ourselves is generally founded on extreme ignorance, and it is not likely to produce any thing of a more liberal or better stamp.' She also attacked the kind of patriotism that depended on undermining other countries:

'We should be ashamed to say, My neighbour's house was burnt down last night, I am glad of it, I shall have more custom to my shop. . . . but we are not ashamed to say, Our neighbours are weakening themselves by a cruel war, we shall rise upon their ruins. . . . Our neighbours have bad laws and a weak government: Heaven forbid they should change them for then they might be more flourishing than ourselves.'

She then embarked upon a sustained attack upon the wars Britain had waged in the past:

'When we carry our eyes back through the long records of our history, we see wars of plunder, wars of conquest, wars of religion, wars of pride, wars of succession, wars of idle speculation, wars of unjust interference; and hardly among them one war of necessary self-defence in any of our essential or very important interests. Of late years, indeed, we have known none of the calamities of war in our own country but the wasteful expense of it; and sitting aloof from those circumstances of personal provocation, which in some measure might excuse its fury, we have calmly voted slaughter and merchandized destruction—so much blood and tears for so many rupees, or dollars, or ingots. Our wars have been wars of cool calculating interest, as free from hatred as from love of mankind; the passions which stir the blood have had no share in them. We devote a certain number of men to perish on land and sea, and the rest of us sleep sound, and, protected in our usual occupations, talk of the events of war as what diversifies the flat uniformity of life.'

She suggested that when it came to setting the army and navy budgets, Parliament should be more honest about what it was doing and set down:

'—so much for killing, so much for maiming, so much for making widows and orphans, so much for bringing famine upon a district, so much for corrupting citizens and subjects into spies and traitors, so much for ruining industrious tradesmen and making bankrupts (of that species of distress at least we can form an idea,) so much for letting loose the daemons of fury, rapine, and lust, within the fold of cultivated society, and giving to the brutal ferocity of the most ferocious, its full scope and range of invention. We shall by this means know what we have paid our money for, whether we have made a good bargain, and whether the account is likely to pass . . .'

This was dangerous talk, not helped by the fact that she then went on to say that: 'In this guilty business there is a circumstance which greatly aggravates its guilt, and that is the impiety of calling upon the Divine Being to assist us in it.' By criticizing the very concept of the Fast Day itself, she was perilously close to criticizing the monarch who had decreed it, but Anna Laetitia was not a woman to flinch from what she believed to be the truth, and thought that people ought to take personal as well as collective responsibility for what was happening. She ended by saying that:

'What ever part we take in public affairs, much will undoubtedly happen which we could by no means foresee, and much which we shall not be able to justify; the only way, therefore, by which we can avoid deep remorse, is to act with simplicity and singleness of intention, and not to suffer ourselves to be warped, though by ever so little, from the path which honour and conscience approve.'

Sins of the Government, Sins of the Nation was received with disgust in loyalist quarters, and the conservative press was quick to try to identify Anna Laetitia with dangerous revolutionary politics. The *British Critic* called her 'This gallicised lady', and accused her of speaking 'the direct language of the present Convention of France'. The reviewer also pointed out that if women entered the masculine field of politics they must accept the consequences; 'when ladies condescend to write political pamphlets, they must condescend also to have their arguments examined.'[12] There is nothing to suggest that Anna Laetitia in any way objected to having her arguments examined, and, though often in more muted terms, she continued to make them for the next twenty years. Though bitterly disappointed by the course of the French Revolution, and dismayed by the British government's relentless repression of reformers and anyone else who disagreed with it, she retained the fundamental pro-democracy, anti-war opinions with which she had started.

In other ways, too, her life had its darker moments. For years her husband suffered from a recurring mental illness, one feature of which was that at times he became extremely violent towards her. She was, understandably given the state of mental health care at the turn of the nineteenth century, extremely reluctant to have him restrained or put into an asylum, but she also found it impossible to care for him herself. Eventually they began to live separately, but although this protected Anna Laetitia from his rages it made both of them miserable. In November 1808, Barbauld was found drowned in the New River. Anna Laetitia was devastated, and grieved for him for the rest of her life.

Despite this, she continued to work, and in 1812, one of the darkest years of the long war, she published her last major political work. Entitled *Eighteen Hundred and Eleven*, it was a long poem that again attacked the war, warning Britain that the idea that it could escape the consequences of the prolonged tragedy was delusional. 'Thou who hast shared the guilt', she said, 'must share the woe'; for her the war was still a shameful evil. She also looked forward to what Britain – and indeed Europe – was likely to become. Like many others, she saw the future as being in the New rather than the Old World, and thought that, eventually, the Old World would become just a kind of tourist attraction for visitors from the New. She envisaged a London in which visitors from many countries would come to marvel at the ruins of an empire that had over-reached itself and fallen, much as they might travel to see the remains of Athens or Rome. Towards the end of the poem she conjured the spirit of liberty sweeping through the world bringing hope and aspiration to even the most oppressed. The recent revolution in Venezuela had reinforced her continued belief in liberty as a life-giving force that even the disappointments of one revolution after another could not quench. Despite the gloom of much of the remainder of the poem she finished it on a high note of hope.

The reception *Eighteen Hundred and Eleven* received was as usual mixed, but at a time when the forces of reaction were in full flow, the balance was against her. She was 'the Cassandra of the state' (the *Monthly Review*), 'unkindly and unpatriotic' (the *Eclectic Review*) and painted a scene which 'a *true* patriot would shudder but to glance at' (the *Anti-Jacobin Review*). The *Quarterly Review* was thunderous in its condemnation.

> '. . . she must excuse us if we think that she has wandered from the course in which she was respectable and useful, and miserably mistaken both her powers and her duty . . . abandoning the superintendence of the . . . nursery, to wage war on the . . . statesmen and warriors whose misdoings have aroused her indignant muse.
>
> 'We had hoped, indeed, that the empire might have been saved without the intervention of a lady-author . . . Mrs Barbauld's former works have been of some utility: her 'Lessons for Children', her 'Hymns in Prose', . . . though they display not much of either taste or talents, are yet something better than harmless: but we must take the liberty of warning her to desist from satire . . .'[13]

Worst of all, poets such as Southey and Wordsworth, who had admired her during their radical youth, were now respectably conservative and unsparing in their hostility. Wordsworth even described her as 'the old Snake Letitia Barbauld'.[14]

In 1812 Anna Laetitia was nearly seventy, and the virulence and sheer nastiness of some of the criticism was highly distressing. *Eighteen Hundred and Eleven* turned out to be the last of her political works. In 1824 she worked with her niece, Lucy Aikin, to put together a retrospective collection of her work, which was published after her death in 1825. It included some of her political work, but by then the upheavals of the 1790s seemed far away, and her reputation was almost impossible to retrieve. The 1820s were as reactionary as the 1790s, and when Lucy contemplated writing a memorial about her father and aunt, she knew all too well how their political views would be received. 'But think', she lamented 'of the age we live in! – think of the Quarterly Review, the Saints, the clergy, the Tories & the canters & tell me how we are to be at once safe and honest'.[15] In the nineteenth century, Anna Laetitia came to be remembered as a rather old-fashioned poet and children's author, at least in part because the Victorian middle classes remembered her children's books from their nurseries and did not care to look at anything else. Since her politics were rooted in religious dissent rather than feminism, she has little appeal for anyone interested only in the history of women as feminists. Yet, as a political writer, she had rare vision, great courage and the ability to convey complicated ideas in straightforward language.

Anna Laetitia Barbauld, Helen Maria Williams and Mary Wollstonecraft all lived through a period of great change both in Britain and around the world, and although they responded to it, recorded it and reflected on it in different ways, they all brought courage, intelligence and ability to the task. But, they were by no means alone, and hundreds of now-forgotten women thought, wrote and argued about the times through which they lived. However, these were almost entirely middle-class women; working-class women's voices were rare. Although many were able to read, far fewer were taught to write, and fewer still had the time to produce pamphlets or books. Despite this, many took a keen interest in what was happening around them, particularly since the war and a fluctuating economy directly affected every aspect of their lives. *Eighteen Hundred and Eleven* was well received in the working-class reading groups of the North of England and the Midlands, where relatively recently urbanized communities were grappling with a hostile economic and political climate. Together with a resurgence of interest in democratic reform, this struggle was driving new (and some old) forms of resistance and protest in which women began to take a more prominent role.

PART TWO

More Turbulent than the Men

Although the principal focus of revolutionary fervour in the 1790s had been in London, it had also spread across the country, and particularly into the industrial areas of the Midlands and the North. In corresponding societies, book clubs, schools, homes, public houses and even churches, revolutionary ideas were discussed with enthusiasm at many levels of society. This was particularly true in the weaving towns and villages of Lancashire and Yorkshire, where a new working class was rapidly springing up in expanding urban industrial centres. Here there were great fortunes to be made from the mechanization of old trades, but the absence of either regulation or welfare provision meant that workers often found themselves caught in a trap of exploitation and appalling working conditions. At the same time, new rural enclosures were driving people off the land and into towns ill-equipped to receive them. Independent craftsmen, such as handloom weavers, who had previously been able to make a decent living on the whole, were now undercut by machines in the factories. Both employers and employees were at the mercy of a cycle of economic boom and bust that brought prosperity in the good times but general misery in the bad. With no safety net other than that which they could provide collectively themselves through benefit clubs and societies, working-class families were at constant risk of being suddenly plunged into penury and starvation. Housing that had been thrown up in haste in places such as

Manchester and Leeds was often badly built, over-crowded and lacking in sanitation. Disease was rife. Moreover, the new ways of working were upending centuries-old social and economic roles. Since time immemorial, spinning had been a female occupation carried out by women and their daughters at home; now, it was done in mills on machinery so heavy and complicated that spinning was increasingly seen as men's work, whilst women were increasingly employed in the traditionally male job of weaving. Children were employed in both, and although most parents hated having to send their children out to work, many families could not survive without the additional wages.

The industrial revolution brought mixed fortunes to the lives of working-class women. The higher a woman's social status, the more restricted her life traditionally was, particularly before she was married. Working-class women tended to marry later than their middle-class sisters, although for both, the average age of marriage was in the mid-twenties rather than the teenage years. Working-class women had often been at work since the age of seven or eight, and might have had nearly twenty years of relative independence before they married. Married women who worked in mills and factories also spent much more time outside their homes and away from their husbands' influence. They were more likely than middle-class women to be able to leave the house unchaperoned. They could be better paid – at least in the good times – than they otherwise might have been, and had more control over the family's money. Arguably, they gained personal freedom and were able to develop an existence independent of their domestic responsibilities. Middle-class people were often intimidated by the fierce and assertive behaviour of urban working-class women, who did not always conform to the stereotypes expected of them.

However, working-class women were also likely to suffer from high levels of domestic violence, drunkenness and poverty, and the new work environments could be dangerous places. The machinery in them often had to be kept working day and night with virtually no regard for safety at all. Employers, foremen and male co-workers might all regard women and girls as fair game, and sexual harassment and assault were rife. Then, as now, women had to carry responsibility for domestic arrangements as well as for work; childcare was rarely available other than through relatives or friends, and menfolk still expected to be fed, looked after and obeyed. Responsibility for housework and cooking was now additional to shifts in the mill. Women in rural areas also found their lives changing for the worse as wages fell and enclosures bit. Young people moving to the town for work often sent money back to keep their parents and siblings afloat. The awful spectre of abject poverty, food shortages and starvation loomed large over almost all working-class lives, wherever they were lived.

Where communities suffered from a lessening of population or industry, women felt the same sense of loss and dislocation as the men, but where employment opportunities increased they usually – though not invariably – did so for both sexes. However, women were usually paid considerably less than men, and employers were quick to take advantage of this. Women were cheaper to employ, and there were complaints about them being used as strike breakers or to deskill traditionally male occupations. There was anxiety about the changing social and domestic roles of women, particularly when they seemed to acquire new levels of independence or when the necessity of earning a wage prevented them from caring full-time for husbands and children. Nor was disapproval of female employment limited to the middle classes. The radical campaigner and reformer Francis Place, for instance, said that he had:

'always deprecated the employment of women in every regularly conducted trade. Women have enough to do to attend to their homes, their husbands, their children, their relatives, and such light labour as can be done at home; their place is home; . . . All is turned upside down, when the woman is turned out of her home and turned into a mill or workshop . . .'[1]

In the absence of votes, representation or voice in public affairs, working-class men and women had always taken to the streets to express their grievances. Both rural and urban populations rioted, often in opposition to specific events or pieces of legislation. The most common riot issue was food in one form or another, particularly when prices were rising. At a time when the amount and cost of food available was heavily dependent on a combination of the weather, the skill and resources of producers, and the reliability of predominantly local supply chains, the prospect of famine if things went wrong was always a reality. One bad harvest could mean shortages and high prices; several bad harvests could spell starvation. On top of this, and despite various legal attempts to control profiteering, prices could always be forced up by sharp practices and the creation of false shortages. Amongst the middle and upper classes there was much hand-wringing over what could be done to mitigate the problems, but there were few solutions. 1790s radicals such as Mary Wollstonecraft and Tom Paine often thought that poverty could be solved by root and branch changes to the way in which land was owned, distributed, managed and taxed, but had relatively few ideas on how to deal with industrialization. Riot could not deal with it either, but it did provide people who were otherwise politically helpless with a sense of power, the possibility of food and (generally) relatively little risk of retribution.

Both Parliament and local authorities were alarmed by riots and spent much time and effort trying to contain the activities of crowds. To this end, the Riot Act, passed in 1714,[2] gave local officials (magistrates, mayors, sheriffs and even the local constable) the power to declare gatherings of more than twelve people unlawful, and to take whatever measures they thought fit in order to disperse them. Before doing so, however, they had to read out to the crowd a very short set form of words warning them to go home peacefully or face the consequences. This was known as 'reading the Riot Act', and unless it was done properly, any actions the authorities subsequently took were illegal. Prosecutions for riot often turned upon whether the Riot Act had or had not been read in the prescribed manner, or even at all. Both judges and juries, particularly by the end of the eighteenth century, were increasingly keen on things being done by the book, and juries often refused to convict if the correct procedure had not been complied with. This does not mean that middle-class men found rioting acceptable, but simply that there was an increasingly strong sense that even the poor should not be condemned without due legal process. Loss of life was generally much greater amongst the protesters than their targets, and punishments could be extreme for the few who were convicted, but despite this riots remained a recurring feature of life, particularly whilst the supply of basic staple foods could be so uncertain.

For many decades the policy of successive governments had been to protect the producers of food rather than the consumers. This was mainly expressed through a series of laws that sought to control the import and export of grain. The new industrial middle classes tended to be advocates of free trade, but since they lacked any presence in Parliament, they were unable to prevent governments protecting the interests of the landowners, many of whom also owned parliamentary seats and could put their own men into the Commons. Legally, grain could only be imported once shortages had pushed domestic prices up to a certain level. This often forced the cost of bread beyond the reach of working-class families, and inevitably hit the poorest hardest, particularly if other factors driving down wages were also at play. In some parts of Northern England, Scotland and Ireland, potatoes had become an alternative source of cheap food, but they were dangerously susceptible to poor harvests when the weather was bad. Butter, always considered a necessity to make hard bread and old potatoes more palatable, could be affected by the milk supply, which was in turn dependent upon grazing. In some years a perfect storm of food shortages, depressed wages and high prices could reduce the labouring classes to destitution. 1812 was one of those years. A series of bad harvests, coupled with the outbreak of war with the United States, rising unemployment, short hours and falling incomes left people desperate. An apronful of flour or potatoes really could make the difference between life and death.

For many women the awful business of trying to feed a family when there was nothing to eat was crushing, and occasionally it is possible to hear their desperation in their own voices. In 1817 a man called Joseph Mitchell was arrested as part of a round-up of radical agitators leaving his wife Elizabeth with six children and no money. In July of that year she wrote wretchedly to him that: 'If you was to see the Clamring around me when sharing thare scanty meal and hear the Cry for more . . . when I have not any to give them it whould make your heart bleed and your Eyes start . . .'[3] Another woman, Charlotte Johnston apologized to her husband, John, for not having written sooner because she had been 'rather indispose(d) with a cold and I rather think it is through getting my feet wet as I have never been able to get a pair of shoes since you have been from me and us'.[4]

These glimpses of women's struggles have only survived because the Home Office was intercepting the mail, but Elizabeth and Charlotte spoke for hundreds of thousands of families for whom grinding poverty was a daily reality. Many middle-class people were sympathetic, and women, in particular, were often involved in providing charitable relief to the starving, but they could not quite bring themselves to understand the helplessness and misery that drove people into the only form of action they felt was open to them. Edward Baines, the editor of the *Leeds Mercury* spoke for many when he observed in August 1812 that:

> 'We know that the distresses of the poor are extreme, and feel most anxious for their alleviation or removal; but that is not to be effected by riot and violence, for it must be obvious to all, that corn will not be made cheap by destroying it, nor the markets better supplied by intimidating the farmers and preventing them from bringing the corn to market.'[5]

The fact that Elizabeth Mitchell and Charlotte Johnston could write to their husbands at all is testament to the level of education achieved by many pre-Victorian working-class people. Both boys and girls were taught to read either in Sunday schools, factory classes or charity schools, and although girls were less likely to learn to write it was by no means uncommon. Literacy levels at the turn of the nineteenth century were, on average, higher than they became later, and this fed the ability of the working class to read and absorb radical and revolutionary newspapers and books. People did not necessarily gather together to hear someone read aloud because they themselves were illiterate, but because the price of printed materials usually put them out of reach for most families and precious copies therefore had to be shared.

Many of the news stories people were reading in 1811 and 1812 were about Luddite machine-breakers. Luddism had first appeared in 1779 when the original Ned Ludd – probably mythical – was said to have smashed a stocking frame in Nottingham in a fit of rage. There had been sporadic outbursts of frame and machine breaking in the years since, in many cases highly organized and with very specific objectives. Because the Luddites ultimately lost the argument, it is perhaps too easy now to forget what their case actually was. Working-class people were by no means opposed to progress generally, but they were dismayed by the deskilling of entire communities, the consequent loss (even if only temporary) of earning power and therefore of living standards, and the loss of personal agency and independence that the unfettered growth of industrialization seemed to bring. Since Luddites rarely left contemporaneous memoirs or accounts of their motives and actions, they tend to be seen only through the eyes of people for whom free trade and unconstrained competition were desirable and even ultimately inevitable. Luddites were often characterized as ignorant, short-sighted and ultimately doomed, and some of this thinking has endured. To this day the word 'Luddite' is understood to mean an ignorant person who resists new technology or ways of working, and refuses to recognize the reality of the future. But in 1812 Luddism was much more about the lack of choice people felt they had about what their future might be and a resistance to the industrial exploitation they were being forced to accept. Much Luddite activity was carefully targeted and planned, and even enjoyed some short-term success.

Very few women were directly involved in machine breaking, though Luddite leaders were by no means unknown to dress in women's clothing and style themselves 'General Ludd's wives' or 'Lady Ludd'. However, there is evidence that women were sometimes involved in the planning and organizing of attacks; in 1788, for instance, a group of women wool spinners in Leicester calling themselves the 'Sisterhood' organized protests against the changes that were happening in their industry. If these were more gradual, they argued: 'the evil would be less; old persons would go off, and young ones be brought up to this new-fashioned employment', but as it was, the masters were employing children to do the work of women, and then sacking them as soon as they had to pay them an adult wage. An unsympathetic response from the employers led to the Sisterhood '(stirring) up all the men they could influence (not a few) to go and destroy the mills erected in and near Leicester . . .'[6] This was not successful in halting the changes, but the Leicester women were not alone in turning to collective action to help solve their problems. Around the country women were setting up benefit societies and trade unions, and although none survived for very long, women were as alive as men to the possibilities of organization. They could also shock 'respectable' middle-class opinion; in 1808, reporting on a weavers' strike in Manchester, The Times correspondent noted that 'The women are, if possible, more turbulent and mischievous than the men. Their insolence to the soldiers and special constables is intolerable, and they seem to be confident of deriving impunity from their sex'.[7]

In 1808 the cause of parliamentary reform was still in retreat after the treason trials of the 1790s and the series of repressive Acts of Parliament. However, by 1812 it had begun to return with renewed vigour, and after the end of the Napoleonic War in 1815 it became the main focus of much working-class activity around the country. This time, however, it was driven, not just by constitutional thinkers and revolutionary enthusiasts, but by women and men who believed that access to political power was their only hope, and that it could be achieved by reforming Parliament and the electoral system.

The parliamentary system as it existed in 1815 was deeply corrupt, and had been so for more than a century. The electorate was tiny, possession of a vote depended on ownership of qualifying property and every constituency had its own rules for who could vote. In theory, the franchise was accessible by anyone in the country, whatever their birth, since all they had to do was raise enough money to buy or rent a qualifying property. In some constituencies, where the requirement was a hearth and a pot to boil on it (the so-called pot-walloper seats), this could be relatively cheap, especially if any local residency requirements could be circumvented. However, the number of properties was severely limited, and for most people the prospect of getting one in practice was vanishingly remote. By and large, Parliament did not either represent working people or see the need to represent them, but as the industrial revolution began to change the face of some parts of the country, the mismatch between population and constituencies grew increasingly obvious, and the venality of the system glaring. This was particularly the case where the geographical nature of the relentless industrial expansion also meant that economic fortunes varied between different parts of the country. Ancient wool towns in East Anglia and the Cotswolds, which had been busy, wealthy and populous under the old methods of manufacture, began to fade as production moved to huge new mills closer to the fast-flowing rivers and streams of Yorkshire and Lancashire. Urban areas expanded exponentially as industries grew. Between 1773 and 1801 the population of Manchester grew from 25,000 souls to 90,000; by 1850 it was more than 400,000. In Leeds, a population of 30,000 in 1800 had sprung up to 150,000 by 1840. Similarly, in 1800 Birmingham accommodated nearly 75,000 people; by 1850 this had become more than a quarter of a million. Across the industrialized areas this pattern was repeated as the building of more and more mills and factories created the need for more and more cheap labour. In an electoral system designed in and for a different age, neither the emerging middle classes nor the burgeoning working classes had any formal presence in the body politic.

To make matters worse, elections themselves were also deeply corrupt. Successful candidates needed either to be very rich, or to have a relative or patron who owned a pocket borough. Voting was carried out in person and in public, and there was no secret ballot. On the contrary, it was observed by large crowds of onlookers, alcohol was often freely available (and paid for by candidates) and it was by no means unknown for there to be violence and even rioting if things got out of hand. Landlords controlled significant numbers of parliamentary seats simply by owning a majority of the qualifying properties in any given constituency. Some of these landlords were women; in 1828, for instance, *The Times* noted that, in the Yorkshire town of Ripon, Sophia Elizabeth Lawrence of Studley Royal owned 'a decided majority' of the 146 burgage properties and 'of course really returns the members sent from this borough to Parliament'.[8] Constituencies and votes had a commercial value, and could be traded, given away or inherited. People who engaged in this trade were often known as 'boroughmongers' and were hated by reformers.

As the long years of the war drew to a close, working men and women began once more to challenge the process by which they were governed. As in the 1790s, however, the political establishment made no effort to understand or negotiate, and every attempt to achieve reform was treated as a step along the road to revolution, and repressed with varying degrees of savagery. The next few years would see an extraordinary flowering of working-class organization, followed by one of the most notorious tragedies of British political history.

Chapter 4

Determined Enemies to Good Order

Late one Friday afternoon in the spring of 1812, a crowd of about fifty people attacked a large factory at Westhoughton near Bolton. Led by two young women wielding mining implements, they set fire to it and cheered as it burned to the ground. Mary Molyneux and her sister, Lydia (later stated to be aged nineteen and fifteen respectively) were seen 'with Muck hooks and coal picks in their hands, breaking the Windows of the Buildings and swearing and cursing the souls of those that worked in the Factory'. They also egged the men on to burn it, shouting: 'Set fire to it! Now lads!'[1] The lads were only too happy to oblige; straw from the stables and a nearby inn provided fuel and it was reported that: '. . . the conflagration was tremendous. The damage sustained is immense, the factory alone having cost 6000l.'[2] Once the mill and its contents were well alight, the crowd moved on to nearby Westhoughton Hall. Here they set fire to the house, though this time with less success since most of it survived. Later there was a small food riot, but in the evening the military arrived, the Riot Act was read, the last of the rioters were dispersed and the perceived 'ringleaders' were arrested.

Over the next few days a dozen or so people, including the Molyneux sisters, were sent north to Lancaster to await trial. This in itself was a miserable process; the radical John Knight, arrested in Manchester a couple of months later, described being 'ironed together, and conveyed to Lancaster, a distance of fifty-five miles, without any other refreshment than a coffee breakfast, and a glass of beer each; and on our arrival we were put among persons accused of robbery, murder, and almost every species of crime'.[3] Lancaster Gaol, where the prisoners awaited trial, was an ancient and fearsome prison housed in the medieval castle. It was over-crowded and unsanitary, and inmates had to endure poor food, bad water and no privacy. Prisoners sentenced to hard labour were set to work on treadmills, whilst those condemned to transportation were sent to prison hulks to await the voyage. Hangings were carried out at the castle gate.

The situation in which Mary, Lydia and the accused men now found themselves must have been terrifying. Their alleged crimes were against the property of precisely such men as would be sitting on the jury sworn in to try them. Two judges, reputedly hand-picked by the Prime Minister Spencer Perceval, were sent up from London,[4] and a Special Commission was set up to try the cases from riots across Lancashire. Each jury was to sit for one day and hear whatever cases were put before it; jurors were required to remain until a verdict had been reached.

Seen from the perspective of the twenty-first century, the courts that tried Mary, Lydia and their fellow defendants on 26 May 1812 had many flaws, including the fact that, even though the charges were extremely serious, the trials took only a few hours and there was relatively little examination of the evidence. Proceedings began the day before with a religious service at which a sermon was preached on the text: 'My son, fear thou the Lord and the king: and meddle not with them that are given to change.'[5] When the trials began, the judge, Baron (also known as Sir Alexander) Thomson, followed this up by addressing the jury and 'exhorting them to use their utmost endeavours, in their respective neighbourhoods, to restore and promote the public tranquillity'.[6] Defendants were tried in batches, and the Molyneux sisters, together with twelve men and boys, were in the first. Proceedings began at 8.00 am and lasted for twelve hours. Since it could not be denied that the defendants had been at the riot, the defence tried to challenge the legal basis of the trial, but once this point had been dismissed, they had to rely on character witnesses and alibis, none of which made for a very strong case.

The jury retired at 8.00 pm and took an hour to reach its verdicts. All of the defendants were charged with offences for which the penalty could be death, and the judge had given the jurymen a pretty clear steer as to the direction in which they should go. However, despite all the evidence to the contrary, they acquitted ten of the accused, including both Mary and Lydia Molyneux. The remaining four – Abraham Charlson, Job Fletcher, Thomas Kerfoot and James Smith – were convicted, sentenced to death and hanged on Saturday, 13 June. Abraham Charlson was just sixteen years old. Another teenager, fifteen-year-old John Bromilow, may have been saved by the fact that on the night in question his mother had spotted him in the crowd and dragged him home with her before the fires were lit.

The sentences for those convicted that day were savage, but the rate of conviction, given that all those charged were manifestly guilty, was relatively low, and this persisted throughout the remaining riot trials at both Lancaster and Chester. Juries tended to convict those they thought were ringleaders and acquit others. They also acquitted those they did not want to see hanged; public unease over the extensive use of the death penalty at this time was growing and it was already becoming unusual for anyone under the age of sixteen to be executed. Mary and Lydia – who had clearly committed exactly the same offences as the condemned men – may have benefitted from a disinclination to hang very young women. But it was also the case that nobody had been killed at Westhoughton, and the jury may well have taken the view that there was no need to be unnecessarily punitive. If the death penalty was applied to one who was guilty, it would have to be applied to them all. The only way of ensuring that that could not happen was to acquit as many as possible.

The lack of any record of Lydia and Mary Molyneux's defence means that there is no explanation available in their own words for why they acted as they did. They must have said something at their trial, yet the only words we know them to have uttered are those urging the men on to arson. Their involvement in riots – or any other form of political action, for that matter – appears to have been an isolated incident; neither of them features again by name in any accounts of Luddite, radical or trade union activity, though this does not by any means mean that they did not participate. Nor do we know very much about what happened to them after their close brush with the gallows, though it is possible to piece together a few likely details about one of them.[7]

The Molyneux family of Westhoughton were not migrants from outside the area, but long-established local residents who had seen huge changes in their village. Many of these had occurred since Mary and Lydia were born in the early 1790s, and would have impacted directly upon their lives. The factory they helped to destroy had only been constructed in 1804, and as children they must have watched it go up and known local men employed in the building of it and the installation of the machinery.[8] Once it opened, local people would have been employed in it, but it would also have attracted workers from further afield. Between 1801 and 1811 the population of Westhoughton increased rapidly from around 3,000 to about 4,000,[9] and as the village grew so the community would have changed, and new people would have brought new customs and accents to the area.

A child called Lydia Molyneux was baptized in Westhoughton in July 1794, which means that she was seventeen rather than fifteen when she was involved in the riot. It was not uncommon for people to lie about their age, and many simply did not know it with any precision. Since it was to her advantage to appear as young as possible, it is hardly surprising if Lydia shaved a couple of years off, and since birth certificates did not exist in England until 1837 there was no way for the courts to check what she told them. After her acquittal, she seems to have returned to Westhoughton, where in 1819 she married John Seddon, a greengrocer of that town, with whom she had at least two children, including a daughter named Mary. She then lived a relatively long and unremarkable life until her death in 1861 at the age of sixty-seven. Of Mary Molyneux, however, there is no further trace. Even more than Lydia, Mary fades all too quickly back into the silent and shadowy history of working-class women and we hear no more of her.

Westhoughton was not the only incident in which women were directly involved. Several days before that attack, for instance, a mob said to consist of more than 2,000 men and women rampaged for two days at Middleton, near Manchester. On the first day the mill-owner, Emanuel Burton, defended his premises stoutly; the military were called out and shots were fired at the crowd. The number of casualties was unknown, but when Samuel Bamford, a radical weaver who worked in Manchester, arrived home he found the streets:

'. . . all quiet, the doors closed, and the alehouses silent. People's minds were however sadly agitated, and fierce denunciations were uttered against "Burton and his shooters," whilst very little anger was expressed against the men who had plundered shops. In the coat pocket of one of the killed was found a half pound of currants, the fruit, no doubt, of such plunder.'[10]

When he got home he was relieved to see his wife and child safe, but appalled to hear that:

> '. . . my wife, in her curiosity to watch a mob, had gone down the town, and with another thoughtless woman or two, had stood at the window of a cottage nearly opposite to the factory, within range of the shot, and only a few yards from the spot where one man was killed. I gave her a lecture for so doing, — the first perhaps since our marriage — and being convinced of her folly, she promised never to transgress in that way again, and I dare say she never has.'

A few years later Jemima Bamford would be one of the women at Peterloo, and would leave her own account of that event, whilst Samuel himself would go to prison for his part in it. In Middleton in 1812, however, he had a living to earn, and so went back to Manchester the next day, presumably leaving Jemima with instructions not to leave the house. The mob reconvened and recommenced the attack on Burton's mill but were again dispersed by the military. Once more there was considerable violence, and over the two days at least ten men were killed and many others injured. One woman was shot through the arm as she looked out of her window to see what was going on.

Emanuel Burton's mill was preserved, but his house did not fare so well, being ransacked and burned to the ground. In his memoirs Bamford said that two sisters, Nan and Clem, whom he described as 'the tall, dark-haired, and handsomely formed daughters of a venerable old weaver', were responsible for setting fire to it.

> '"Come," said one to the other, "let's put a finish to this job," and taking up a shred which lay on the floor, she lighted it at the fire which had been left burning in the grate. In a moment the sofa was on fire . . . at the expiration of probably half an hour, not a beam nor a board remained unconsumed in the whole building.'[11]

Nan and Clem escaped arrest and therefore were not prosecuted; hence we know nothing about them other than Bamford's account.

However, six men were charged with various offences and tried at Lancaster the day after Lydia and Mary Molyneux were acquitted. Their trial had the same judge but a different jury, which included a man referred to as 'Mr Ewart'.[12] Mr Ewart seems to have had strong views about the death penalty and had no intention of allowing the six men in the dock before him to be hanged if he could help it, and help it he did. According to the Attorney General's exasperated report to the Home Office:

> 'There were six others acquitted of the clearest case of arson, to the utter dissatisfaction of the whole Court, Mr. Ewart, . . . the Foreman of the Jury and the *sole* cause of the Mischief, having kept the Jury out an hour, before he could bring them over to his opinion.'[13]

The acquitted men were immediately charged with lesser offences for which they received jail sentences. A couple of days later Ann Butterworth,[14] Anne Dean, Alice Partington and Millicent Stoddard were sentenced to six months in prison apiece for being part of a crowd that attacked the houses of two men suspected of having fired on people outside the mill on the first day of the riot. Furniture was broken and burned, and a considerable amount of damage done, but nobody was injured or killed. Another woman, Ann Hamer from Barton-upon-Irwell, who had stolen an apronful of flour, was fined and sentenced to six months hard labour despite having turned herself in to the constables and having a blind mother to look after.

As we have seen, working-class women were rarely able to recount their experiences in these events for themselves. Occasionally, however, it is possible to hear the voices of other women involved. On 14 April, a large crowd of people appeared at the gates of a factory at Edgley, near Stockport. Conditions in the area were dreadful; not only was food scarce and prices high, but many of the weavers were Irish immigrants who were not eligible for what little help indigenous families could get from parish poor relief. The community had been simmering uneasily for weeks, and only ten days earlier the factory owner, John Goodair, had been shot at through the window of his house near the mill. The charitable interpretation of his immediate departure for London is that he went to enlist help, but he obviously thought it safe enough to leave his wife and family behind. Mrs Goodair knew what danger they were in, however; in her account of events published in *The Times* a few days later, she said that her household had been 'for some days under great apprehension of the mob'. Their unease was fully justified. The crowd surged around the gates and 'remained there for nearly an hour, calling to us at intervals to open our windows, and throwing stones in order to compel us to comply with their wishes'. When the windows remained firmly shut, the crowd moved off to Stockport, but later, and now swelled to about 3,000 in number, they returned in a much uglier mood. This time she noticed that they seemed to be headed by two men in women's clothes who were referred to as 'General Ludd's wives'. Mrs Goodair had to act quickly and so:

'On perceiving them from our cottage coming down the road, I assembled the children and nurse in the parlour, and fastened the windows and doors; the gardener presently rushed into the room. and conjured us to fly that moment, if we wished to save our lives. It was with difficulty I could speak; but each snatching up a child, we escaped at the great gate just in time to avoid the rabble. . . . Every thing, I have since learnt, was consumed by the fire, and nothing left but the shell.'[15]

In the wool-weaving districts of Yorkshire, the Luddite campaign seemed more organized than in Lancashire. Larger mills near Leeds and Wakefield were attacked and burned, and those which remained were often fortified like castles. William Cartwright of Rawfolds near Cleckheaton was even said to have a tub of oil of vitriol ready to be tipped onto any unwary assailants, and William Horsfall of Huddersfield had a cannon mounted on the roof of his mill. At the beginning of April, a couple of weeks before the riot at Westhoughton in Lancashire, the Luddites mounted a midnight attack on Cartwright's factory, as they did so marching stealthily past the farmhouse where the young curate Patrick Brontë lodged. He later told his children how he had heard the tramp of many feet passing by; years later his daughter Charlotte used the incident as the basis for her novel *Shirley.*[16] Cartwright had a handful of employees and soldiers to help defend the mill, and was well-prepared for the assault. Despite their greater numbers, the attackers could not break in, and when they retreated they left two wounded men behind them. Both subsequently died. Cartwright's victory had demonstrated that resistance backed up by force could succeed.

At the end of April, William Horsfall was murdered as he rode home from Huddersfield cloth market. The subsequent hunt for the ringleaders was lengthy, but in January 1813 a total of seventy men were tried at York for their part in the various events of the previous spring. Fourteen were hanged. However, Luddite activity had already begun to diminish, though general unrest was by no means extinguished, and the newspapers remained full of stories of arms raids and groups of men practising military drill on the moors. The *Leeds Mercury* reported in June 1812 that:

'On Saturday night, about ten o'clock, a number of men, with muskets, were seen performing the military exercise, . . . and about two o'clock on Sunday morning, 47 of them, all armed, passed through the village of Gawthorp, near Osset, where they obtained some guns, and several sums of money, which they are now in the habit of demanding.'[17]

There is no mention of any women involved in these events, perhaps because the level of organization involved required secret meetings in pubs and workplaces, but also because nocturnal quasi-military activity would have been more or less impossible for most women, even had the men been prepared to allow it. Food riots, however, were a different matter, and in the spring and summer of 1812 they erupted around the country. At Skipton in April, women pelted a potato seller with his own stock and at Knottingley, near Wakefield, a crowd of several hundred women tried to intercept barges on the Aire & Calder Navigation Canal. When that failed, they went into the town and forced flour sellers to lower their prices, the new ones being advertised by the town crier.[18] In Carlisle there were extensive riots during which several people, including one woman, were killed, and in April there was unrest in Sheffield when:

'a number of mischievous people assembled in the Market-place, where they seized the potatoes, fish and some other commodities exposed for sale, and threw *(them)* about the streets in most tumultuous manner; . . . they afterwards broke open several cellars in which potatoes were deposited, and threw the contents at each other, in doing which many windows were broken . . . it was now insinuated by some evil-disposed persons, that the fire-arms belonging to the Sheffield Militia should be destroyed . . . the mob proceeded to the Wicker, where the said arms were deposited . . . About one hundred stand of arms and the drums were broken and other damage committed.'[19]

Amongst those sent to York for trial was a woman called Mary Gibbons, who had allegedly stolen some military breeches and gaiters from the arms store. She was sentenced to a year in prison in York Castle for riot and theft. In August the *Leeds Intelligencer* reported that:

'In our Corn-market, last Tuesday, a spirit of insubordination and tumult was evinced by a mob of women and daring lads, which, if persisted in, must produce incalculable damage. . . . A woman, stiled *Lady Ludd* headed the mob; they hooted at every passenger who had the appearance of a farmer or corn-dealer and shouted and huzzaed opposite the bakers and meal-sellers shops. . . . On Thursday some potatoes were seized and *Lady Ludd* ordered the different shopkeepers to lower their prices.'[20]

In Lancashire there were riots in most towns at one point or another, including, in April, several days of disturbances in Manchester. Flour, potatoes and butter were all targeted, as were the houses and mills of producers or sellers who were thought to be overpricing. The rioting lasted for several days, beginning on the morning of 18 April in the markets at New Cross and Shudehill. Some food was looted, but a good deal was resold, particularly the potatoes. Several arrests were made and at least one person was shot; the following day was quiet. On 20 April, however, the trouble began again and was more extensive. A 54-year-old woman called Hannah Smith encouraged a crowd of about 100 people to stop potato carts and remove the contents. At one point she managed to upend a cart herself and, having filled her apron with potatoes, ran away with them. Later that day she was leading an even larger crowd that forced a Mr Lomas to sell his goods at a reduced price. She stopped butter and milk carts on the road and threatened to raise a mob to steal the contents if the owners did not sell them cheaply. Later she implemented the threat, selling 20lb of butter at less than its market value. She returned to the fray a day or two later, with much the same result. Crucially, and for her, fatally, she did not pass the proceeds of the sales back to the owners of the produce she commandeered. When she was arrested she was charged with highway robbery and tried at Lancaster on the same day as the Middleton rioters. In her own defence she seems to have denied nothing except the potatoes. 'I never touched a potato', she said, 'nor had one in my apron'.[21] Once she had been convicted the only sentence legally available was death. Condemning her the judge felt neither sympathy nor understanding.

'You, Hannah Smith, have been found guilty of a robbery on the highway . . . This circumstance seems to prove that you were one of the most determined enemies to good order, and it is fit to be understood, that sex is not entitled to any mitigation of punishment, when the crime is of such a nature as to deserve it . . . and may all within these walls, and without, wherever these tidings may reach, take warning from your example, and observe, that they cannot, with impunity, conspire to disturb the public tranquillity . . .'[22]

Hannah Smith was executed on 13 June alongside the four Westhoughton men and three other rioters from Manchester. So far as is known, she was the only woman to be hanged as a result of the 1812 riots, though several were killed by troops as various mobs were dispersed. It is hard to tell why she alone should have been singled out for such a fate. Other women seem to have been more fortunate; Betty Wood, Mary Ellis and Mary Wright from Horbury, near Wakefield, for instance, who had also been charged with highway robbery, were acquitted at York despite clear evidence of their guilt. Had they been convicted they would have been hung as well. Accounts of Hannah's actions during the riots suggest a forceful woman who did not take kindly to being told what to do. When, at one point, somebody threatened to send for the constable she was alleged to have replied that she 'would have him to mind *(take care)*, or he will be hanged, I know he will'.[23] Perhaps she had previous form, or perhaps she was argumentative and uncompliant whilst in gaol awaiting trial. At this distance, and with nothing but a courtroom account of her to go by, it is impossible to tell.

Portraits of working-class men from this period are rare, and those of women rarer still. However, there does exist a line drawing of Hannah Smith awaiting execution at Lancaster Castle.[24] Clothed in a plain, short-sleeved dress, she seems small and unprepossessing, her head bent and her hair covered in a kerchief. Her hands are folded in front of her, and her thin wrists are heavily manacled. She casts her eyes down, possibly in shame, but possibly also to prevent us from seeing what she is really thinking. She does not gaze at us across the centuries, nor does she challenge us to feel anything in particular at her fate. She is ordinary, nondescript, not at all romantic or remarkable. She may well deliberately have been depicted in this way by the artist so as to make her seem penitent, or as an awful warning to others to avoid her example, but somehow this is not the impression that crosses the intervening years. Whatever her faults and mistakes, she seems a woman crushed by a system she could not ultimately resist. Her lowered eyes may be a symptom of remorse, or they may conceal the embers of the rage that propelled her into action in the face of such overwhelming odds. It is impossible to say. The male voices of the courts and the newspapers tell us what she did and how she was punished for it; her own voice is almost inaudible because it was not thought worth hearing.

Just as the Luddism of 1812 was at its height, the parliamentary reform movement, more or less in abeyance during the long Napoleonic wars, began to re-emerge, and on 26 May, the same day as that upon which the Molyneux sisters were tried at Lancaster, a series of events were set in train that would come to a climax a few years later on the field of Peterloo. A group of men in Manchester, some of whom, like their leader, John Knight, had been involved in the radical societies of the 1790s, set up a new Parliamentary Reform society. In his youth, Knight had had revolutionary ideas, but the new society was intended merely to petition the Prince Regent and the government. Now in his late forties, Knight was a well-liked, intelligent and stubborn man who knew he was right and refused to accept what was wrong, but he was no longer the revolutionary firebrand he had been twenty years previously. However, this made no difference to a government already alarmed by the riots. Despite the qualms of many Whigs, lawyers and sections of the public, the Home Office made widespread use of spies, informers and *agents provocateurs.* They took the view that if men detained or convicted on such evidence were not guilty of one offence, they were certainly guilty of another, so that it all came to the same thing in the end. On the basis of information from one of their spies, therefore, they arrested thirty-eight members of Knight's new society and sent them for trial at Lancaster on charges of administering and swearing secret oaths.

These were serious accusations because they carried a mandatory sentence of seven years' transportation to Van Dieman's Land.[25] The Manchester group had, in fact, not been swearing oaths; apart from anything else they knew what the risks were and did not intend to take them. Indeed, rioters convicted of precisely this offence at the Luddite trials were on their way to the convict ships even as Knight and his friends arrived at Lancaster. For the state, the problem was not necessarily the oath itself – that might be perfectly innocuous – but the secrecy of the circumstances in which it was taken. An oath taken in public meant that people knew who had sworn what and to whom, but an oath taken in secret meant that entire hidden networks of loyalties and pledges could and did exist in the shadows, and that these oaths could (and did) prove to be stronger than those sworn in public. Oaths of secrecy often underlay the refusal of communities to give information to the authorities; it took months, for instance, to find the men responsible for the murder of the mill owner William Horsfall in Huddersfield because local people refused to admit to knowing anything about it.

Convictions that involved transportation or death did not just affect those standing in the dock. The consequences also fell upon the families they left behind, who found themselves without a breadwinner and facing ruin. Had John Knight been convicted in 1812 he would have been leaving behind his wife, Elizabeth, and several teenage children. His first stint in prison had been in 1794 when Elizabeth had found herself alone with four children under the age of eight and no visible means of support. By 1812 the children were old enough to work, but still finances were precarious, and although Knight probably did not devote a great deal of his time to earning his living even when free, he could devote none at all whilst locked up in solitary confinement. The uncertainty of what was happening, the shortage of money and the awful prospect of their husbands being transported and possibly never returning must have made it a very stressful time for both Elizabeth and the other wives and children.

In the event a robust and ultimately successful campaign was fought to get the Manchester Thirty-Eight acquitted. The case against them rested entirely on the evidence of one informant, and the conditions under which they were kept whilst awaiting trial at Lancaster prison were grim. Knight recorded that at one point he was 'ordered into solitary confinement in a dungeon, in the tower, where I remained upwards of fifty hours: eighteen without either fire, candle, or book, and forty-two without pen, ink or paper, though I had repeatedly applied for them'.[26] Their case was raised in Parliament and when the case came to court the evidence was found to be so thin that even the judge found it less than credible, virtually directing the jury to acquit all thirty-eight, which they duly did. An account of the trial was published in October with an introduction written by Knight, who succinctly explained the reformers' case:

> 'I have been informed, that a prejudice exists against us, in the minds of some respectable persons, . . . on account of the lower classes interfering in political affairs. The poor, I am persuaded, feel no wish to usurp the place of their superiors . . . but so acute, so long continued and severe have been their sufferings, that the apathy and indifference of the middle and higher classes, on subjects of the most vital importance to their welfare, and even existence, have rendered it imperiously necessary for them to come forwards.'[27]

Undaunted by his experience, Knight continued to work for parliamentary reform. His high-profile trial had brought him into contact with leaders of the national reform movement, including Major John Cartwright, who had been campaigning for annual parliaments and universal (male) suffrage for more than forty years, and had founded one of the earliest reform societies in 1780. Now in his seventies, he had been touring the North of England trying to drum up support for the formation of Hampden Clubs (named after the seventeenth-century Civil War leader and parliamentarian, John Hampden). Cartwright and the reform movement's most famous orator, Henry Hunt, had grasped that the momentum was now outside London, and they spent a considerable amount of time over the next few years visiting clubs, creating networks and addressing increasingly vast public meetings. In 1816 John Knight was one of the founders of the Manchester Hampden Club, and there were others in industrial towns across the north.

In January 1817, Cartwright and others called a meeting of representatives of as many reforming societies as possible at the Crown

& Anchor inn[28] on the Strand in London. This meeting was ostensibly to agree a way forward for the campaign, but in fact it became a tussle of wills over the meaning of the term 'universal suffrage'. Cartwright took the traditional view that the basic social and political unit was the family, and that votes should therefore be allocated to householders, who would use them on behalf of family members living in their houses. Henry Hunt favoured universal (manhood) suffrage based on individuals. Hunt won. The meeting also passed resolutions demanding annual parliaments, equal constituencies, secret ballots and payments for MPs. There was no demand for female suffrage, and any proposal for one would have received short shrift from the men present. Over the next few weeks more than 700 petitions in support of reform were presented to Parliament. Back in Lancashire a plan was hatched for a mass march to the capital to present a petition to the Prince Regent asking for help for textile workers. Carrying blankets – and hence known as Blanketeers – the men set off in early March, but they were intercepted and dispersed by cavalry, the leaders having been arrested in Manchester at the mass meeting sending them off.

The government was now seriously worried by the nature and scale of radical and reformist activity, and believed that there was a significant chance of revolution emerging from the unrest. At the end of March the government passed the Seditious Meetings Act, which limited – but, crucially – did not prohibit, mass public meetings, and habeas corpus was suspended. As a result, long-standing legislation prohibiting indefinite detention or imprisonment without trial was temporarily in abeyance, and the authorities were able to round up and incarcerate radical leaders and agitators, particularly in the manufacturing towns of the North of England.

John Knight was arrested at his home in April 1817 and sent to Reading Gaol. He was later moved around the country, and at no time during the nine months of his imprisonment was any attempt made to charge him with an offence. Kept as he was away from home and often in solitary confinement, it was difficult for him to know what was going on elsewhere and what was happening to his family. He was technically allowed to write and receive letters, but these were often intercepted and sometimes never got through at all. Elizabeth knew that since their correspondence would almost certainly be read by government agents, she should be careful not to write to him about political matters. But it was hard not to speak her mind, and her letters contained a good deal of political comment. She was also not above telling her husband when she thought he was wrong; in a postscript to one missive she remarked with some asperity:

> 'Your new plan of taxation must be absurd you know well enough we have taxes enough and too many; we want a new plan for the lessening of taxes – this only can do us any good at Manchester.'[29]

Unlike some of the other prisoners' wives, Elizabeth was probably not going to starve, but like them she had to worry about how to pay the rent and buy food. Even if she laid it on a little thick for the benefit of readers in the Home Office, the force of both her personal commitment to the cause and her apprehension for what might happen is clear:

> ". . . it may be easily supposed that the nobler feelings of humanity are nearly overwhelmed by the daily struggle with Poverty Want and despair; all this must have been sustained even had your Political conduct been culpable; but knowing as I do the purity of your motives, the extreme moderation of your public speeches and unwearied attempts to procure a Reform in the Commons House of Parliament; it does indeed add greatly to the misery of my condition; and whether I can long survive the accumulation of misery, God only knows, but I much fear I cannot, then what is to become of our family?'[30]

Some women shared their husbands' letters from prison with local radical groups, both to encourage them and to try to raise money. Not all husbands were happy with this, and when Hannah Wolstenholme of Sheffield passed her husband James's letters on to be read aloud he objected. She wrote back with some irritation to say:

> 'I think I told you in my last that your letters should never be withheld but be always open to the inspection of all our Friends at their request *(and I)* can assure you that so far from your letters being kept secret they always exerts *(sic)* interest and curiosity enough throughout the whole kinds of your acquaintance to make them public enough all are anxious to hear from you and none are forbidden access.'[31]

She went on to point out that life was now very difficult:

'I hope you make me some allowance I pray take this into consideration that instead of the simple part in life I was wont to take I have now two parts which to me is a perpetual round of fatigue, having me scarcely a leisure moment . . .'

The letters of women such as Elizabeth Knight and Hannah Wolstenholme suggest that they were politically acute and committed as well as literate and articulate, but they were not members of the new reform clubs and societies. Certainly women could attend public meetings, but only as spectators, and they could not take any prominent part in them or vote for or against the resolutions that were proposed. There was a widely held view, even amongst many radicals, that women should remain in the background and be loyal but silent. However, as women were increasingly active outside the home, and as radicals began to make links between the economic and the political, it was inevitable that some women would begin to consider how they might contribute to the struggle in a more active way. The result, in June 1819, was the creation of the first Female Reform Societies.

Chapter 5

The Most Abandoned
of their Sex

With the advantage of hindsight, it is easy to see the development of female political organisations as natural and inevitable, but at the time it seemed unlikely and even bizarre. Women were known to riot, and female benefit societies and even very short-lived trade unions were by no means uncommon, but it was a big leap from that to setting up formal political groups. However, in 1818 a step was taken that brought the prospect of women's public political participation closer. In May of that year, a series of increasingly large public gatherings were held after the release of the men detained during the suspension of habeas corpus. One of these was on the windy heights of Saddleworth Moor. In his memoirs, the radical Samuel Bamford said that he proposed that the women as well as the men should be able to vote on the resolutions being put. He claimed that during his speech he:

'insisted on the right, and the propriety also, of females who were present at such assemblages voting by show of hands, for, or against the resolution. This was a new idea; and the women who attended numerously on that bleak ridge were mightily pleased with it. The men being nothing dissentient, when the resolution was put the women held up their hands amid much laughter; and ever from that time females voted with the men at Radical meetings.'[1]

Given that Bamford's wife, Jemima, was an active and committed reformer who, the following year, would attend the meeting at St Peter's Fields in Manchester despite Samuel's reservations, it is impossible not to suspect that Bamford's enthusiasm for women voting might have originated with her rather than him. But, even though Jemima wrote her own contribution to her husband's memoirs, she did not mention this particular incident, and thus the credit ever since has gone to Samuel.

A year later the government rejected a large reform petition from Stockport, and the reform leaders decided on a new tactic designed to draw attention to their demands and demonstrate the widespread support for them across the North of England. They organized a series of weekly open-air rallies in the mill towns of Lancashire and the West Riding of Yorkshire. These were addressed by prominent local and national speakers, and passed resolutions in support of parliamentary reform. They were almost all held on Mondays, because Monday, for many working people, particularly weavers, was traditionally a day off. Some of the meetings were relatively small and local, but some were huge, with people flocking to them to pledge support and to see and hear famous speakers. National figures such as Major Cartwright and Henry Hunt joined local leaders such as John Knight and Samuel Bamford to urge the crowds on to greater enthusiasm, unity and determination. Newspapers carried detailed accounts of these meetings, and they were very successful in generating a sense of excitement and purpose. They also helped to create the conditions in which a single mass-action organization could develop, and although there was some disagreement about how this should be done, there was a general view that it was necessary.

It is not known whether, during the early months of 1819, there was any discussion about how women might best be involved in the campaign. Hitherto, they had attended the public meetings but not joined the reform clubs, but that was about to change. On 18 June a group of women got together at Blackburn and, at a meeting chaired by John Knight, drew up rules and membership requirements for a Blackburn Female Reform Society. Members were drawn from the local area and paid a subscription of a penny a week; since the object of the Society was to 'assist the male population of this country to obtain their rights and liberties', it is perhaps hardly surprising that the funds raised were to be used to support the work of the men's reform organization. However, the Female Reform Society had its own officers and meeting schedule, and remains the first known working-class women's political organization run by the women themselves (once Knight had handed over the Chair). They invited women in other towns to follow their example, and their invitation was accepted with alacrity.

On 5 July the Blackburn Female Reformers took part in another historic occasion, becoming the first working-class women to have a formal role at a political event. Their performance had been well-planned in advance and had a theatrical feel to it that other parts of the programme may have lacked. The reformer colours were green and white, and the women all wore white dresses and bonnets with green sashes and cockades. This not only identified them as a group, but also enabled them to stand out from the darker, more drab colours worn by the crowd. At an agreed point, the women gathered at the edge of the huge assembly and waited until the stewards had indicated their presence to John Knight, who was in the Chair and was one of the main speakers. He then beckoned to them to come forwards. The crowd, being instructed by Knight to 'make way for the ladies' and sensing that here was something new and possibly entertaining, parted to allow them through and cheered enthusiastically as they went. Arriving at the platform, they mounted it to more cheers and cries of 'God bless the women'. Mrs Alice Kitchen now advanced towards Knight and 'with becoming diffidence and respect' presented him with 'a most beautiful Cap of Liberty, made of scarlet silk or satin, lined with green, with a serpentine gold lace, terminating with a rich gold tassel'.[2]

This was a gift full of meaning for everyone who saw it or heard about it later. Like the middle-class and aristocratic women who had presented banners to regiments leaving for the Napoleonic Wars, the female reformers of Blackburn were urging their men on to greater deeds, but they were also reinforcing a sense of common identity and purpose. The excitement and anticipation being generated by the long series of monster Monday meetings leading up to the middle of August was palpable, and for many people it already seemed almost inevitable that some great trial of strength was coming. The Cap of Liberty, with its revolutionary connotations and its dangerous past, entirely reflected the febrile atmosphere that was slowly brewing. Nor were the reformers the only people to see this. The Home Secretary, Lord Sidmouth, was seriously alarmed by the Cap's reappearance in public, and as early as June had been writing to the magistrates in Manchester that:

'This symbol gives a character to these meetings which cannot be mistaken, & leaves no room for surprize at the disgust of the well affected inhabitants of Manchester. If it shall be displayed again with impunity, it will be a deep subject of regret.'[3]

Having handed over the Cap, Alice Kitchen then abandoned the traditional female role of modest silence in the public space and made what was described as a 'short emphatic speech'. She said that the Cap was 'a token of our respect to those brave men who are nobly struggling for liberty and life', and passed to Knight the Blackburn Female Reform Society Address, which she requested him to read out, and which she said 'embraces a faint description of our woes, and may apologise for our interference in the politics of our country'.

Although the Address was not read out by a female voice, it represents one of the earliest political pronouncements from a public platform made by a group of women – and especially northern working-class women – in Britain.[4] As usual, it was subsequently claimed that it had been written by a man – either Joseph Mitchell, who may or may not have been related to Alice, or John Knight, who had been involved with the fledgling society from the start, and who now used his powerful voice to read the speech out to the crowd. Given Elizabeth Knight's ability to write coherently about political issues, it may even have come from her pen. Whoever wrote it, it was a very effective piece of work. After some introductory flourishes about the presentation of the Cap, the women said that they had:

'the avowed determination of instilling into the minds of our offspring a deep rooted abhorrence of tyranny, come in what shape it may; ... and particularly of the present borough-mongering[5] and Jesuistical system, which has brought the best artizans, manufacturers, and labourers of this vast community to a state of wretchedness and misery, and driven them to the very verge of beggary and ruin.'[6]

The Address then proceeded to outline the suffering being caused by the post-war depression, the poor harvest[7] and, in particular, by the taxation system, including the new Corn Laws, which kept the price of bread artificially high. The women said that:

'our houses which once bore ample testimony of our industry and cleanliness, and were fit for the reception of a prince, are now, alas! robbed of all their ornaments; and our beds, that once afforded us cleanliness, health and sweet repose, are now torn away from us by the relentless hand of the unfeeling tax-gatherer, to satisfy the greatest monsters of cruelty, the borough-mongering tyrants, who are reposing on beds of down, while nothing is left us to stretch our weary limbs upon but a sheaf of straw, laid on the cold ground, with insufficient covering to shelter us from the inclemency of the weather. But above all, behold our innocent wretched children; sweet emblems of our mutual love! how appalling are their cries for bread! . . . We cannot describe our wretchedness, for language cannot paint the feelings of a mother, when she beholds her naked children, and hears their inoffensive cries of hunger and approaching death.'

The men were entreated to:

'come forward and join the general union, that by a determined and constitutional resistance to our oppressors, the people may obtain Annual Parliaments, Universal Suffrage, and Election by Ballot, which alone can save us from lingering misery and premature death. We look forward with horror to an approaching winter, when the necessity of food, clothing, and every requisite will increase double-fold . . .'

Finally, the women concluded by pledging to do everything they could to support the cause. Given the length at which the men tended to speak, and the florid nature of much of the language employed at this time, it was in its way a little masterpiece of a speech, containing a call to action, an explanation for the reasons for that call, an appeal to the emotions as well as to reason, and, finally, a pledge to act themselves. At the end, and to much applause, a vote of thanks to them was proposed and passed, following which the women stayed on the platform for the remainder of the meeting. When all the speakers had been heard and all the resolutions passed, both male and female members of the platform party adjourned to the nearby General Wolfe inn, where they ate what *The Manchester Observer* described as a 'frugal but substantial and excellent dinner,' after which many toasts were drunk, the first being 'The Female Reformers of Blackburn, and may their example be speedily followed throughout the united kingdom'.

The Blackburn women had invited women elsewhere to follow their lead, and many soon did. The Stockport Female Reform Society was begun early in July, and its second meeting attracted quite a lot of attention. It began with the election of officers, including, as president, a young woman called Mrs Hallworth. The women were meeting in the same venue as the men's Reform Society, and men had turned up to attend – perhaps to show solidarity but probably also to enjoy the novelty. In her inaugural address, Mrs Hallworth's first act was to ask them to leave. It was, she said, with perhaps a little irony:

> 'not done with a view to transact any thing of a secret nature, for it is commonly said that women can keep no secrets, but merely with a view that if in our debates (for it is something new for women to turn political orators), we should for want of knowledge make any blunders, we should be laughed at, to prevent which we should prefer being by ourselves.'[8]

Faced with this appeal to their understanding the men left and went to sit in the taproom downstairs. Mrs Hallworth then went on to make the kind of speech familiar to women everywhere, the one in which the woman elected describes how unworthy she is whilst proving exactly the reverse. Her short remarks are worth quoting in full.

> 'Ladies, you have this evening placed me in a situation which I never occupied before. I kindly thank you for the honour you have done me, but cannot help observing that I am a very unfit person for the office; but as you have placed me here to protect order and peace, I will perform the task as well as I am able. I assure you that I am determined to dedicate to Liberty, my heart, body, yea, my very life. *(Unbounded applause, with cries of Liberty.)* I am young, but ladies, young as I am, I can assure you that the Borough villains have furnished me with such a woeful life of wretched experience, that I can feel for myself, and equally with myself, feel for my injured, plundered country-women. This feeling is so acute that, an eternal war is waged betwixt us, which will never end, but in the

emancipation of a distressed and overburdened people from slavery to liberty—*(Reiterated applause.)*— These are sentiments I imbibed when almost child, and as I grow older, the grumbling spirit grows stronger. *(Laughter.)*—I thank you. Ladies, for your kind attention, but assure you I do not look for your applauses. Applaud me not, it cannot please me, for I consider it my duty to use every ability in the cause without receiving any reward at all for my weak endeavours. It is a good cause, it is the cause of God—for it is the cause of the people, and the voice of the people is the voice of God—we therefore are sure to triumph. Seeing then, that it is the common cause let us all unite, and never cease from persevering in a cause so just and holy, until we fully possess those constitutional liberties and privileges which are the birth-right of every English man and woman.'[9]

Unlike Alice Kitchen addressing a predominantly male audience in Blackburn, Mrs Hallworth made no mention at all of women's domestic duties, of houses bearing testimony of industry and cleanliness or of apology for her temerity in speaking. The speech seemed immediate and present in the room in which it was made; Mrs Hallworth was directly responsive to her audience, and they to her. She made her political position clear, but she was also known to her listeners in a personal way; when she refers to her 'grumbling spirit' it is still easy to hear the laughter of people who knew it all too well, and who thought that it was precisely what made her suitable to be their president (or, as she was referred to by another speaker, 'worthy Presidentess').

Despite Mrs Hallworth's references to the constitutional rights of women, however, the cause for which women were signing up in substantial numbers was not female suffrage. The battle was for universal male suffrage, and it would have been extraordinary if large numbers of working-class women had suddenly begun to argue for votes for themselves. This did not mean that they were either supine or unable to speak and think politically. Nor did it limit their self-belief; Charlotte Johnston, whose husband was still imprisoned under the suspension of habeas corpus, wrote to him: 'I dare say you have seen by the Observer if you have it now that the women have taken it in hand, and you will see that they will do something, for one woman will do more than five men.'[10]

Elsewhere, there was deep disapproval of what the northern women were doing. One disgusted Blackburn correspondent wrote to *The Morning Post* in London that:

'Our Female Reformers had a Council Extraordinary this morning, which I am told was very numerously attended. With the names of the Chairwomen and different lady speakers it would be idle to trouble you: they can never shine brighter than by being left in their native obscurity. The business of the day was to consider the best means of forwarding the great object for which they have abandoned their proper domestic cares, and given themselves up to the mania of mending Constitutions, to the neglect of the more befitting occupation of mending their husband's breeches.'[11]

Disapproval was insufficient to halt progress, however, and on 10 July 1819 a small advertisement appeared towards the back of *The Manchester Observer*. It advised readers that:

'The Public are respectfully informed, that the members of the Manchester Female Reform Society, will meet on Monday Evening next, at 8 o'clock, at the Union Rooms, George Leigh-street, for the purpose of taking down the names of such Persons as are willing to become Subscribers to this Institution, and to submit a string of Resolutions for their adoption or rejection.'

On 12 July – the 'Monday Evening next' of the notice – a deputation of Blackburn women, including Alice Kitchen, travelled to Manchester to show solidarity and support. They 'paraded different parts of the town . . . in the costume which made such an impression on the late Blackburn Meeting'. They then attended the meeting at the Union Rooms, where, the unimpressed *The Morning Post* reported, 'Mrs. I_, Mrs. W—, and other Radical Amazons, harangued the audience on the usual topics, and at considerable length', rather querulously adding: 'Might not women be better employed?'[12]

For the reformers, however, the meeting was highly successful, and it was reported that no fewer than 1,000 women 'were present to enrol their names, against our borough-tyrants'.[13] The President of the Society, Mary Fildes, and the Secretary, Susannah Saxton, were two women who would both have prominent roles to play in the approaching events.

Mary Fildes was an Irish immigrant in her late twenties, and was later described by Henry Hunt as a handsome 'married woman of good character . . . though rather small, she was a remarkably good figure, and well dressed'.[14] She and her husband, William, had been married for a little over a decade and had five sons, including one named Thomas Paine after the famous revolutionary. Her youngest child had been born only recently, in April. William was a reedmaker by trade; reedmakers made the combs used in weaving machinery and he may therefore have been an independent artisan or employed in a small workshop. Mary Fildes is unusual in that, although she was married, next to nothing is known about her husband other than his name and occupation. He was not himself a radical leader, nor did he appear as a witness at any of the inquests or trials after Peterloo. Mary Fildes appears to be one of the first married women of any class who established, however briefly, a political identity separate from that of her husband.

Susannah Saxton's husband, on the other hand, was a well-known journalist and campaigner. The couple came originally from Chesterfield, where John Thacker Saxton had run a bookshop, before moving to Sheffield where he had earned his living as a radical printer. They had arrived in Manchester only in 1818, and Saxton had quickly got himself noticed as a firebrand who was prepared to take risks. Together with John Knight and others he co-founded *The Manchester Observer* as a radical voice for Manchester reformers. Another founder, John Wroe, became editor and took Saxton on as chief reporter. By July 1819, Saxton had a name as a good speaker and a writer of combative and occasionally inflammatory prose and doggerel verse.

On 20 July, the Manchester Female Reformers published their own Address. This was not presented at a public meeting for the simple reason that the Manchester mass meeting was not intended to take place until 9 August, and presumably the Manchester women wanted to get something out quickly. Their Address, the text of which was published in *The Manchester Observer* on 31 July, was addressed to the 'Wives, Mothers, Sisters, and Daughters of the Higher and Middling Classes of Society'. On one level, given that the reform movement was heavily working class, this seems a slightly odd opening, but there was purpose in it. Susannah, Mary and the other women on the Committee were trying to establish the idea that all women shared a common experience, and that an evil done to one group could easily happen to all. Beginning 'Dear Sisters of the Earth', it opened by laying out the plight in which the working-class women of Manchester found themselves as they tried to deal with food shortages and poor trade.

> 'Our minds are filled with horror and despair, fearful, on each returning morn, the light of heaven should present to us the corpse of some of our famished offspring, or nearest kindred, which the more kind hand of death had released from the grasp of the oppressor. . . . Every succeeding night brings with it new terrors, so that we are sick of life, and weary of a world where poverty, wretchedness, tyranny, and injustice, have so long been permitted to reign amongst men.'

The Address then went on to suggest to the women of the middle classes that if things continued in this way they themselves would be the next to suffer.

> 'Dear Sisters, . . . You may then fairly anticipate, that when we are mixed with the silent dust, you will become the next victims of the voracious Borough Tyrants, who will chase you, in your turn, to misery and death, till at length, the middle and useful class of society, is swept, by their relentless hands, from the face of the creation.'

The only remedy for this was access to political power, and the female reformers urged their readers to 'exert your influence with your fathers, your husbands, your sons, your relatives, and your friends, to join the Male Union for constitutionally demanding a Reform', or face miserable consequences. The recent unpopular wars, the women said, had been fought:

> '. . . for the purpose of placing upon the Throne of France, contrary to the people's interest and inclination, the present contemptible Louis, . . . this war, to reinstate this man, has tended . . . to load our beloved country with such an insurmountable burden of Taxation, that is too intolerable to endure longer; it has nearly annihilated our

once flourishing trade and commerce, and is now driving our merchants and manufacturers to poverty and degradation.'

However, there was hope on the horizon, the progress of Liberty and Truth was irresistible, and people of all classes were banding together to demand reform.

'The beam of angelic light that hath gone forth through the globe hath at length reached unto Man, and we are proud to say that the Female Reformers of Manchester have also caught its benign and heavenly influence; it is not possible therefore for us to submit to bear the ponderous weight of our chains any longer, but to use our endeavour to tear them asunder, and dash them in the face of our remorseless oppressors.'

The Address concluded with a flourish by saying that 'corruption, tyranny, and injustice, have reached their summit; and the bitter cup of oppression is now full to the brim'. It was signed by Susannah Saxton 'By Order of the Committee'. A postscript informed those interested that: 'The Committee will sit every Tuesday Evening, from six to nine o'clock, for the purpose of enrolling the Names of such Members, and transacting other Business.'

As with similar addresses, the Manchester Address is sometimes represented as having been written by a man, the most obvious candidate in this case being John Thacker Saxton. In November 1819, the magistrate James Norris stated that Saxton had written the Manchester Female Reformers' Address to the famous radical William Cobbett to welcome him back to England from his exile in America.[15] Joseph Mitchell, present on the platform at the Blackburn meeting, claimed that Alice Kitchen's Address – 'that fine address of the females' – had been written by 'my valued friend, James Mitchell'.[16] Letters to the press were certainly sometimes written by men masquerading as women, but then men also wrote under a wide range of other pseudonyms, too, usually classical in some form.

Saxton himself does not seem ever to have claimed to have written the Manchester Address. It is often pointed out that the language of the Manchester and Blackburn Addresses (and others) is similar to that used in *The Manchester Observer* and in the speeches of the male reforming orators, but this was the language of the times and of the campaign as a whole. The fact that articles written by different men used similar arguments does not usually lead to the suggestion that individual men could not have written their own material. It is also hard to know what other language the women either could or should have used. They were Manchester residents, active in an all-absorbing movement and surrounded by the arguments they put. It seems unlikely that a group of working and lower middle-class women, none of whom had been involved in any campaigning previously, would spontaneously produce a whole new way of looking at their world and a whole new language for describing it. Moreover, to suggest that they should have done so is to detract from the Address's real strengths. It is one of the first occasions upon which one class of women calls upon another to take political action. That the action was limited in scope is both a reflection of how women saw their role and of what they knew to be practicable. Middle-class women, so much more sheltered and hedged about with convention than many working-class women, were not going to take to the streets or join mass crowds of men to demand their rights. But, they could perhaps be persuaded to have sympathy with starving women and children, and to talk to their menfolk about it.

Women related the political and economic situation in which they found themselves to their domestic experiences, but the later idea that this makes their activism of less value is part of what obscures them from our view. Women, then as now, were held responsible for the welfare of their families, and to be forced to watch children become weak and ill from lack of food was as distressing then as it would be now. To suggest that women should not, or could not, argue from this direct and dreadful personal experience to the political is to devalue their struggles. The daily battle to find enough food was real, and impacted forcefully upon families, sometimes with tragic consequences. Men also made appeals about this aspect of their lives – Samuel Bamford spoke and wrote about it repeatedly – but the fact that they did so is not used to undermine the validity of their opinions or actions. To minimize the domestic is to diminish the political experience of women who were doing something new and untested. The Female Reform Unions were the first avowedly political working-class women's organizations. How they defined those politics was bound to relate to the world they knew, the experience of it they had, and the language available to them at the time. Susannah

Saxton and her committee were certainly capable of writing the Manchester Female Reformers' Address; to assume that they did not is to deny them their voice once again.

Certainly, the Lancashire Female Reformers were not feminists, but it is unhelpful to try to read twenty-first century feminist sensibilities back into nineteenth-century pioneering events. Susannah Saxton, Mary Fildes, Alice Kitchen and their sisters did not challenge the status quo of their inferior legal, economic or political status, nor did they position themselves as the equal of men. Faced with the disaster of food shortages, depressed wages and an establishment that only too clearly cared nothing for them, their children or their collective fate, most women accepted the interpretation of the situation put forward by the men whom they had been taught to regard as their masters.[17] Women had little history of independent political thought at this stage; and although many would have been aware of Mary Wollstonecraft's *Rights of Woman* they were more likely to be familiar with Tom Paine's *Rights of Man*. In the endless struggle to keep themselves and their children alive, they had no time to reinvent the world. But, despite this, they were true pioneers. They stepped outside the role society assigned them and began to claim for themselves a place in the political sphere. It was not long before they found out precisely how unwelcome there they were.

The events in the cotton towns, particularly the ceremonial of the Blackburn mass meeting, were widely reported and commented on, with predictably different slants depending on the standpoint of the different outlets. *The Manchester Observer* regarded the appearance of the Female Reformers as 'interesting and enchanting'. However, anti-radical papers were unanimous in their condemnation, and, since the unregulated press of the early nineteenth century had much in common with the unregulated social media of the early twenty-first, there was very little limit to what they could publish. *The Times*, for instance, reported 'with repugnance':

'one novel and most disgusting scene – a Deputation from the Blackburn Female Reform Society mounted the stage, to present a cap of liberty and an address to the meeting. . . . These women then mixed with the orators, and remained on the hustings during the rest of the day. The public scarcely need be informed, that the females are women well known to be of the most abandoned of their sex.'[18]

This was a coded way of calling the women prostitutes, and would have been well understood by *The Times'* readers. Elsewhere, there was criticism of both sexes; speaking of the Stockport meeting, the *Bath Chronicle and Weekly Gazette* remarked:

'That these wretched creatures in their eagerness to display their persons, and let loose their tongues, should forget how much more women are protected than restrained by the barrier which separates them from the toil, and obloquy, and hazard of public business, cannot but surprise any one who reflects upon the predominant influence of female vanity in low life. But what can be said of the feelings or morals of the fathers, and husbands, and brothers, who have permitted or encouraged this violation of that sacred female privacy, of which they are the appointed guardians? Happy indeed will they be, if they only find that their wives, sisters, and daughters, return to the domestic commonwealth, with powers of eloquence sharpened by practice, and notions of sovereignty confirmed the contemplation of their collective importance.'[19]

Some newspapers reported the Stockport meeting in rather more lurid terms than others. The *Yorkshire Gazette* informed its readers that when the men left the meeting they:

'took with them their pipes and porter. One of them, we understand, was detected in conveying out of the room a bottle of brandy, but Mrs. President Hallworth insisted that they could not go on without it . . . Miss Whalley, seizing hold of it by the neck, twisted it out of the grip of the possessor, and deposited it (in) triumph by the side of the chairwoman. . . . *(After the speeches)* They all sat down and filled out a glass of brandy. A Committee of twelve were next appointed to act for the Union. . . . About this time the bottles were emptied, and it was carried by acclamation that another should be ordered in, and chalked up to the male Reformers below. It was also put to the vote, and unanimously adopted, that pipes for three should be allowed . . . The meeting dispersed at half-past ten clock, and the several members assisted each home, as a symbol of that sisterly union and mutual support, to which they had reciprocally pledged themselves.'[20]

Another tactic was to suggest that the women were not as poor as they sought to portray themselves: one report of a public meeting at Leigh alleged that the women's 'dress and appearance bore no marks of that misery and want which were said to prevail in Leigh and the neighbourhood'.[21] Other papers reported with horror that, after one member of the platform party was arrested, 'The Chairman left his station, which, for the remainder of the meeting was filled by a woman!' At the end of the report it was alleged that:

> 'On Monday last, Mary Bradshaw, alias Moll Nush, was apprehended . . . on a charge of felony, at Chorley. This is one of the Ladies who adorned the stage at the much-talked-of Reform Meeting in this town, when the Cap of Liberty was hoisted.'[22]

Newspapers at the time reproduced one another's reports freely and without attribution, so that accounts like this could and did appear in many local publications. But all this was mild compared to a cartoon produced by George Cruikshank, the famous satirist, which was published in mid-August and called 'The Belle-alliance: or female reformers of Blackburn!!!' The women on the platform are depicted as corpulent hags with their skirts tucked into breeches; their leader, who waves a rolled up copy of the Address is shown without a nose, signifying syphilis, a disease with which prostitutes were often afflicted. A speech balloon contains her remarks which begin 'Muster Chairman & Brother—will you accept this token of our Love & by placing it on the head of your pole . . .' All of the women are depicted as grotesque and most wield daggers or alcohol. One is drawn with a bottle in each hand and a baby tucked under her arm as she shouts to the men that 'we are some of the right sort, my lads'. Children brandish knives, and one man wears a petticoat. The whole scene is presented as both ludicrous and an alarming and monstrous inversion of the natural order.

Even radical men could be equivocal about women's new role, and were, for neither the first time nor the last, prone to reporting women's activism in ways that either distorted its scale or used it to pursue other agendas. Thomas Wooler, for instance, the editor of the radical, widely read and influential *Black Dwarf*, had not previously been entirely sympathetic to women, using them more as a means of satirizing the government than anything else. In one piece in 1818 he envisaged the idea of women holding government office as something ridiculous, if only because the men could then be made to work at 'the deserted wash-tubs, the ironing boards, and the scrubbing brushes . . . Those who have nursed the nation into a consumption may make some recompense by nursing ricketty children into good health'. In his final flourish, Wooler told women that since the men had let them down they themselves should take the lead.[23] This piece is sometimes quoted as showing Wooler's support for women, but in point of fact it is a satire using the familiar idea of the world turned on its head to attack the establishment. Less than a year later, however, Wooler's report of the Female Reformers at the Blackburn meeting was much more sympathetic, perhaps at least in part because the women had positioned themselves as being in support of, rather than in competition with, the men.

During July and early August 1819, new Female Reform Societies sprang up across the North of England and beyond. In Yorkshire towns such as Leeds, Yeadon, Pudsey, Halifax and Hull, in Lancashire in Oldham, Leigh, Rochdale and Ashton, and further afield in Midlands towns, such as Nottingham, women came together to pledge support for the cause. In Scotland, societies appeared in textile towns, such as Paisley. A woman called Elizabeth Russell wrote to *The Manchester Observer* to report the founding of the West of England Female Reform Society 'to shew that the flame of liberty from the North has reached the West'.[24] One after another, women's groups attended public meetings and presented Caps of Liberty and formal Addresses to their male counterparts. They also defined and defended what they meant by educating their children to hate tyranny. Mary Hallam, the Secretary of the Stockport Society wrote to *The Manchester Observer* to refute the allegations of the editor of the *Liverpool Courier* who had accused the women of inculcating revolutionary principles. She said that:

'WE WILL instil into the minds of our children what he calls revolutionary principles, but what we call principles which will safely carry them through the maze of political ignorance which now pervades the circle of the HIGHER ORDER.'[25]

The great mass meetings at which the women appeared to such effect were intended to culminate in a monster meeting in Manchester in August, and for this event the radical women of Lancashire now began to plan. As with all the meetings, it was organized by a remarkably small number of people, in this case the editorial board of *The Manchester Observer*, who wrote to invite Henry Hunt to speak at a public meeting on Monday, 9 August. Hunt accepted, but only on condition that it was to be for the whole of Lancashire rather than just Manchester. In practice, this meant people from the nearby cotton towns rather than further afield, but even so it opened the event up to a much wider audience. In the meantime, three large meetings around the country added to the build-up. In Birmingham on 8 July tens of thousands of people tried to 'elect' the radical landowner Sir Charles Wolseley to represent them in Parliament, whilst in Leeds on 19 July another large meeting at which John Knight and the editor of the *Leeds Mercury* spoke agreed to elect someone as well. On 21 July, 10,000 people gathered at Smithfield in London to hear Henry Hunt and the Rev. Joseph Harrison, the radical pastor from Stockport, argue for reform and advocate direct action to achieve it if necessary. During the meeting, Harrison was arrested because of a speech he had made in Stockport in June. Far from being seen as risky, the removal of speakers from platforms in front of thousands of their supporters was a common tactic, one which was later to be employed with disastrous consequences.

Meanwhile, preparations for the Manchester meeting were in hand, and on 31 July *The Manchester Observer* carried a notice that indicated that, amongst other things, it would 'consider the propriety of the "Un-Represented Inhabitants of Manchester" electing a Person to represent them in Parliament'. The magistrates promptly declared the meeting illegal and banned it, since electing or proposing to elect an MP without a writ having been moved in Parliament was an offence, and arrests on those grounds had already been made in Birmingham. John Thacker Saxton was dispatched to Liverpool to consult Fletcher Raincock, a radical lawyer who had represented the Luddites at Lancaster in 1812. He gave it as his opinion that, if the meeting tried to elect representatives it would be breaking the law, and could even be seditious. As a result it was decided to abandon the first event and organize a new one, without the electoral element, for Monday, 16 August. This was the gathering that was to become known as Peterloo.

Chapter 6
Persistent Amazons

The shocking events of Peterloo are often presented as having been unforeseen, but in fact there were apprehensions about the meeting on all sides. The magistrates, already alarmed about radical activity, believed that the country was on the point of revolution, that pikes were being manufactured and concealed, and that people coming into Manchester from neighbouring towns would be armed. There was not much evidence for this, except that in some areas the military drilling of men on the moortops had continued. This would – and did – come in handy for marching in on the morning of the meeting, but some of the drills were accompanied by threatening language and the mock firing of guns, and the magistrates were convinced that there was a serious intent to use violence. There had already, in February, been trouble at Sandy Brow in Stockport, when the magistrates had sent a contingent of constables and yeomanry into a crowd to seize the Cap of Liberty with disastrous results. The crowd had fought them off with stones and fists, and there had then been a running battle through the streets. The Riot Act had to be read twice, and the Cap itself was successfully defended by the reformers. John Knight had been one of the speakers on the platform, as had John Thacker Saxton, who had been chairing the meeting, and was said by Samuel Bamford to have been in the thick of the fight, blackening the eye of one constable and giving 'his jaw a welter'. Thus, there can have been no illusions on either side about what might happen if the Manchester magistrates took the same line.

In July, *The Manchester Observer* reported that the Manchester & Salford Yeomanry, which had been set up following the difficulties of dispersing the Blanketeers March in 1817, had sent their sabres for sharpening. Spies and informers were, as usual, very active, feeding back both fact and speculation to the magistrates and the Home Office. The magistrates were also in direct and rather anxious contact with the Home Office themselves. The Home Secretary, Lord Sidmouth, urged caution. On 4 August his private secretary wrote to Sir John Byng, the general commanding the troops in the North of England that:

> 'even if they should utter sedition or proceed to election of a representative Lord Sidmouth is of opinion that it will be the wisest course to abstain from any endeavour to disperse the mob, unless they should proceed to acts of felony or riot. We have the strongest reason to believe that Hunt means to preside & to deprecate disorder.'[1]

Unfortunately, the Manchester magistrates were unable to accept this advice, and continued to prepare for what they believed would be a violent confrontation which, once it had begun, would be their responsibility to deal with.

From the reformers' side, there was no shortage of the kind of revolutionary rhetoric by which loyalists were so alarmed. Both through the radical press and at successive meetings, sentiments were expressed that could certainly be interpreted as incitement. The women were well to the fore in this. The Female Reformers of Stockport, for instance, declared that they expected their menfolk to 'imitate the ancient Romans . . . who fought to a man in the defence of their liberty', and required their 'daughters and female friends to imitate the Spartan women' who, when waiting for the return of their men from the wars, 'would rather have heard of the death of any of them, than their deserting the standard of liberty'.[2]

Thus, as the day approached, there was an increasingly feverish atmosphere of anticipation, apprehension and fear. Despite the cancellation of the original meeting, Henry Hunt had arrived in the town on 9 August, and issued a statement asking for calm and for people to come to the meeting unarmed and to resist provocation. Not everybody thought his peaceful approach was wise. Samuel Bamford, who was to be one of the speakers in Manchester and also foresaw trouble, wanted 'a party of men with stout cudgels' to accompany the banner and Cap of Liberty, but this was vetoed by Hunt and the local organizing committee.[3]

Others were uneasy about what might happen to the women who were also busy planning for the part they were to play. On the Sunday morning before the meeting, as John Thacker Saxton was passing the Union Rooms where the Manchester women were finalizing their arrangements, he suggested to fellow radical George Swift, who was walking with him, that they should go in and tell the women not to go, 'for it will be a bloody day, every Yeoman's sword is ground on purpose'.[4] If he was prepared to talk like this to Swift it seems highly unlikely that he had not discussed the dangers with Susannah, and that Mary Fildes and the other women were not therefore aware of the risks they were running. This sense of foreboding existed outside Manchester, too, and the picture later projected by the reformers of women and children happily setting out as though for a day's holiday is somewhat diluted by the recollections of women such as Bamford's wife, Jemima. In her memoir she remembered that she had been uneasy about what might happen, but that she:

'was determined to go to the meeting, and should have followed, even if my husband had refused his consent to my going with the procession. From what I, in common with others, had heard the week previous, "that if the country people went with their caps of liberty, and their banners, and music, the soldiers would be brought to them".'[5]

However, not everyone shared this apprehension, or was prepared to believe that force really would be deployed against them. Archibald Prentice, a reformer who watched the incoming processions from a friend's house and wrote one of the first published accounts of the day, said later that he had 'occasionally asked the women if they were not afraid to be there, and the usual laughing reply was—"What have we to be afraid of?"'[6] People were used to the authorities trying to make life difficult for them, and must have found it hard to believe some of the more alarmist rumours they heard, particularly if they lived some distance from Manchester and were not as aware as Saxton and his readers of the yeomanry's sharpened swords.

Monday, 16 August dawned as a warm, sunny summer's day, with a light breeze relieving the heat for those marching in from any distance.

At an early hour groups of reformers began to gather with their banners at the meeting places and to form themselves into ranks. Speakers reminded them of the importance of the event and the need to remain peaceful. One after another, as the early morning light grew stronger, processions of people began to leave the towns surrounding Manchester, marching in good order and carrying banners and Caps of Liberty. Some had serviceable walking sticks, but there was no sign of the pikes the authorities had been worrying about, nor did there seem to be any firearms. As the central columns marched, they acquired followers and hangers-on, but by and large order was maintained and gradually the streams of people began to merge as they reached the main roads leading into Manchester. Innkeepers, pub landlords and farmers' wives did a good trade in refreshments as the day began to grow warmer; later there were claims that some people were drunk by the time they got to St Peter's Field.

Almost every cotton town within what would then have been considered reasonable walking distance of Manchester sent its own contingent. From Stockport came about 1,500 people, described as walking well in step with time being kept by 'about thirty stout lads' in the body of the column. Forty women marched in the middle, with a member of the Committee, Mary Waterworth, carrying a banner that read, 'Success to the Female Reformers of Stockport'. Organized groups of women also came from Oldham, Royton, Bury, Rochdale, Ashton and Stalybridge, and more from other towns and villages. We do not know whether Alice Kitchen was with the Female Reformers of Blackburn when they set out; they were expected to attend but the distance was greater than most and they may not have arrived in time. The men marched alongside the women, often surrounding them as a protective guard, but women also sometimes led the columns. Almost all the Female Reformers wore the white dresses and green sashes that had become their trademark. Other women walked with their families or just joined because they thought it might be a good day out. Once the processions reached Manchester they were joined by women from that town, whilst the Manchester Female Reform Society itself and the Manchester Patriotic Union gathered at the place where Henry Hunt and his party were waiting to set off.

Considerable thought had gone into how Hunt, the star attraction of the day, should arrive at St Peter's Fields. As on other occasions, he would travel in an open carriage with prominent local reformers, and a contingent of local supporters would provide an escort. A novel feature of this plan was the presence of organized companies of women, and it was intended that the Middleton Female Reformers should march ahead of the vehicle and the Manchester women behind, with the men surrounding them. Hunt, who had an eye for the dramatic, had (by his own account) the idea for one of the most striking images of the day. According to him:

'We very soon met the Manchester Committee of Female Reformers, headed by Mrs. Fildes, who bore in her hand a small white silk flag. These females were all handsomely dressed in white, and they proposed to lead the procession to the field, walking two and two, but as, in consequence of the crowd, this was found to be impossible, they fell into the rear of the barouche, which position they maintained with some difficulty, during the whole way till we arrived at the Hustings. Mrs. Fildes, who carried the flag, was taken up at my suggestion, and rode by the side of the coachman, bearing her colours in a most gallant stile.'[7]

Another man thought Mary was 'the most beautiful woman I ever saw'.[8] The bookseller and polemicist Richard Carlile, who had come up from London for the meeting, described her as:

'an interesting looking woman, *(bearing)* a standard on which was painted a female holding in her hand a flag surmounted with a cap of liberty, whilst she trod underfoot an emblem of corruption, on which was inscribed that word. She was requested to take a seat on the box of the carriage, (a most appropriate one) which she boldly and immediately acquiesced in, and continued waving her flag and handkerchief until she reached the hustings, where she took her stand at the front, on the right.'[9]

The Manchester Chronicle was rather less enthusiastic, however, describing how:

'At a quarter before one o'clock a *Body of Women*, in treble files, marched in with music; and soon after, a great number of men, four or five deep, marched in, with drum beating, music playing, a red pole, with the Cap of Liberty hoisted; . . . At a quarter past one, a very large Procession advanced from Deansgate, headed by an open carriage, with a *Woman* in front, who bore and brandished a Flag with an inscription. In the Car were five persons, one of whom gave a signal for a general shout on approaching the Hustings.'[10]

Not all women approved of what was happening, either; *The Times* reporter noted:

'. . . a group of the women of Manchester, attracted by the crowd, came to the corner of the street where we had taken our post. They viewed these Female Reformers for some time with a look in which compassion and disgust were equally blended; and at last burst out into an indignant exclamation—"Go home to your families, and leave sike-like matters as these to your husbands and sons, who better understand them." The women who thus addressed them were of the lower order in life.'[11]

When the various processions arrived at the field, they were marshalled by stewards who told the columns of female reformers to gather around the platform or hustings. Samuel Bamford's wife, Jemima, related that the woman with whom she was walking, a Mrs Yates, held onto her arm and 'would keep hurrying forward to get a good place, and when the crowd opened for the Middleton procession, Mrs. Yates and myself and some others of the women, went close to the hustings, quite glad that we had obtained such a situation for seeing and hearing all'.[12] Some women were to be on the hustings itself, to present banners and Caps of Liberty and hand over – possibly even read - Addresses. As the field filled up, other women were scattered amongst the crowd, sometimes in groups, sometimes with their menfolk, even a few on their own. Richard Carlile described the wind ruffling their long hair amidst a general air of sunny anticipation.

There has subsequently been much discussion of how many women were on the field of Peterloo, and in what capacity they got there. After the event, the authorities tried to say that there had been very few, but hardly anybody else agreed with them. The radical leaders, on the other hand, were keen to assert that the intent had been peaceful and suggested that women were there with their families almost as though for a holiday outing. However, this also does not exactly square with contemporary accounts. Careful analysis[13] of the various claims has resulted in the current view that women (amongst whose number children were included) constituted about an eighth – roughly twelve per cent – of the assembled crowd. Estimates vary, but somewhere between 60,000 and 80,000 people gathered on St Peter's Field that day, of whom only something between 7,500 and 9,000 were women, and many of those had arrived as part of organized groups. Women were certainly present in unusually high numbers, and their visibility and level of organization were also for many a provocative novelty, but the crowd remained overwhelmingly male in both number and tone.

Hunt's carriage took a long time to make its way through the streets to St Peter's Field. At every stage it was held up by the crowds, but it kept moving slowly along until it arrived at the edge of the space where the huge throng awaited it. At this point the brass bands that had been entertaining the crowd struck up 'See the Conqu'ring Hero Comes' from Handel's *Judas Maccabaeus*, a tune well-known by everybody. Hunt stood up in the carriage and waved his trademark white hat as the cheering crowd made way for him. The carriage was parked next to the hustings and Hunt and his companions got out and mounted the platform. The Manchester women joined the other Female Reformers at the front. One woman, Elizabeth Gaunt, was pregnant and exhausted, and Hunt suggested that she rest in the carriage. According to evidence given later at the Peterloo trials, Susannah Saxton was also seated in the carriage. Mary Fildes and several other women climbed onto the hustings with their banners and Caps of Liberty, where Richard Carlile saw that Mary:

> 'was elevated at one corner in the front, with a banner in her hand and resting on a large drum; a most singular and interesting situation for a female at such a Meeting; but a completer heroine never figured in any situation before. Joan of Arc could not have been more interesting.'[14]

The stage was now set.

The platform party that faced the vast crowd was large and consisted of several different groups. First, there were the reformers, who constituted the main element and most of whom intended to speak. As well as Hunt himself, there was John Knight, Joseph Johnson and several others. Then there were the female reformers, probably about eight or ten of them, ready to play their part in the proceedings and providing a very noticeable, very dramatic and rather unsettling demonstration of solidarity. One carried a white board with 'Order! Order!' painted on it, and several carried Addresses to be presented to Hunt. But there was also a small contingent of journalists, not just from Manchester, but also from London, who had come to observe what everyone knew was, for one reason or another, going to be a significant event. The Manchester meeting was the first of its kind to attract national attention and to make London-based newspapers think it worth actually sending someone to a place that took more than thirty hours to reach by coach, rather than depending on second-hand accounts many days, or even weeks, later. What happened next, as these people all crammed onto the limited space on the hustings, would reverberate around the country in a new and immediate way.

There was some difficulty in getting the crowd to quieten down and listen, but eventually it was achieved. Hunt took the chair and stood at the front to begin his speech. After a moment, John Knight tried to tell him something, but Hunt shook him off. Then things began to happen rather quickly. There was a commotion at the edge of the crowd; according to Samuel Bamford, some people thought it was the Blackburn contingent arriving. In fact it was the Deputy Constable, Joseph Nadin, accompanied by the mounted Manchester and Salford Yeomanry.

In the days and weeks leading up to the Manchester meeting the magistrates had not been idle. They had recruited hundreds of special constables who had been used to police the arrival of the crowds during the morning. They had stationed both the Manchester and Cheshire Yeomanries nearby, as well as regular infantry, cavalry and artillery troops in the side streets leading into the field. There were even two long, six-pound cannon in Lower Moseley Street, near where the Bridgewater Hall now stands. In all about 1,500 troops were encircling St Peter's Field, some of whom, in the case of the largely young and amateur yeomanry, were not entirely sober. Once the meeting started, the magistrates became solely responsible for what to do about it. They decided that it was seditious and a threat to public safety, and that Hunt and the rest of the platform party should be arrested. As we have seen, the notion of arresting people in the middle of meetings was not new, but it was risky. The magistrates thought the risk worth taking, withdrew the police constables from the field, and sent Nadin and the Manchester and Salford Yeomanry into the crowd.

The first casualties of Peterloo, however, were not actually on the field at all. Ann Fildes (probably no relation to Mary) had been out on an errand and was accidentally knocked down by a straggling cavalryman trying to catch up with the others. Ann was seriously injured, and her two-year-old son, William, whom she had been carrying, fell from her arms and was crushed under the horse's hooves. Ann survived, but William died that evening; the first, and the youngest, casualty of the day.

Meanwhile, the magistrates, seeing that the yeomanry were having difficulty getting through the press of people to the hustings, allegedly read the Riot Act. However, nobody in the crowd actually heard them do it, and they themselves subsequently declined to swear on oath in court that they had, so there was later considerable scepticism about their claim. Once the Riot Act had been 'read', however, the authorities were entitled to take any steps they thought necessary to break up the meeting, and this they did.

When the soldiers arrived at the hustings, the captain of the yeomanry, a mill owner called Hugh Birley, tried to arrest Hunt and Joseph Johnson. Hunt replied that he would surrender to the properly constituted civil authority, but not to the military, whereupon Joseph Nadin showed him the warrant. Hunt and Johnson jumped down from the platform and were hustled ungently away. Nadin also had warrants for others, including John Knight, but Knight disappeared in the mounting confusion and was arrested at home later. At this point the regular cavalry arrived and began to clear the field. These troops were more experienced, less likely to panic, and less concerned with capturing trophies, but they were also more efficient. Where the yeomanry used the edge of their blades, the Hussars used the flat; people injured by them were less likely to have open wounds but much more likely to have serious bruising and broken bones, though in fact at least as many injuries were caused by trampling and crushing as by blades. The crowd broke and fled, but the exits from the field were now all blocked by the military in one form or another. Nineteen-year-old William Joliffe, a lieutenant in the Hussars, later recalled that the charge:

'swept this mingled mass of human beings before it; people, yeomen, and constables, in their confused attempts to escape, ran one over the other; so that by the time we had arrived at the end of the field the fugitives were literally piled up to a considerable elevation above the level of the ground.'[15]

The Manchester Yeomanry had been instructed to arrest Henry Hunt, and that had been achieved. They had also been told, however, to seize or destroy every banner, placard and Cap of Liberty, and this they and the constables now proceeded to do, 'cutting most indiscriminately to the right and to the left in order to get at them'.[16] Women with their flags and caps had been concentrated around the platform, and they were treated as mercilessly as the men. Richard Carlile was standing next to Mary Fildes on the hustings and tried to reassure her, but he 'found her above everything like fear'. He helped some of the other women to escape through a gap between the two carts that had been pushed together to form the platform, crouching with them behind the wheels, just inches from the horses' hooves.[17] The constables were still trying to arrest people on the platform, including Mary, who now found herself attacked by men with weighted truncheons. Speaking in the third person in a petition to the House of Commons asking for a public inquiry she later recalled that she was:

'. . . violently assailed by a person of the name of Heiffor a special constable, who knocked the petitioner down with a truncheon heavily weighted, she believes, for the purpose of destruction, the blows of this man being followed up even after she was struck prostrate to the ground; Heiffor then forcibly wrenched out of her hand the pocket-handkerchief, with which she was wiping the blood from her forehead, and accompanying the act with the most dreadful oath, put the handkerchief into his own pocket.'[18]

John Thacker Saxton saw what happened and wrote in *The Manchester Observer* that:

'The lady who carried an elegant flag from the Manchester Female Reform Society, which she defended from the brutal attacks of a special constable with Amazonian intrepidity, was hurt in the forehead by this cowardly poltroon; who, however, was sufficiently collected, to deliberately pocket the white handkerchief, which [had] buffeted the air as she went along.'[19]

Other reporters also noticed Mary and her struggle. John Smith from the *Liverpool Mercury* said that she carried a flag and 'resolutely stuck to it until cut and when the staff was wrested from her, she kept hold of the drapery, and as she fell, twisted it round her waist'.[20] Edward Baines, the nineteen-year-old son of the editor of the *Leeds Mercury* was horrified by what he saw and reported that:

'One woman . . . who stood by her colours to the last, was cut down by a trooper. We should not state this, as thinking it totally incredible, had not our reporter seen the woman and flags fall together from the hustings, while the soldiers were cutting round them; and afterwards seen at least four or five women dreadfully wounded, conveyed to the Infirmary'[21]

As Mary either fell or tried to jump from the platform her dress or, if it was still wrapped round her, perhaps the flag itself, caught on a nail and she was left hanging and helpless. A man on horseback slashed at her with a sabre, and she was probably lucky not to have been killed. Somehow or other she freed herself or was freed, and, according to her 1821 petition statement, went home covered in blood and was unable to leave her room for a fortnight.

As she staggered away from the hustings she had to pass through dreadful scenes. Because of the size of the crowd, the geography of the field and the speed with which it was cleared, people were being knocked down, trampled and sabred. Many were stumbling, falling and being crushed by the weight of others either trying to run over them or falling on top of them. Women would have been particularly prone to these injuries because they could not run as fast as the men; they were more likely to be dragging or carrying children, and their movement was more restricted by their clothing. They had to run in ankle-length dresses over rough terrain, and most of them would also have been wearing corsets. Seventeen-year-old Ellen Harvey of Pendleton was reported as having been 'Struck on the stomach by a Yeoman's sabre which cut through her stays and broke a piece of whalebone two inches wide and a quarter of an inch thick'.[22] Neither youth nor childhood offered protection; Ellen Harvey's sisters, Elizabeth and thirteen-year-old Isabel, were trampled by horses and struck with the flat of sabres. Horrified, Richard Carlile reported that:

'A woman who was near the spot where I stood, and who held an infant in her arms, was sabred over the head, and her tender offspring DRENCHED IN ITS MOTHER'S BLOOD. Another was actually stabbed in the neck with the point of the sabre, which must have been a deliberate attempt on the part of the military assassin.'[23]

Many people were injured when they were forced up against the railings of the houses bordering the field on one side. In places these railings gave way, and people fell into the areas (often described as cellars) of the houses. This happened to 38-year-old Martha Partington and her friend Judith Kilner, who that morning had walked in together in the sunshine from Eccles. A man called John Brierley, a hatter from Oldham, recalled Martha's head lying on his shoulder whilst she 'cried most piteously'.[24] Martha died of suffocation, whilst Judith, who was pregnant with her sixth child, sustained a serious back injury.[25] Jemima Bamford, who had no idea where her husband Samuel was and feared that he might have been either arrested or hurt, had earlier got into the actual cellar where she sat appalled as she saw:

'. . . all the dreadful work through the window, and their exclamations were so distressing, that I put my fingers in my ears to prevent my hearing more; . . . The front door of the passage . . . soon after opened, and a number of men entered, carrying the body of a decent, middle-aged woman, who had been killed. I thought they were going to put her beside me, and was about to scream, but they took her forward, and deposited her in some premises at the back of the house.'[26]

Many people just ran for their lives, but some fought back. Despite Jemima's fears, Samuel Bamford was still free and had taken refuge near the Quaker Meeting House with some other people who began throwing stones at the oncoming cavalry. He recorded that:

'A heroine, a young married woman of our party, with her face all bloody, her hair streaming about her, her bonnet hanging by the string, and her apron weighted with stones, kept her assailant at bay until she fell backwards and was near being taken; but she got away covered with severe bruises.'[27]

When Mary Fildes finally got home she had to go into hiding whilst the constables scoured Manchester for her. They were determined to arrest everyone who had been on the hustings, and in the end only Mary and Richard Carlile escaped them. Carlile went straight back to London to publicize what had happened, but the hunt for Mary went on for some time. Initially there was confusion over which woman might be what the *New Times* contemptuously called the 'persistent Amazon' who had carried the flag on Hunt's carriage. The loyalist Wheeler's *The Manchester Courier*, for instance, reported that:

'Shortly two Females, who had come to the meeting under such ideal pomp, and with a demeanour the reverse of every thing that man delights to see in woman, were brought forward. One of them, Elizabeth Gaunt, had borne a standard in the carriage of Hunt; the other was much bruised, having received a contusion in the face.'[28]

Elizabeth Gaunt had been, together with Susannah Saxton, Mary Horton and others, in Hunt's carriage when the chaos began, but not when it entered the field. None of them were able to get away, and they were an easy target for the Manchester Yeomanry. They were beaten by the constables and one was stabbed in the throat with the point of a sabre. Despite being quite badly injured, Elizabeth Gaunt was dragged from the carriage and arrested.

John Tyas, the reporter from *The Times*, was also detained. As he approached the magistrates' house under guard he saw that 'the constables were conducting Hunt into it and were treating him in a manner in which they were neither justified by law nor humanity, striking him with their staves on the head'.[29] Tyas was taken into the parlour of the house where he found Hunt, Saxton, Knight and others, including Elizabeth Gaunt 'in a fainting condition'. Some of the magistrates present were 'assembled over wine, which they appeared to have drunk to the point of inebriation; on her asking for a glass of water, they refused it her, accompanying the denial by a language too brutal and indecent to state'. Later the prisoners, including Elizabeth, were marched from the magistrates' house to the New Bayley Prison just on the Salford side of the river; Tyas related that: 'The staffs of two of Hunt's banners were carried in mock procession before him.'

During the evening there were a number of outbreaks of violence, the most serious of which was at New Cross, where a shopkeeper displayed Mary Fildes's blood-stained banner in his window as a trophy. A crowd of women and boys gathered to protest, there was some stone throwing and abuse, and constables and soldiers were sent in to disperse the riot. Several people were shot, one fatally. One of those arrested was the 'uncontroulable (sic) woman, whose tongue no human effort could check'.[30] Another was Ann Scott, the wife of a boatbuilder, who was beaten and kicked by a constable, and hauled off to the New Bayley where she was held for nine weeks without trial. The conditions in which she was confined were so bad that she eventually became ill and had to be removed to the infirmary.

Meanwhile, having arrived at the New Bayley, Elizabeth Gaunt and the others were put into separate cells to await their court appearances. A number of other women had also been taken. Both Mary Waterworth from Stockport and Elizabeth Gaunt had been arrested on suspicion of being Mary Fildes, but Mary Waterworth was soon released on the grounds that she and Elizabeth could not both be the same woman. Ann Coates and Martha Conroy were released after a few days, but Elizabeth Gaunt and Sarah Hargreaves (who had been on the platform), were charged with treason, as were Henry Hunt and the other men. In her later petition to the House of Commons in support of a public enquiry, Elizabeth said that she was 'confined in a solitary cell, and suffered to remain a day and a half without any kind of food'. Her husband tried unsuccessfully to get in to see her, and he was also not allowed to send a doctor to examine her. Elizabeth was subjected to continuous questioning, being 'dragged many times a day from her cell up a flight of stairs to be exhibited', interrogated and then returned to her cell. By the end she was too weak to walk or even talk. Ten days after her arrest she and the other prisoners were taken to court where she was allowed to sit down and 'answered to her name but feebly, being unable to speak out from a tendency to faint'.[31] The court released both her and Sarah Hargreaves. Soon afterwards Elizabeth lost the child she was expecting.

Although there was no public inquiry into what happened that day, there were inquests and some people did try to pursue cases through the courts. The inquests were brief and often ignored the evidence of witnesses before arriving at verdicts of 'accidental death'. At Martha Partington's inquest, Judith Kilner tried to argue that her friend had been murdered, but the coroner was having none of it, and though he conceded that she had been smothered, the jury dutifully decided that it had been an unfortunate accident.

Judith Kilner's baby seems to have survived its mother's grim experience, but others were not so lucky. Bridget Hagan of Manchester miscarried as a result of being 'rode over by cavalry'. Catherine Oxley of Manchester and Elizabeth Mellor of Ancoats both miscarried as a result of being knocked over and trampled by the crowd. Catherine was also deafened by the blows to her head. Ellen Wood's child survived but was born blind, which the doctor said was caused by the injuries she had received. Mary Heys was dreadfully injured and suffered fits for weeks before dying in childbirth when her baby was born prematurely.

Many of the women injured were young, but age was no protection. Mary Orm, aged sixty-eight, had her hip dislocated by being 'thrown down and much trampled on', 71-year-old Alice Kenyon's ear was sliced almost completely off and Betty O'Neale, aged seventy-nine, had both external and internal injuries and was 'taken from the ground in an insensible state but was afraid to apply to the Infirmary, expecting to be sent to the New Bailey'. It is likely that many other people besides poor Betty failed to report injuries through fear of reprisals, and the number of those hurt was probably much higher than reported.

Since the state was clearly not going to help either the casualties and their relatives or those arrested, a subscription fund was set up to provide relief, and this raised quite a large sum. However, most of it went on paying the legal fees for Hunt, Knight, Saxton and the others at their trial early in 1820, and relatively little was left for the injured or bereaved. Unfortunately, the monies were distributed by people who clearly had little understanding of working-class life and the devastating effect the injuries received could have. People who had been permanently disabled were allocated the equivalent of a few weeks' wages, and the bald statements of their plight fail almost completely to convey the pain and suffering involved. Moreover, whilst the compensation scheme dealt with physical injury, there must have been terrible mental scars, too. These are almost impossible to track with any certainty, but occasionally they surface. 16-year-old Mary Ward[32] had not intended to go to the meeting at all, but she had been told that there would be music and entertainment, and so walked in from her home in Fallowfield with her cousin. When the attack began, Mary's white dress was splattered with the blood of a man sabred near her. Later she found herself tearing strips off her skirt to use as bandages. She was physically unhurt, but so traumatized that she never recovered.[33] There must have been many more such cases, but they went almost entirely unheard and unrecorded in an age in which trauma was very little understood, particularly when it came to working-class women.

In all, a total of 654 people are known to have been injured at Peterloo, of whom 168 – about a quarter – were women. Eighteen people were either killed or died soon after, including four women. These were Martha Partington, Mary Heys, Sarah Jones from Salford, who died from head injuries and Margaret Downes from Manchester, who died from chest wounds. Others may well have succumbed from their injuries later. At the time it was claimed that women were disproportionately targeted, particularly by the Manchester Yeomanry, and there is some evidence to support this. In many respects it was inevitable once the attempt to arrest the speakers began. The various female reform groups were very closely clustered around the hustings, and many had banners and emblems that the magistrates were keen to see destroyed. The women in the carriage, however, were not carrying anything, yet all were attacked and injured. The sight of women in a public space, unaccompanied by husbands and expressing political opinions, went against all the socially acceptable forms of behaviour for women, and seemed to many men – even in some cases to reformers – to challenge the whole structure of society. In a spectacular piece of victim-blaming, the coroner and jury at Martha Partington's inquest 'lamented the indiscretion of females wantonly throwing themselves in the way of harm, and said they must under such circumstances take the consequences'.[34] Women were particularly likely to be cut about the face and breasts; Henry Hunt reported visiting a woman who had her 'left breast taken clean off, leaving her ribs bare'.[35] Women were also vilified in the press. According to *The Morning Post*, for instance:

'Two noted female Reformers, of the names of Partington and Killer *(sic)*, left their homes at Eccles, along with their husbands, on the morning of the rebellious meeting at St. Peter's. They stopped at a public house by the way; and whilst drinking there, Partington stood up before the whole company with a glass of liquor in her hand "hoping to God she might never go back again alive, if they (the Reformers) did not carry their point that day".'[36]

A month later, a 'Manchester resident' refuted this in *The Morning Chronicle*, saying that the women had never been into 'any public house on the way, nor did they hear any such expression anywhere from Mrs Partington'.[37] But, by then it was too late, the story had been repeated by loyalist papers around the country.

With the exception of Richard Carlile, pro-reform reporters and artists tended to portray the women as helpless victims rather than active participants, to minimize their involvement in the political aspect of the day. Anti-reformist loyalists, on the other hand, continued to characterize women who had attended as morally lax, socially disreputable and displeasing to men. Even Henry Hunt felt obliged in his memoirs (written in prison after his conviction at his trial in early 1820) to justify the presence of Mary Fildes on the carriage, saying that as she was 'a married woman of good character, her appearance in such a situation by no means diminished the respectability of the procession, the whole of which was conducted with the greatest regularity and good order'.[38] The dividing lines on how political women should be represented in the press as well as in wider society were thus set, and unfortunately they had serious implications for women's activism in radical movements in particular. The reformers chose to defend women by characterizing them as helpless, innocent, respectable, victimized and weak. Cartoons and engravings designed to portray the horror of what had happened often showed women as the prey of male violence, crushed by the cavalry and assaulted by sabres. Most famously at the time, perhaps, George Cruikshank, whose cartoon of the Blackburn Female Reformers not six weeks earlier had attacked political women as sexual, venal and drunk, now produced '*Britons Strike Home!!!*', which had at its centre a kneeling woman trying to protect her child from a corpulent, red-faced cavalryman brandishing a sabre. This image of woman as the weaker sex to be defended was now baked into the radical view of women's place in reformist movements, and would have consequences when both the next wave of reform campaigns and the later Chartist movement came into being. In the meantime, the Female Reform Societies continued to exist, but much reduced and largely without their public role on platforms.

Richard Carlile, on the other hand, was very forcibly struck by the audacious courage of the women he had seen, and by Mary Fildes in particular. When he returned to London, he commissioned an unknown artist to produce a picture that he dedicated to Henry Hunt and the Female Reformers of Manchester. It shows the hustings with several figures on it rising above a tangled mass of horses, soldiery, swords and unarmed people. In the centre of the platform, Henry Hunt, with his famous white hat, stands with his arm outstretched as if trying to calm things down. Near him is Mary Fildes, her banner surmounted by its Cap of Liberty fluttering above her and a sprig of green in her straw bonnet to signify peace and reform. To the modern eye, her bonnet and white gown are oddly reminiscent of those worn by Jane Austen characters in books that were being written at exactly that time. Mary is shown raising one hand as if to ward off what is coming, and below her she can see her friends in the carriage being sabred by the troops. She is the only woman on the hustings, and all the other female figures in the image conform to the stereotype of victimhood. But Mary's upright, horrified, defiant figure remains for posterity one of the enduring images to come out of that day, an emblem of all the working-class women who came to St Peter's Field in both body and spirit to claim their place on the political stage, and paid, both then and in the future, such a terrible price.

Figure 1 Thomas Rowlandson The Contrast 1792, Which is Best? (©Getty Images).

Figure 2 Mary Wollstonecraft (©Getty Images).

Figure 3 The March to Versailles (©Getty Images).

Figure 4 Helen Maria Williams (©British Museum).

Figure 5 Anna Letitia Barbauld (©Alamy).

Figure 6 Edmund Burke running the Literary Gauntlet. Helen Maria Williams is in profile at the left, and Anna Laetitia Barbauld third from left, with Richard Price between them (©Getty Images).

Figure 7 George Cruikshank, 'The Belle-alliance: or female reformers of Blackburn!!!' (@Mary Evans Picture Library).

Figure 8 To Henry Hunt . . . and the Female Reformers of Manchester at Peterloo, (cartoonist unknown) (National Portrait Gallery).

Figure 9 Manchester Female Radical Society (By kind permission of Cheethams Library, Manchester).

Figure 10 Anna Doyle Wheeler (National Portrait Gallery).

ELIZA SHARPLES CARLILE ("ISIS").

From a Crayon Copy of an Oil Painting.

Figure 11 Eliza Sharples.

Figure 12 Leeds Reform Meeting 1832 (By kind permission of Leeds City Libraries).

PART THREE

Monsters in Female Form

Richard Carlile left St Peter's Field determined to tell the world about what he had witnessed. Having got himself back to London as rapidly as the chaos (and initially getting into the wrong coach) would allow, he wrote and published an excoriating account of what had happened. He was particularly enraged by the treatment meted out to the women who, he wrote, 'appear to have been the particular objects of the fury of the Cavalry Assassins'.[1] He changed the name of the paper he ran from *Sherwin's Political Register* to *The Republican,* and immediately started to escalate the running battle he had been waging with the government ever since he had first become involved in reformist politics in 1817. But Carlile was much more than just a reformer, and after Peterloo he was scarcely a reformer at all. He saw himself as a republican, a revolutionary, and above all, an infidel[2] and a freethinker, and he wielded the press as his primary weapon against the oppression he saw all around him.

In the aftermath of Peterloo, the government mopped up radical leaders as fast as they could. Except for Mary Fildes and Richard Carlile, all the speakers and organizers of Peterloo were arrested on one pretext or another. In Carlile's case, however, it was not necessary to hunt him down, for by the end of the year he was safely locked up in Dorchester Gaol anyway, having been convicted of blasphemous libel and sentenced to two years imprisonment and a hefty fine. Everyone else was pursued by the government with enthusiastic attention to detail. James Wroe, the editor of the *The Manchester Observer*, was convicted of several counts of seditious libel and sentenced to a year's imprisonment. However, this was not the end of it. The men Wroe employed in his shop were prosecuted, as well as both his brothers. His wife, Jane, found herself serving six months' hard labour, and not even his children were exempt, his seventeen-year-old daughter being fined £5 and his eleven-year-old son sixpence.

Despite the graphic reporting of the massacre and the outrage of middle-of-the-road papers such as *The Times* and the *Leeds Mercury*, the magistrates and the military were lauded by Tories and loyalists. There were congratulatory dinners and resolutions, and in November, despite Whig opposition, Parliament passed the notorious Six Acts – generally known as the Gagging Acts – banning unauthorized political meetings, outlawing flags and insignia such as the Cap of Liberty, giving powers to magistrates to search houses for arms, banning military drill and speeding up trials for political offences. Significantly, the Acts also tightened up the laws on unstamped newspapers and increased the penalties for publishing blasphemy and sedition; this was to have a direct and catastrophic impact on radical publications.

The Gagging Acts were, collectively, regarded either as necessary and appropriate (by Tories and conservatively minded independents such as William Wilberforce) or a hugely repressive over-reaction (by Whigs, radicals, reformers and many working-class people). Some of the legislation, such as the Seditious Meetings Act, had a sunset clause built in, which meant that it expired after a set period. But this did not apply to all of it, and the Unlawful Drilling Act (though by then disused for any real purpose), was only finally repealed in 2008. The Blasphemous and Seditious Libels Act, shorn of some of its penalties and more outdated clauses and renamed the Criminal Libel Act, remains in force to this day in England and Wales.[3]

For Carlile, the stamp tax posed particular problems. Together with periodicals that published news, newspapers had been subject to a stamp tax since 1712. In 1797 it had been increased, and it had to be paid on every copy printed, regardless of whether or not it was sold. In 1815 it had gone up again to four pence, which, together with a heavy tax on paper, effectively put newspapers out of the reach of most working-class people. However, the law left an ambiguity that meant that if papers published commentary and satire, they could avoid having to pay the tax; both Thomas J Wooler's *Black Dwarf* and Carlile's *Republican* had exploited this omission to the full and thus been able to attain their relatively wide readership. The Six Acts firmly closed that loophole and additionally required editors to pay bonds that could be forfeited if they broke the rules. The stamp applied to any paper published at least once a month that cost less than sixpence, a net which caught almost all the newspapers and magazines of the time. In many cases, the tax was actually more than the cost of the paper. The Act had the desired chilling effect on the distribution of news as well as the development of both national and regional publications. Many radical papers either closed or went underground. *The Manchester Observer* lost the battle for survival in 1821, and the *Black Dwarf* in 1824. *The Republican*, which at one point had a wider circulation than *The Times*, finally ceased publication in 1826, after years of being produced by Carlile under, as we shall see, some extraordinary conditions.

By the time the Peterloo leaders went on trial at York in March 1820, the political climate had shifted. King George III died in January 1820 and his son, the unpopular Prince Regent, ascended the throne as George IV. It soon became clear that the question of his relationship with his wife, Caroline, was going to blow up into a serious constitutional issue. She had been living abroad for some years, completely cut off by George from their daughter, Princess Charlotte, of whose marriage in 1816 and subsequent pregnancy and death in childbirth in 1817, she heard only by chance. When George became King, therefore, there was immediate apprehension in some quarters and speculation in most as to what Caroline would do. She was now regarded by popular opinion – and particularly by women – as a virtuous Queen wronged by an immoral and vicious husband; the rather more scandalous details of Caroline's life abroad, which would emerge later, were not widely known at this point, though rumours were rife. On the other hand, both George and the government found the prospect of Caroline arriving to claim her rights utterly horrifying, and many believed that when it came to it she would stay away. Communications being unreliable, nobody knew whether she was coming or not, or what she would do if she did. The King was desperate to keep her away and wanted a divorce, which the government was equally desperate to avoid, since it would bring all the salacious details of both royal lives into the public domain. Attempts were made to pay Caroline to stay away, and the excitement and uncertainty over what might happen next was palpable.

The developing crisis occupied public attention almost to the exclusion of everything else, but other factors were also beginning to change the political landscape. The economy was starting to recover after its post-war dip, and food prices were falling. The combination of the reactionary aftermath of Peterloo, the improving economy and the perennial fascination of an almighty royal row began to drain energy from the reform movement. Meanwhile, another focus of public attention was the arrest in February of the Cato Street conspirators, who were accused of plotting to murder the whole Cabinet. In fact, although there was indeed a plot, it had hardly been a well-kept secret, and had easily been infiltrated by a government *agent provocateur*, George Edwards, whom the leader of the plotters, Arthur Thistlewood, had actually made his deputy. When the conspirators read in the loyalist *New Times* of a dinner to be held for government ministers in Cato Street, they decided to use it to assassinate them. Unfortunately for them, the dinner was a hoax set up by Edwards and the Home Office, and the conspirators were arrested. Although the trial was not due until April, there was much rumour, counter-rumour and speculation about the whole affair.[4]

Despite all this, the Peterloo trials were widely reported. In the end the charges were not capital, so Hunt and the others stood in no danger of the noose, but most were sentenced to terms of imprisonment. John Thacker Saxton was acquitted on the grounds that he had, as a journalist, been there merely to observe and report; this was one of the earliest occasions upon which the courts accepted that the press had the right to report events without penalty. Hunt was sentenced to two years and dispatched to Ilchester Gaol in Somerset. The rest received a year apiece. By this stage almost the whole of the radical leadership was now either in prison or bound over for good behaviour for enormous sureties. For the time being, the radical reform movement was disabled and its press increasingly silenced.

Henry Hunt, however, was determined to continue the fight, and from his Ilchester gaol cell he oversaw the establishment of the Great Northern Union (GNU). This was a national body that was to organize itself in local branches and collect subscriptions from members. The money would be used to buy five or six seats in the House of Commons, thus getting reformers into Parliament. Hunt himself was to take the first seat, which was to be Preston. Carlile was scathing about this plan, thundering that: 'Their talk about Radical Reform . . . is a greater delusion than any thing that has yet been practised upon any nation comparatively civilized and intelligent. The Great Northern Radical Union is a cheat that picks the pocket and corrupts the mind, . . . It will end in nothing, . . .'[5] In this last prediction he was right, but his own solutions to the problem were no better. He took the principles of Tom Paine to be almost biblical in their infallibility, and he gave very short shrift indeed to anyone who disagreed with him. Where Hunt retained a respect for the institutions of the country and a belief in the Christian religion, Carlile detested them and raged continuously against both church and monarchy. He was didactic, self-righteous and sectarian, and unfortunately for the reform movement, Hunt could match him in all of these. Neither was prepared to concede an inch, and between them they amply demonstrated Anna Laetitia Barbauld's observation twenty years earlier that too many reformers wanted 'people to be happy their way; whereas every one must be happy his own . . .'[6] From their respective gaol cells, they bellowed at one another about everything, including whose prison conditions were worst. Most infuriatingly of all to Carlile, Hunt accused him of cowardice at Peterloo. It was an unedifying quarrel and showed neither man at his best, although some allowance has to be made for the possibility that both were suffering from some form of post-traumatic stress disorder following the harrowing experience of Peterloo. Unfortunately, it also reflected a fundamental split in radical politics and would never be resolved.

Hunt was undoubtedly by far the most popular of the pair with radicals and reformers. He had a much better understanding of what people wanted and how they thought, and despite his ego and more than occasional arrogance, he was widely held in respect and affection, particularly in the North. To mark his birthday in 1820, no fewer than nine Mancunian babies, including Mary Fildes' youngest, were named after him in a mass baptism. Despite the government's best efforts to paint all radicals as ungodly and irreligious, most were rather shocked by Carlile's infidelism and appalled by the violence of some of his opinions. But all the characteristics that could make him impossible to deal with either personally or politically, came into their own when he began his battle with the government and the courts for freedom of thought and of the press. Then his dogged refusal to concede even the most minor of points wore down a highly reactionary and determined government and scored one of the few radical victories of the 1820s.

The fight that Carlile picked with the religious and political establishment was ostensibly over the publication of the works of Tom Paine, but was in fact about the use of religion as a political and economic weapon against the working class. Religion was part of the fabric of society, but it was also perceived by the governing elites as a useful mechanism for controlling the behaviour of the lower orders. Ridiculing Christianity, treating it with contempt, or suggesting that the Church of England was corrupt, venal or absurd could all lead to a charge of blasphemy or blasphemous libel. However, the government did not have the necessary machinery with which to seek out and prosecute deviant thought, and the police service existed in only the most rudimentary form. Into the vacuum, therefore, stepped vigilante organizations committed to stamping out wickedness in all its forms, and, in particular, to the silencing of deist or atheist thought and revolutionary ideas. The Society for the Suppression of Vice (generally known as the Vice Society) was founded in 1802 by Anglicans, and soon attracted evangelicals and, in particular, William Wilberforce, Hannah More and the Clapham Sect, all keen to enforce conformity on the wider public, particularly in London. The Vice Society had a variety of offences in its sight, including 'blasphemy, profane swearing and cursing, lewdness, profanation of the Lord's Day, and other dissolute, immoral, or disorderly practices'.[7] Amongst these was the publication of obscene literature, the definition of which included the works of deists or anyone believed to be atheist, or to have atheist tendencies. Prime amongst these were the works of Thomas Paine, banned by the government since 1792, but still much read and sought after under the counter.

Very early on in its existence, the Vice Society and its sister organization the Constitutional Association for Opposing the Progress of Disloyal and Seditious Principles (known by radicals as 'the Bridge Street gang' from the location of their headquarters), acquired a controversial reputation for the use of spies and *agents provocateurs*. They paid people to buy things from shops on Sundays, for instance, so that the Society could then bring a prosecution for Sunday trading with their own employee as the chief witness against the defendant. In their first couple of years they brought a total of nearly 700 prosecutions in London, of which more than 600 were for Sunday trading in one form or another.[8] Most of the defendants were small shopkeepers supplying local needs, so it is hardly surprising if the idea quickly sprang up that the Vice Society was persecuting working people. Despite several attempts to do so, this was a perception the Society never managed to throw off. It seemed to be, as the editor of the *Edinburgh Review*, Sydney Smith, called it 'a Society for supressing the vices of persons whose income does not exceed 500l per annum'.[9] Remarking on the natural propensity of societies promoting virtue to descend into something rather less acceptable, Smith observed:

'Beginning with the best intentions in the world, such societies must in all probability degenerate into a receptacle for every species of title-tattle, impertinence, and malice. Men, whose trade is rat-catching, love to catch rats; the bug destroyer seizes on his bug with delight; and the suppresser is gratified by finding his vice.'[10]

In 1817 the journalist and publisher William Hone had scored a famous victory against the government when he was triumphantly acquitted of three separate counts of blasphemy, but this only spurred the Vice Society on. Agents of the Society regularly visited bookshops asking for a copy of one of Tom Paine's works; any bookseller supplying them was prosecuted. A conviction might result in a fine, but it might also result in a prison sentence. On their side the Society had money, the law and the support of highly respected pillars of society such as Wilberforce and Hannah More. Ranged against them were largely working-class women and men who persisted regardless of the penalties. The reactionary press supporting the Vice Society were particularly offended by the women; in 1822 the *New Times* raged against 'these monsters in female form *(who)* stand forward with hardened visages . . . to give their public countenance for the first time in the history of the Christian world to gross, vulgar, horrid blasphemy'.[11]

In fact, the women who stood to oppose the might of the Georgian state did so, as we shall see, from a variety of motives, not all of which were either radical or particularly sympathetic to modern sensibilities. But they were united in a feeling that the state had no business trying to control what they or their families thought, and they doggedly refused to give in in the face of seemingly insuperable odds. In many accounts of the movement for freedom of thought and of the press, these women are treated as marginal characters, but when they take centre stage they turn out to have remarkable stories, and to have made conscious and material contributions to the fight for freedom of thought.

Chapter 7
Beyond Expression Horrible

In the spring of 1813, Jane Cousins, 'the daughter of a humble cottager, in a sequestered part of Hampshire' who had 'reached the years of maturity without any, the least education',[1] was living in Alverstoke, near Gosport. She was 'not without accomplishments as to personal appearance',[2] and she was intelligent and hard-working. She was quick-tempered and did not suffer fools gladly but she was also warm-hearted with a great dislike of injustice. In religion she was on the whole conventional; to politics she gave no thought. We do not know in what trade she earned her living, but she must have had one, since rural working-class families could not afford to support single daughters who did not work. At thirty she was old to be unmarried, and must almost have given up hope of ever finding a husband, but early in April 1813 she met a 23-year-old itinerant tinplate worker called Richard Carlile. She married him in May in the parish church at Alverstoke. Richard signed his name in the register, but Jane simply made her mark with an 'X'.

Richard Carlile had been born and brought up in Devon, but was now on his way to London to look for work. Once married, the couple travelled on to the capital, where Carlile found a job fairly easily, and they moved into lodgings in Holborn. Over the next six years, Jane gave birth to three sons, Richard, Alfred and Thomas Paine. It is possible that, during those years, Carlile taught his wife to write; certainly he taught his sister, who at some point came from Devon to live with them and help with the children. He later approvingly described Jane as having 'most of the qualifications necessary to a good trades man's wife',[3] and initially he settled happily into the routine of a relatively well-paid trade and a contented home life. 'I was not', he later said:

> 'that idle, drunken, brutish character, that would do any thing to be rid of a wife and family, or run into any thing as a freak; I was a regular, active, and industrious man, . . . and when out of the workshop, never so happy any where as at home with my wife and . . . children.'[4]

At this stage he had few political interests. However, all around him he heard talk of revolution, radicalism and reform, and slowly he began to imbibe new ideas. The peace of 1815 brought a downturn in the tinplate trade, and as food prices rose rapidly, he found himself struggling to keep his little family housed and fed. In London, as elsewhere, there were riots, demonstrations and reform meetings, and Carlile began to read the radical press, in particular William Cobbett's *Two-Penny Trash*, the first mass circulation paper aimed at working-class people and hugely influential in politicizing a generation. Although Cobbett was radical in politics, however, he had started life as a Tory, and his views on society and religion were very conservative. Carlile would soon go far beyond anything he found in *Two-Penny Trash*.

If his conversion to political activism was relatively late, his progress to notoriety was astonishingly rapid. Many people became radicals or reformers after 1815, but in Carlile's case it seems to have struck him with particular force. Urgent action was needed. He began to bombard people such as Cobbett and Henry Hunt, and the editors of radical newspapers, with extreme political ideas and ill-considered proposals for action. To a man, they were unimpressed, one noting contemptuously that 'Half-employed mechanic is too violent'.[5] Then, in March 1817, and probably to Jane's horror, Carlile abandoned the tinplate trade altogether and threw himself into a new venture selling ultra-radical publications. 'When I first started as a hawker of pamphlets', he said later, 'I knew nothing of political principles; I had never read a page of Paine's writings; but I had a complete conviction, that there was something wrong somewhere, and that the right application of the Printing Press was the remedy'.[6] Through hawking, he met William Sherwin, who, at the tender age of eighteen was writing and publishing *Sherwin's Political Register* from a shop in Fleet Street. With remarkable speed, Carlile persuaded

Sherwin to install him there to manage the business. He was by now convinced that the government should be challenged at every turn, and as soon as he took over the shop he was spoiling for a fight. He got one by publishing an early Painite poem from the radical youth of the now highly respectable poet Robert Southey, followed by pirated versions of parodies written by the author and bookseller William Hone, then awaiting trial on blasphemy charges. As commercial ventures they were hugely successful, and in August 1817, whilst habeas corpus was still suspended, Carlile was arrested and consigned to the King's Bench Prison for an indefinite period.

The King's Bench was a notorious hotbed of anti-government feeling. Carlile – at this point still in his twenties – had begun to be radicalized by a combination of what he was reading, what he could see happening around him and the feeling that, no matter how hard he tried, he was always going to be at the mercy of forces he could not control. Prison completed the process. When someone gave him illegal copies of Thomas Paine's *Rights of Man* and *Age of Reason* their effects were profound, and he was an immediate convert to both republicanism and deism. As a result, he decided to reprint all Paine's banned works, an action that was bound to infuriate the authorities and could even incur a capital charge of high treason. However, William Hone's courtroom triumph, followed by the acquittal of the Spa Field defendants of charges of high treason,[7] had made the government cautious, and in London as in Lancashire, juries were insisting on exercising their own judgement in political trials. Although Carlile's combative approach was unlikely to win him friends in a court of law, he thought the risk worth taking. In December, he was released from prison, still poor but having 'got a name of being a good fellow, a bad fellow, a daring fellow, a dangerous fellow, . . . a fortune is half made when a name is made'.[8]

By the time he wrote this in 1823, Carlile had been in Dorchester Gaol for more than three years, but the exhilaration of his discovery of his life's work was still evident. He was by nature a controversialist, and the conviction of the rightness of his own opinions and actions would bear him up through vicissitudes that would have broken other men. He fell out at one time or another with almost everyone he met, but he had intelligence, principle and resolve, and he fought a repressive government with single-minded courage and endurance. Unfortunately, as we shall see, he expected everyone around him to do the same, and his commitment to women's rights, which he fully believed to be genuine, did not necessarily extend to affording them to the women with whom he lived.

The government turned out to be disinclined to arrest him for treason, but the Vice Society was very happy to oblige him with a prosecution for blasphemous libel, an offence which was often used to try to silence religious debate. Almost everybody in the country was Christian, and the majority were members of the Church of England. Deists, who believed that reason and nature rather than divine revelation provided the only valid evidence for God's existence, were few and far between, and outright atheists even fewer. Religious ceremonies marked all the rites of passage such as birth, marriage and death, and membership of the established Anglican church – effectively the state religion – gave access to legal and civil rights. Marriage was a sacrament; there was no civil marriage ceremony and no religious divorce. Civil divorce was effectively impossible for ordinary people to get, since it required a substantial amount of money and an Act of Parliament in each individual case. Even then, only men could initiate it; women had no rights whatsoever.

In all kinds of ways, the Anglican church was the glue that held society together. It taught people their place in the world, and enforced a sense of duty and obligation that kept them there. The ruling classes were fully aware of this; speaking in 1823 the then Home Secretary, Robert Peel, observed in the House of Commons that, 'The law of the country made it a crime to make any attempt to deprive the lower classes of their belief in the consolations of religion; and while this law remained unrepealed, he should think himself wanting in his duty, if he shrunk from applying and enforcing it'.[9] Educated middle- and upper-class men objected to being lectured by people they considered their inferiors. One judge at a blasphemy trial, referring to Carlile and apparently forgetting that Jesus had been a carpenter, asked with disgust, 'What, are we to take our religion from a tinman?'[10] The courts were routinely used to enforce conformity, as was the education provided for those who could afford it. For everyone else, the charity schools that taught the labouring-classes to read and write were often run by churches, religious organizations or philanthropic Christians, whilst those provided by mill owners had an obvious interest in teaching subservience and obedience as religious as well as civil duties. Members of the evangelical Clapham Sect, who were leading lights in the movement to abolish the slave trade, also supported the extension of education, prison reform, the reduction of the use of capital punishment and limited parliamentary reform. However, they were implacably socially conservative, believing that the working classes should remain in that estate into which God had called them, and that women had no place in the public realm and ought to be subordinate to their husbands. Even when it came to the anti-slavery movement, Wilberforce had reservations about the role of women in it, writing to a friend that 'for ladies to meet, to publish, to go from house to house stirring up petitions – these appear to me proceedings unsuited to the female character as delineated in Scripture'.[11] Hannah More wrote many tracts on the necessity for the labouring classes to accept and even embrace their lowly estate. The complex intertwining of civil and religious rights meant that an involvement in religion was very difficult to escape, even for those who, like Richard Carlile, rejected it. Despite everything, and possibly thanks to Jane, all of their children were baptized into the Anglican church; failure to do this could have jeopardized their future civil and political rights.

For women, religion governed their lives at every turn and was widely believed to be what kept them on the straight and narrow. Women's obligations to their fathers, husbands and children were regarded as sacred, and from birth they were surrounded by a cultural as well as religious reinforcement of their position. In a system that was almost Orwellian in its ability to invert reality, women were taught that the laws that deprived them of their rights were in fact there for their protection, and that the religion that told them that St Paul's dictum that 'Women should remain silent in the churches. They are not allowed to speak, but must be in submission, as the law says',[12] was in fact in their interests. Women's silence, and their retreat into the background of any situation, was not just an obligation, but a positive attraction. 'I must own', said the young Mary Wollstonecraft in her book *Thoughts on the Education of Daughters*, 'I am quite charmed when I see a sweet young creature, shrinking as it were from observation, listening rather than talking'.[13] There was much discussion of the types of silence that women might adopt, when female speech was permissible and how women should guard, moderate and control their voices, both privately and in public.

For middle- and upper-class women, acceptable public spaces in which they could appear were the church, respectable social gatherings and occasional set pieces, such as, during the wars with France, the presentation of military colours to regiments. Working-class women usually had to earn a living from a very young age, and many would have to go on working all their lives, but they were often just as committed to the accepted idea of sacramental marriage and the duties it incurred as their middle-class sisters. They tended to marry later, and it was by no means unusual for them not to marry until they were pregnant, but once the knot had been tied all the same restrictions and expectations applied. When Jane Cousins married Richard Carlile, she understood with absolute clarity that to be a 'good' woman she would have to keep her promise of obedience, not just with diligence, but with joy. This obedience was, in all classes, regarded as one of women's great glories and fulfilment of it in challenging circumstances an admirable virtue. Even radical and republican women found it impossible to break away from this view of marriage. Most women accepted that their place was divinely ordained and could not be changed, indeed, that it was wicked to question it at all.

Long before Karl Marx described religion as the opium of the people, Tom Paine, Richard Carlile and others like them had come to much the same conclusion. But they were in a tiny minority, and the open expression of their opinions was a risky business. This was particularly true when it came to women, whose role in society was so profoundly connected with religion that any questioning of it seemed blasphemous, and vice versa. The editor of the *New Times* was deeply reactionary, but he undoubtedly spoke for the majority when, in 1822, he said that 'Blasphemy from any lip is shocking, but from those of a female it is beyond expression horrible'.[14]

Despite all this, the English, in particular, believed themselves to be living in a tolerant country where freedom of thought and of the press were basic rights guaranteed under the constitution. Thus, they were even more outraged when that perception was contested, or when radicals used the liberties granted to them to bite the hand that fed them. The charge of blasphemy,[15] which could result in a term of imprisonment, was useful for attacking people such as Carlile. On the other hand, a charge of blasphemous libel could also be very useful to publishers and writers in terms of publicity, and so Carlile found it. By the end of 1818 his editions of Paine's works were selling out at least in part because of the notoriety of their publisher.

However, this did not necessarily lead to prosperity or an easier life. Although he was making large amounts of money, Carlile had also borrowed quite a large sum to buy the lease on William Hone's old bookshop at 55 Fleet Street, which he described as being:

> '. . . in a ruinous state; not a stove, a lock or a fixture in it. Glass much shattered, stair-case falling down; shop floor quite rotten, in fact, with the exception of an excellent shop front, the house was a barn, and such as no one would live in, but for the sake of the shop. . . . Having possession of my new worn-out house, I soon felt that I was got into the right sphere for action.'[16]

By this stage Jane had three little boys under the age of seven to look after, and may or may not have been pleased at the prospect of living above a shop so dilapidated that no-one else wanted it. However, it was her duty to make the best of it and she did what she could. But waiting for Carlile's case to come to court, combined with the long hours she was working and the conditions in which she was living, were very stressful, and things deteriorated still further when, in March 1819, the baby died at the age of eleven months. Jane was then already expecting her fourth child, and when Carlile, still locked in his very public running battle with the legal system, went up to Manchester in August 1819 she was six months pregnant. In November he was finally tried, convicted, sentenced to three years' imprisonment, plus the payment of a huge fine of £1,500, and dispatched to Dorchester Gaol, leaving Jane with two small children to support, another about to be born and the shop to run. She had a very good head for business and was more than capable of keeping things going on her own, but as she did so she must have known full well that her husband's plan was that she also should be prosecuted. The birth (of another boy, named Thomas Payne like the baby who had died in March) was difficult, made worse by the Sheriff raiding both the shop and the living quarters and taking everything, including the furniture. This was ostensibly done so that Carlile's possessions could be auctioned in part-payment of the fine, but actually his goods were impounded so to prevent payment, since if the fine was not paid his sentence could be almost indefinitely extended.

In January, Jane travelled through dreadful weather to Dorchester with two-month-old Thomas and the bookshop accounts for Carlile's inspection. The loss of (according to Carlile) £2,000-worth of stock, together with almost all of their furniture had hit them hard, but despite this Jane had got things going again. Before his conviction she had managed to save 'a few hundred pounds', but this was now all spent on medical and travel expenses, printing bills, paying bail and fines, and buying back from the Sheriff, at a cost of £55, some of her own furniture, including her bed, which had been removed from under her by the Sheriff's men within hours of her having given birth. By the time she returned from her trip to Dorchester, she had just £30 with which to pay the outstanding bills. Carlile was full of admiration for her business abilities, but he freely admitted that when it came to money he himself was careless. 'For my own part', he said, with what sounds like misplaced pride:

'I can say, that I never kept fifty pounds in money in my possession one week, up to this day, and never troubled about money for myself beyond the current wants from week to week, or sometimes, I may have had a month's supply.'[17]

In Dorchester Gaol he was kept separate from the other prisoners so as not to contaminate them with his wicked ideas, but he was allowed writing materials, newspapers and books, and he worked tirelessly to keep *The Republican* in print. He kept up a steady stream of instructions to Jane from his cell, and was dismayed when she did not greet them all with enthusiasm. Supporters of the cause of free speech, republicanism and deism turned up at the shop to help and bombarded her with advice. Some wanted her to 'let her shop to some person that would better stand prosecution'. Carlile described her as 'doubting and distracted, not knowing what to do, or which way to look', whilst the Sheriff and the Vice Society were 'threatening immediate prosecution if she followed my business and instructions'.[18] She was constantly harassed by the authorities, being arrested and required to find bail, and never knowing at what point they would actually charge her. Against Carlile's wishes, she did not sell books that had already been condemned by the courts, but everything else was available as it had been before, and the tone and content of *The Republican* continued unchanged.

Despite all this, however, by April she had paid off the debts and made a surplus of £200. Carlile promptly spent it on printing a deluxe edition of the works of Thomas Paine, which plunged the business back into debt again.

In June 1820, Jane was finally charged with publishing seditious libel. This was in the form of a letter from Carlile in his prison cell in Dorchester to the Reverend William Wait in Bristol, in the course of which he had advocated the assassination of tyrants, amongst whose number he included ministers of the Crown. Jane had published the letter in *The Republican*, a copy of which she had sold to an agent of the Vice Society. Thus on 19 January 1821, she found herself before the Lord Chief Justice and a special jury at the Guildhall. The prosecuting lawyer was the Solicitor General in person, a man who, by an ironic little quirk, was also the MP for the constituency of Ashburton, in Devon, where Richard Carlile had been born.[19] Jane did not appear alone, however; some of Carlile's friends were in court to support her and she had her baby in her arms. She had no lawyer, but she did have a statement that was to be read in her defence; she was effectively intending to defend herself. Women did not usually make speeches in court, and were certainly not permitted to practice as lawyers, but a famous case in 1818 had provided Carlile with an example he thought his wife should follow. A Cornish woman called Mary Ann Tocker had successfully defended herself against a charge of libel brought by a lawyer whom she had accused of electoral corruption and extorting money from clients. She was, in fact, the first woman to act as a lawyer in her own or anyone else's defence, and when she won the case she provided the reform movement with a stunning victory. Richard Carlile had been hugely impressed, writing that 'the lady's fame . . . shall remain unsullied, when the name of her oppressors shall be buried in oblivion'.[20] Mary Ann Tocker, however, had the advantage of being a literate middle-class woman whose brother was a solicitor, and whilst she had indeed conducted her case entirely herself, she had not done so from Jane's position. However, Jane's inability to turn herself into a lawyer overnight was no impediment to Carlile, for whom success was not necessarily defined as acquittal.

For her defence, Jane had a lengthy speech that resounded with her husband's voice and had hardly an echo of hers. Neither was it hers in any physical sense, either; she handed it to the Clerk of the Court who read it out, which must have robbed it entirely of any life or spontaneity it might otherwise have had. Carlile was a polemicist rather than a speechwriter, and Jane's plea reads more like an article from *The Republican* than an address to the court. It began, predictably enough, with a denial of responsibility for the content of the letter.

> 'I assure you, Gentlemen, that I have neither the power nor the ability to undertake any alteration in the manuscript transmitted for the press, and I never read it until printed. I may be told that this can form no excuse for me, and that it is a misplaced confidence. I would answer, Gentlemen of the Jury, that I proceed in it as a matter of conjugal duty . . .'[21]

The speech then went on to expound, in some detail, the right of the oppressed to rise up against tyrants as expounded by 'the best authorities, and from such authorities as no man in this Court would rise to decry'. Referring (amongst others) to Moses, Plato, Aristotle, Solon, Cicero, Tertullian, St Augustine and Sophocles, and even the Bible, Carlile outlined his case, at one point even breaking into verse. He attacked the government over its handling of recent events, including the repeated suspensions of habeas corpus and the massacre at Peterloo. If, he declaimed:

> '. . . studiously and openly to corrupt the representatives of the people be not tyranny: if to imprison men for months and years without any specific charge, and then to liberate them without trial, be not tyranny: if to seek Indemnity Bills for admitted violations of the laws, be not tyranny: if to encourage the assassination of a peaceable and legally assembled multitude, such as was the Manchester Meeting, on St. Peter's Plain, on the 16th of August, 1819; and to shelter the murderers, by screening them from justice, be not tyranny: if the late Bill of Pains and Penalties against the Queen be not tyranny: then, indeed, I am ignorant in what tyranny consists . . .'[22]

A few more flourishes brought him to the end of the peroration, whereupon the Solicitor General correctly said that it could not possibly have been Jane's work, and that it was 'nothing more than an aggravation of the libel: its stile and tendency are calculated to produce still more mischief'. His summing up was a model of brevity, as was that of the Chief Justice, who backed the Solicitor General up to the hilt, and virtually instructed the jury as to what verdict they should bring in. It took them precisely fifteen minutes to comply, and Jane Carlile was duly found guilty. However, before the verdict was announced she had left the court; defendants who remained were all too likely to find themselves sent to prison immediately, and she already knew what the verdict was going to be.

On 3 February, she returned to the Guildhall, again carrying her baby son[23] and accompanied by friends. She had submitted a statement that sounded much more like something she would have written, and which emphasized her compliance with what was expected of a virtuous wife. She said that she had:

'acted entirely from a sense of conjugal duty, with out consulting my own interest, or my own ideas of right and wrong. I stand before your Lordships as the instrument of my husband in this publication. I know . . . that he would as gladly bear any punishment that may fall upon me; but if this cannot be the case, I must be content to share his sufferings as I have shared his prosperity. For better, for worse, is the motto of the altar, and I am happy in giving my husband this instance of my regard and affection. I have already suffered all the misery that can befall a wife and a mother, and I have to entreat that your Lordships will not further agonize my mind by separating me both from husband and children.'[24]

This was a plea that could – and indeed did – resonate with many people. In radical circles, in particular, Jane came to be regarded as the model of a good wife, sticking with her husband through thick and thin, and prepared to suffer any hardship in his cause. However, the judge found it almost unbelievable that a woman could publish blasphemy and remain virtuous, and her pleas fell on deaf ears. Sentencing her he mused that whilst he found the whole situation very painful, he 'could not but be astonished at seeing a woman stand forward as the opponent of that system from which everything valuable to woman was derived'.[25]

After 'a moments consideration, during which the Judges enjoyed a laugh',[26] she was condemned to two years imprisonment to be served with her husband. No fine was imposed because as a married woman she could not have any property with which to pay it, but she – or rather, Carlile – was required to provide sureties for good behaviour after her release of £200.

Once Jane had been removed, responsibility for the shop devolved to Carlile's younger sister, Mary-Ann. She is often described as being more enthusiastic about Carlile's views than Jane was, and so she may have been, although other than the transcript of her trial there is little evidence for her opinion either way. She was, as she later pointed out, a working-class woman who had received a very basic education. In childhood she had been taught to read but not write; this skill Carlile himself taught her after she arrived in London. Helped by a growing band of supporters, she now took over the shop, and early in March sold various items to agents of the Vice Society. She was charged with two counts of blasphemous libel, and her trial was eventually set for 21 July 1821.

For her defence on the first charge, she had a lengthy and very detailed defence prepared by her brother which, like Jane before her, she handed to the clerk to be read aloud to the court on her behalf. However, when the Clerk of the Court arrived at a passage in which Carlile said that the prosecution was founded upon 'what they call the common law, but which I shall make appear plain to you, Gentlemen, is nothing but a common abuse',[27] the judge intervened on the grounds that he 'could not permit the laws of the country to be reviled in his presence', and he advised Mary-Ann to expunge all such material from the speech. Well-primed, Mary-Ann replied, 'I have no other defence'. The judge suggested that one of the gentlemen present might help her, but she declined this. Eventually she left the court for a few minutes to think about it, but soon returned with a written sentence that said that, 'If the Court means to decide that an English woman is not to state that which she thinks necessary for her defence, she must abide the consequence of such a decision'. The judge said that he had said no such thing, but Mary-Ann stuck to her line that she had no other defence. The judge 'without the least hesitation' summed up. The jury did not bother to deliberate at all, but simply gave a verdict of 'Guilty'.

This was not the end of proceedings, however, because the second charge was heard in the afternoon. This was going to be a rather different affair from that of the morning; Mary-Ann was represented by a barrister called Henry Cooper, and this meant that, apart from anything else, the reading services of the Clerk to the Court would not be required. Cooper was in his mid-thirties and after struggling earlier in his career was now beginning to make a name for himself. The second charge Mary-Ann faced, although much the same as the first on the face of it, also had new hazards. The Gagging Acts provided that whilst for the first conviction the sentence was imprisonment and a fine, for the second it was transportation. Buying tracts on two separate days, and trying the cases separately, left it open to the judge to interpret the Acts in a draconian way and impose a much more extreme sentence.

As before, the trial began with a statement of the charge, followed again by the two witnesses to whom Mary-Ann had sold the offending material. Cooper cross-examined them both at some length as to whether or not they were paid by the Society, what their jobs were and why they had left previous posts. In both cases he was able to cover them in a vague miasma of untrustworthiness. He then moved on to his speech in Mary-Ann's defence. This was very different from Carlile's peroration, and contained much more law and less theology. The judge was also much less able to interrupt him or put him off his stride. Even so, however, the speech was long, the courtroom very crowded and hot, and the stress for Mary-Ann, who had been in the dock all day, very great. Part way through Cooper's speech she fainted and had to be taken out of the room. Undeterred, the judge continued the trial, becoming visibly more irritated as the afternoon wore on. Eventually Cooper finished with a final flourish to suggest to the jury that they would be doing a good deed by acquitting Mary-Ann:

> '. . . you will, by your verdict of Not Guilty, give security to the free expression of public opinion, compose our dissensions, and protect both yourselves and posterity; since in calling on you to acquit the Defendant, I call on you to protect the freedom of the Press, and with it the freedom of the country; for unless the Press is preserved, and preserved inviolate, the political liberties of Englishmen are lost.'[28]

The judge summed up with as much bias as he could decently employ, and sent the jury out at 4.00 pm. Forty-five minutes later they returned to say that they could not agree on a verdict. Four of the jurors were being 'obstinate'. One of the jurors objected to this, saying: 'I throw back the charge of obstinacy in the teeth of the Foreman. *He* is obstinate.' Another juryman, clearly already fed up of the wrangling, wearily confirmed: 'My Lord there is obstancy.'[29] The judge told them that they must find an agreement and sent them back to the jury room. At 8.00 pm they had still not agreed, so the judge ordered that they be locked up together for the night. In the morning the court filled up again but still there was no news. At 9.30 am a replacement judge appeared on the bench and a message was sent from the jury saying that they had no prospect of reaching a verdict. After some discussion, prosecution and defence agreed with the judge that the jury could be discharged. The jury was bought back, the trial came to an end and the jury left the court to loud cheers from the assembled crowd.

This was a rare victory for the radicals – the first since the introduction of the Six Acts – and there was a considerable amount of jubilation. Mary-Ann herself must have been very relieved to have escaped the threat of transportation. However, she had still to be sentenced on the count on which she had been convicted, and this was now delayed. She was released and returned to the shop, presumably anticipating that she would be brought back to court quite quickly. But this did not happen for more than four months, and in the meantime she was left in an agony of uncertainty as to what was going to happen to her. Inevitably, this began to tell. A friend called Benjamin Jones recounted that when he dropped in to visit her as usual at the Fleet Street shop on Saturday evening he found her:

'. . . in great trouble, when I inquired "what was the cause of her trouble?" Her answer was, that "next week she was to surrender, to receive sentence of the Court, and be imprisoned. Then the House in Fleet Street would be closed, and they would be starved in prison". It struck me forcibly that this would most probably be their fate, knowing the apathy that generally follows after a person gets into prison. It completely staggered me for the moment, that I hardly knew how to answer, for I saw that what she anticipated would inevitably be the case.'[30]

Jones was, however, essentially a man of action, and he immediately organized a meeting for the following Monday to decide on a plan. A committee was set up, and a public meeting held to start to raise the funds that would be necessary to keep the family going. Everything that did not go to the support of the prisoners was to be spent on printing. Volunteers took over the day-to-day running of the shop. One of the people who came forward was a friend of Jane Carlile's called Susannah Wright, who, according to Jones, undertook that when Mary-Ann was imprisoned she would 'take charge of the House, and attend to the business at all risk, and we, on our part, agreed to support her'.

On 15 November, Mary-Ann returned to court for sentencing. There had evidently been some discussion about this behind the scenes, for the sentence was punitive. The year in prison she was given was not so bad, but she also had to pay a fine of £500 before she could be released. This was a colossal sum for a working-class woman with no source of income, and was thus effectively a sentence of indefinite imprisonment. Mary-Ann had no hope of paying it, and, indeed, so unusual was the scale of the fine that it caused some public unease; even *The Times* noted that 'Mary Ann Carlile stood before the Court a pauper as well as a criminal', and asked:

> '. . . if upon such a person the imposition of a fine of five hundred pounds should appear to be nothing less than a sentence of perpetual imprisonment, is there no danger that an undue degree of compassion for the sufferer may dull the edge of public abhorrence for the sinner?'[31]

By this time, however, Mary-Ann was already on her way to Dorchester to join her brother and sister-in-law, where, for the foreseeable future, she would now have to live as a prisoner.

Chapter 8
This Infatuated Family

When Jane Carlile was sentenced in February 1821, she and little Thomas were removed from the court and taken to the Kings Bench Prison to await transfer to Dorchester. The older children had been sent to her sister in Hampshire, but the baby, who had just been weaned, became ill in the gaol and Jane was terrified that he would die. Nevertheless, she was made to carry him nearly two miles across London in the cold night air to the Saracen's Head inn at Snow Hill, where the coach departed for Dorset at dawn. When she arrived at Dorchester Gaol she was put into the same cell as her husband. She remained in a state of mental exhaustion and physical collapse for some weeks, and although baby Thomas survived his ordeal he also needed time to recover.[1]

Dorchester Gaol was one of the more modern prisons in the British penal system. It was still less than twenty years old, and had been built along progressive lines, as a result of which, unlike the more old-fashioned prisons, it was relatively clean, and less prone to disease. Rather than being kept in communal wards, prisoners were separated into cells and subjected to a regime of hard, physical work. Punishments were less brutal than in older prisons, but still included flogging. However, political prisoners were largely exempt from hard labour, and Richard Carlile had been put into a cell by himself to prevent him contaminating other prisoners. This was effectively solitary confinement, but it also meant that the conditions in which he was kept were relatively comfortable; he reported that his cell was:

'large, light, and airy . . . I have a complete water-closet attached to the room, and a water pipe and sink in the room, so that I have the enjoyment, nay the luxury, of hot and cold baths at pleasure, having provided myself the necessary bathing machines, both for shower and open baths. Bathing is a wholesome recreation to which I am particularly attached, and I now enjoy it to satiety.'[2]

This makes his imprisonment sound almost restful, although he did also say that he had spent so much time alone that his voice had become weak from lack of use. However, he had a fire in the room, together with a sofa and a writing desk, and as much food as he felt he needed which, since he was abstemious, was not much. He filled his time with activity, reading, thinking and writing, publishing furious attacks in *The Republican* on both the Christian religion and his enemies, including Henry Hunt, with whom he now disagreed about almost everything. When Jane and the poorly baby arrived, the available space in the 'large, light and airy' cell became less, but had to do more. Carlile could no longer spend his days just thinking and writing, and although he was probably glad of the company, and relieved that little Tom soon got better, the lack of privacy, the constant intrusions of the gaolers and the lack of air and exercise were depressing. He engaged in a series of running battles with the prison authorities over issues such as exercise, the frequent searches to which he was subjected, and the water closet, which was locked at night. This last one infuriated him more than anything else, and it seems to have been a bone of contention throughout his time in prison. On one occasion when he complained, the authorities 'only laughed at it, and seemed to say, the question with us is how we can annoy you most'.[3]

Given Carlile's prickly and controversialist nature, annoying him was fairly easy, and the constant friction probably helped him to cope, but for those locked up with him it must have been very wearing. Perhaps the most extraordinary feature (to the modern eye) of his incarceration was the ease with which he was able to maintain contact with people outside the prison and continue writing and publishing. Against all the odds, and as other radical papers foundered and fell, *The Republican* kept going and, except during 1821, was published regularly throughout Carlile's years in prison. However, it was a constant challenge both to fill the columns and to pay for the printing and distribution, and fundraising took up much of his time.

For content, he used anything that came to hand. He wrote furiously himself, but this was not enough to fill the paper and he had to turn to many other sources. Anyone who wrote to him, to Jane or to Mary-Ann was liable to find their letter in print, together with replies and sometimes extensive comment. Lists of donors to the relief fund that was set up for the prisoners also took up a good deal of space, as did speeches, accounts of trials, articles sent in by supporters and even legal documents relating to the family's cases. Many of his arguments were carried on through *The Republican's* columns, with Carlile energetically rebutting any criticism and making (sometimes outrageous) counter-allegations. Readers got an eclectic mix of politics, religion, economics and polemic; eventually it was virtually the only radical or republican paper still going, and that it did so is a tribute to Carlile's extraordinary combination of ability and obsession.

While he was alone in the cell he could organize himself in whatever way suited him, but once Jane arrived things became more difficult. The baby was only just over a year old and subject to all the usual ailments of a child of that age. Carlile was at this point refusing to take his daily exercise in the yard, but the baby needed fresh air, and in the end he paid a woman to come and take Thomas out for a couple of hours a day. As Jane recovered slowly from the ordeal of the trial and realized that she faced two years being locked in one room with a husband whose primary focus was his work, and a baby who needed constant attention, her heart must have sunk.

A few months later, Mary-Ann arrived and was put into Richard and Jane's cell for the daytime. However, at night she was removed to a cell elsewhere in the prison, which caused her constant anxiety. She never knew where she would be sleeping; sometimes she was housed with other women, sometimes on her own, and sometimes in less populated parts of the prison where she felt vulnerable and afraid. On one occasion there was a fire in the chimneys and a huge volume of smoke and ash poured into the cell in which she was sleeping. The smoke got into her throat and her frantic hammering on the iron door was either not heard or actually ignored. Eventually the door was opened, but when she stumbled out half suffocated she was accused of starting the fire herself. In the end she was taken to the infirmary, where she was ill for some time, but the poor physical conditions, coupled with the anxiety and stress of believing that she might never get out, continued to undermine her health and her brother began to be seriously concerned for her. He made it clear that when there was enough money he would pay her fine before his, but it was hard to see how this point would ever arrive. Mary-Ann seems to have spent most of her time in prison ill, frightened and depressed as her life passed her by.

By the autumn of 1821 Jane was pregnant, and this caused new problems. She suffered badly with sickness and diarrhoea during the early stages, and it was therefore even more urgent to have access to the water closet at night. Accordingly, Carlile asked the visiting magistrates, part of whose job it was to determine the conditions in which prisoners were held, if the closet could be left open. The magistrates 'tittered and laughed, saying, they would go below and talk about it'. After waiting a couple of days for a decision, the Carliles were told that 'if Mrs. Carlile wanted any further accommodation that way, she must buy a close-stool pan'. As they had anticipated, 'Mrs. C. suffered dreadfully . . . we had frequently to beg the matron to violate her duty and not to lock the door, which she sometimes would and sometimes feared to do'. After Jane had the baby the water closet was always left open. 'I leave the reader to comment', concluded Carlile, bitterly.[4]

The long months of the pregnancy must have been very difficult for all of them. Little Tom was starting to toddle and get into mischief, Mary-Ann was constantly unwell, and Jane was sick and worried about how she was going to manage the birth with no help and no way of summoning it if she went into labour at night. At one point Carlile even wrote directly to the Secretary of State, Robert Peel, to ask him to consider Jane's pregnancy as 'a circumstance to justify a remission of the remainder of her sentence', as 'the nature of her confinement, and the double dread of danger, and probable want of necessary assistance on such an occasion in a Prison, preys heavily on her mind'. He added what was probably also true, that in mitigation of her offence she 'never was a principal in my business, and that . . . she had, speaking in the character of a husband, no choice, and saw nothing of the pamphlets intended for publication until they were ready for sale'.[5] This prompted a chilly reply from Peel who resolutely declined any assistance other than the rather depressing assurance that 'the Officers of the Prison will afford her every assistance which is consistent with the nature of the place'.[6]

Outside the gaol there was much support for the family from republican and reformist circles. Women, in particular, thought that

Jane had been very shabbily treated and was now being punished for a fidelity to her husband which, in any other circumstances, would be considered a virtue. Women wrote to thank her for her staunch adherence to her marriage vows; when, in May 1822, the Female Republicans of Manchester expressed their support, they began by thanking her 'for doing what every honest and virtuous woman considers to be her duty, namely, to obey the voice of her husband, according with what every married woman promises in her marriage ceremony . . .'[7] When Jane wrote to a correspondent that 'neither my children or myself will ever have occasion to blush at the cause of my incarceration', she almost certainly meant that she had done her duty in a way that almost every other woman in the country would understand. Since then this remark has often been interpreted by historians as meaning that she felt that she had done her duty by the cause of free thought, and she may indeed also have meant this, but at the time she was more honoured for her iron observation of her duty to her husband and her marriage vows.

Once Jane was known to be pregnant, women felt particularly protective of her. When republicans gathered in Manchester in January 1822 at a dinner honouring the immortal memory of Tom Paine, they drank a toast to 'Jane Carlile, and her infant Son, Thomas Pain', but it took the women to add 'A Safe Delivery with the Next'.[8] Elizabeth Gaunt, who had herself lost a baby in the aftermath of Peterloo, wrote to 'condole with you for what you endure from the infliction of those who preach passive obedience whilst they profess it to be in good will towards mankind'. Explaining that she had 'witnessed the blood-stained field of St. Peter's, and suffered eleven days incarceration in one of the Boroughmongers' Bastiles because I was exposed to the sabres of a ferocious Yeomanry Cavalry, whilst I was performing what I then conceived and now conceive to have been my duty', she went on to hope that Jane would have an easy delivery and avoid further illness. She also sent her a small gift of a little pair of shoes she had made for the baby, which, she thought 'will be more acceptable to you than if they were diamonds from a tyrant'.[9] Jane replied with thanks, adding at the end that she had never been either a politician or a theologian but:

'a sentence for Two Years has roused feelings in me that I might never have otherwise possessed. I have been made to feel the necessity of reforming the abuses of the Government; as I am sure, that under a Representative System of Government no Woman would have been sent to Prison for Two Years, for publishing an assertion that tyrants ought to be treated as dangerous and destructive beasts of prey. I have been made to think it, as well as to publish it.'[10]

Whether Jane really had been politicized by her experience is an interesting question. In court she had told the judge that she had not consulted her 'own ideas of right and wrong', but this may well have been a very sensible attempt to deflect her guilt onto her husband. Decades later, Theophila Carlile Campbell, Carlile's daughter from his later relationship with Eliza Sharples, observed that Jane 'had absolutely no sympathy with Carlile's aims and ideas . . .', and accused her of being interested only in money.[11] Theophila was writing at the end of the nineteenth century and was keen to present her own mother in as good a light as possible; she is therefore not an entirely credible witness when it comes to Jane. George Holyoake,[12] who was a friend of Carlile's and wrote a biography of him, said that 'Mrs. Carlile, as well as his younger sister . . . did it rather from natural resentment at the injustice practised for his destruction, than from any sympathy with his opinions. But, in this respect, they behaved with a bravery worthy of their name; they resolutely refused to compromise . . .'[13] However, at the point at which the Carliles separated, Holyoake was a teenager in Birmingham, and did not meet Carlile until much later. Whatever Jane's motives, they were likely to have been mixed; she probably could have got out of managing the shop had she been determined to, and there was certainly no shortage of men willing to take over. A decade later she was running a bookshop on her own account where she chose to sell radical publications. She may well have been strongly motivated by marital duty, but that alone does not preclude political commitment.

Carlile himself did seem to recognize that he might bear some responsibility for the pain and anxiety Jane suffered. In 1822 he wrote that he was:

'. . . in duty bound to observe, that I consider the prosecutions have caused Mrs. Carlile a greater punishment and suffering by a hundred degrees than they have caused me. There is nothing in the shape of mental anguish, but she has suffered; whilst I have never suffered a moment's uneasiness in that shape. But this is the peculiar characteristic of religious persecutions; the suffering of the individual persecuted bears no comparison to the mental anguish, the privations suffered by his family.'[14]

However, it is impossible not to note that in his mind it is he who is 'the individual persecuted' and that Jane had merely sustained collateral damage. The idea that following him into prison might have been a choice Jane made for herself, and that she had thus been doubly persecuted – once by the state and once by the expectation of conjugal obedience – does not seem to have crossed his mind.

Outside the gaol, women rallied to Jane and Mary-Ann's support. The Female Republicans of Manchester wrote enclosing a collection of two pounds and two shillings. A list of sixty-six donors – all women – was attached; most had signed their names and none had been able to give more than three shillings. Many had only been able to give pennies. One had signed herself 'Margaret Clarke, a real Deist, but hath the misfortune to be the wife of a Christian . . .' Another, Mary-Anne Rhodes, said that her father was serving a two-year prison sentence 'as the only way to learn the blessings of Christianity'. In their covering letter the women said that they wished:

'by subscribing their mites together, as far as their situation in a land of oppression and taxation will admit, first to shew a token of humanity and respect towards you; and in the second place, to convince our enemies that we approve of your conduct, and glory in your spirit; we are not ashamed to come forward and prove to the people of England that there are yet women possessed of common sense and reason.'[15]

These letters, and others like them, have been preserved only because of Richard Carlile's dogged determination to keep his newspaper going and to prove that he had a steady stream of support from around the country. As a result, it is possible to hear in his pages the voices of working-class women who would otherwise be unknown, and to recognize their generosity, their solidarity and their ability to organize. The Manchester women were by no means the only ones to send gifts and encouraging messages, and Jane was so grateful that after her release she visited some, including the Manchester group. Men also wrote and sent gifts, but it is the letters from women that are most striking, the most unusual and the most moving. Addressing the prisoners as 'Beloved and Highly Esteemed Sisters', or 'Noble Minded Women', they express both admiration and affection, and are expressions of solidarity and sisterhood from literate and political working-class women. When Mary-Ann was convicted, *The Times* remarked that 'No impudence in our opinion, can exceed the impudence of this infatuated family',[16] but for ordinary working women up and down the country, the Carlile family's resistance to the tyranny of the system seemed heroic, and all the more so in the case of the women because of the additional pains and perils they had to undergo. Women sent pennies from their subsistence-level wages because something about the situation in which the Carlile women found themselves spoke to them about the condition of their own lives. It also presented them with examples of real-life heroines, who, like them, had had to work all their lives and live in obedience to everyone around them. Whether Jane and Mary-Ann themselves rejected Christianity as Carlile and many of his followers had done, did not really matter. Women who signed themselves as deists still praised Jane's example of adherence to wifely duty and Mary-Ann's loyalty to her brother. Jane and Mary-Ann's replies also sound like letters written by themselves rather than Carlile, often detailing the frustrations and problems of their daily lives. In their letter to the Manchester women, they complained about the circumstances in which they were allowed exercise:

'Would you believe that if either of us walk out alone, during the hour we are allowed to walk, a man is appointed to watch us and dog us until we are locked up again. We are not only denied the satisfaction of sympathizing with or relieving any poor female in this place, but we are forbidden to speak or to give a compassionate look to any of them, and to effect this object, we are always, when unlocked, under the watching of a sentinel.'[17]

Later we get a glimpse of Carlile's way of dealing with the over-crowding in the cell while he was working: 'Were we to say that we like imprisonment, we should not speak the truth; and being incessantly locked up in the same room with Mr. Carlile, whose affairs and duties often require a sort of silence that is not most agreeable to us, makes us feel it more than we otherwise should.'[18]

Carlile himself, on the other hand, was also suffering from the conditions. Writing furiously in February 1822 to Henry Hunt, with whom he was conducting a vehement argument about a number of things, he complained:

'Here we are, self, wife, and sister, locked up in one room by day, in which we have no alternative but to attend to every call of nature in the presence of each other, or by drawing a curtain across our little water closet, and at dusk in the evening my sister is removed to a distant part of the Prison, after the female felons and others are locked up, . . . and during this absence of hers from my apartment, the water closet is locked up and unlocked when she returns.'[19]

Carlile and Hunt were at this point quarrelling about several bones of contention, one of which was their respective actions at Peterloo. Carlile maintained that Hunt was at least partially responsible for the massacre, since he had told people to come to the meeting unarmed. Hunt, unsurprisingly enraged, accused Carlile of cowardice. Into this war of words waded Mary Fildes, who had contributed to Carlile's relief fund but also remained a staunch supporter of Hunt. In March 1822 *The Manchester Observer* printed a letter from her to Carlile that was scathing, and which cut him to the quick. He had lauded Mary as a heroine whom he had tried to help; now she turned furiously on him.

'*You* charge him [Hunt] with cowardice . . . you have said, that where the post of danger is, there is the post of honour, and that this alone induced you to come and show us an example! But what sort of an example did you show? Not the example of the man whom you call a coward, for at approach of the Yeomanry, your countenance betrayed those symptoms of fear and cowardice, which marked your conduct during the remainder of the day! . . . With respect to myself, I did not expect such a flattering compliment as you have been pleased to pass upon me but I must be candid enough to confess, that when you speak of offering me comfort, I thought at the time, by the quivering of your lips and the faultering of your tongue . . . that you stood in more need of comfort than I did. The part which

I took, I consider as nothing more than my duty as a wife and mother; and may the curses of the rising generation pursue the cowards that deserted the standard of liberty . . .'[20]

Carlile replied in kind, claiming that the letter had been written by John Thacker Saxton and that Mary had only 'put her name' to it; this was backed up by Mary Walker, another veteran of Peterloo. It is impossible now to know what the truth of this was, but it was a sad postscript to Mary Fildes' heroism and Carlile's admiration of it.

On 4 June 1822, after a miserable pregnancy and a long labour, Jane gave birth to a daughter, whom Richard named Hypatia, after Hypatia of Alexandria, a gifted mathematician, astronomer and philosopher who in 415 CE had been beaten, burned and torn to pieces by Christian monks. By naming his child after a pagan martyr rather than a Christian saint, Carlile was making clear his view of where civilization did and did not lie. What Jane thought of this choice is, of course, unrecorded. Crammed into a cell with a newborn baby, a toddler, a husband who spent his time writing his newspaper and a sister-in-law with whom she may or may not have got on particularly well and who was constantly ill, she may not have had much time for dwelling on it either.

By the autumn, Mary-Ann was becoming increasingly desperate. Her year's sentence was due to expire in the middle of November, but she could not be released unless her fine was paid, and there was no prospect of this happening. She and Carlile drafted a Memorial to the government explaining yet again that she had no money and asking for her to be released at the end of her sentence. She emphasized that she had only been helping her brother out, that she had not been allowed to make her defence in court and that she had only ever been paid subsistence wages for any job she did, pointing out that 'at no period of her life did she ever possess property of one tenth of the value of the fine imposed upon her; and, that at this moment, she has no prospect of ever being able to pay it'.[21] She also said that she feared the effect of another winter on her already delicate health. In the middle of December the government turned her request down.

Since Jane did not have a fine to pay, she and the two children were released at the end of her sentence in January 1823. After going to Hampshire to see her family, recover from her ordeal and collect her two older sons, she embarked on a tour of Northern towns to thank the women there for their support. She was received as a heroine by the remaining radical and reform societies, for whom she represented a model of both commitment to the cause and wifely obedience. Then she returned to the shop in London, where temporary shopmen were still being arrested, though she herself was more or less left alone.

This left Carlile and Mary-Ann still imprisoned with no prospect of release. Carlile had already served more than the three years to which he had been sentenced, and Mary-Ann had served her year. They now tried the route of petitioning Parliament directly. The plea they made was short and to the point, which suggests that Mary-Ann rather than her brother may have had the major hand in it.

Describing herself as 'twenty-nine years of age, of irreproachable character, and [having] for the last twelve years, previous to her confinement in Dorchester gaol, maintained herself by her industry, . . . having no property whatever, nor any other reputable means of obtaining a livelihood', she outlined again the injustice of her conviction, the unreasonable nature of the fine and the likelihood of it leading to 'perpetual imprisonment' if something was not done. Claiming to be 'a very extraordinary case, and one of singular hardship',[22] she asked the House of Commons to intervene on her behalf and secure her release. The petition was presented in March by Joseph Hume, the MP for Aberdeen who had started his political life as a Tory but was now an energetic and often successful campaigner for reformist and radical causes. On this occasion, however, it was hopeless. One after another, members of the Vice Society and their supporters got up to oppose him. The Attorney General, who was outraged that judges should be criticized, believed that Mary-Ann should show some remorse before being released; 'If', he said, 'the petition had set forth the reformation and contrition of that woman, he should know on what grounds he would receive it, but it contained no expression to that effect'. A series of men rose to give an opinion about a woman they had never met in a situation they found shocking. William Wilberforce defended the Vice Society, and referred to Mary-Ann as an 'unhappy woman', and 'fallen and wretched . . . without one ray of hope to cheer amidst the dark and desolate prospect of eternity'.[23] He said that he thought that: 'If such offences as hers were not to be visited by the arm of the law, the attorney-general might as well be absolved at once from all care of the public morality and religion, and every thing be suffered to go to wreck and ruin'.[24]

The petition was denied, and Mary-Ann's imprisonment dragged on through the summer. However, outside things were beginning to change. Throughout the Carliles' incarceration an extraordinary procession of (mainly working class) people had been staffing the bookshop and accepting the consequences. They came from around the country to take their turn behind the counter, knowing perfectly well that, often within days, they would sell a pamphlet or book to a member of the Vice Society and find themselves in court. Collectively, however, they were defiant. In early 1822, for instance, a placard appeared outside the shop proclaiming:

> 'Two shopmen arrested . . . by the Bridge Street Gang, the same obnoxious pamphlet shall be sold in spite of them: tis a right noble cause: they shall not with all their combined powers shut up the Temple of Reason . . . "This is the mart for blasphemy and sedition".'[25]

Each trial was faithfully recorded and reported in *The Republican*, complete with speeches attacking the church, the state and the legal system. The cumulative effect of this was becoming evident. In introducing Mary-Ann's petition to Parliament in March, Joseph Hume observed that the Vice Society had in fact:

> 'increased the mischief which it pretended to remove. No fewer than thirty-two victims had been dragged by this Society before courts of law, every one of whom it was their boast that they had convicted; and what was the result? Why, as fast as the prisons were filled with victims, individuals pressed forward eager to become martyrs, and oppose a system of persecution by a participation in the sufferings inflicted by their oppressors.'[26]

It had become an elaborate game of cat and mouse, the outcome of which was always certain, but in which the overall balance of power was always inexplicably out of the cat's control. Ingenious ideas were developed for preventing Vice Society agents from being able to identify who was selling books to them; these mechanisms may or may not have been effective, but Benjamin Jones later recalled that Carlile had:

'formed a plan to sell the books down a spout, so that the person purchasing the books could not see the person that sold them. . . . There was a little door on the counter, which the person wanting a book had to rap at, when the door opened, and the purchaser asked for the book which he wanted. Then a small bag was lowered down for the money. When it was drawn up, the book with the change—if any was required—was lowered down to the purchaser. By this system the informers were baffled . . .'[27]

To the great irritation of their persecutors, the booksellers often adopted the language of Christian martyrdom, regarding themselves as willing sacrifices for the great cause of freedom of thought and of expression. Carlile wrote his long, detailed, provocative defences for the men as well as the women, and took an active interest in everyone who was prosecuted. One after another, they trooped through the courts and the columns of *The Republican* doggedly claiming their right to think, write and speak as they liked. In all, about 150 people were convicted and served sentences of anything from a few months to three years.[28] Some of the sentences were even more punitive than the Carliles', involving long periods of hard labour in the appalling conditions of Newgate. Carlile made no secret of the scale of the sacrifice required, which included virtually no remuneration and the risk of transportation if convicted a second time. Despite this, however, the courts were clogged with blasphemy cases and the gaols with people who persisted in regarding themselves as political prisoners and martyrs for free thought. As Home Secretary, Robert Peel was nothing if not pragmatic, and he could see that common sense needed to prevail if an even more protracted, expensive and ultimately unsatisfactory battle was to be avoided. He must also have known from his own sources that warnings about Mary-Ann's health were more than just Carlile's usual rhetoric, and that public opinion would turn against the government if women were going to start dying in gaols just because they could not pay impossible fines. His solution was simple. The government paid Mary-Ann's fine and she was released in November 1823 having served exactly double the term of her sentence. Rather than return to London, she seems to have gone to a sister in Devon to recuperate, and beyond a few events to celebrate her release took no further part in public affairs. According to an extract from a letter published by Carlile's daughter Theophila towards the end of the century, Mary-Ann married a Methodist army officer in 1837,[29] but other than that nothing else is known.

Gradually the Vice Society and the Constitution society, which had to bear the costs of the prosecutions, began to run short of funds. By 1825 the government had had enough, and prosecutions ceased. There was a smaller second wave a few months later, but effectively the battle was over. It was a stunning victory. A little band of working-class men and women, led by a tinplate worker from Devon, had defeated the combined might of the establishment, from Wilberforce and the Clapham Saints, through the might of the courts, to the power of one of the most repressive British governments in history. Carlile himself was released in November having served six years in his Dorchester cell and never having conceded one inch to anybody. He was jubilant and emerged a hero to his followers, apparently unbowed by his experience and ready to take on all comers. However, the world he was re-entering was very different from the one he had left in 1819. The Peterloo leaders had all served their terms and dispersed. Some, such as Henry Hunt, were continuing the fight, but others had receded into the background and others still had given up altogether. The veteran John Knight, who had first been arrested for radical activity in 1794, was still going, but now he was beginning to concentrate on trade union activity rather than parliamentary reform. Thomas Wooler, whose *Black Dwarf* had folded in 1824, was editing a radical weekly, but also building up a practice as a defence lawyer; within a few years he would quit politics altogether.

There were other changes, too. Carlile's older two sons were almost strangers to him, having spent much of their childhood split between London and Hampshire, and having visited him only occasionally. But perhaps the biggest change was in Jane. It is hard to tell at what stage her tolerance of the life she had had with her husband broke, but perhaps it was with the loss of two-year-old Hypatia who died of whooping cough in February 1825. It must have been evident to anyone who knew him that Carlile was not going to stop fighting authority, and that it would only be a matter of time before he was back in gaol again. Jane must have found the prospect of having to follow him there almost unbearable. She had committed herself in her marriage vows to obedience to her husband, and she had gone to extreme lengths to honour this vow and to be what even revolutionary society expected in a good wife. But two years cooped up in one room with a husband who, though heroic in some respects, could be selfish and demanding in others, must have taken its toll.

Almost all of the information we have about how – and even when – Jane and Richard Carlile separated, comes through Theophila Carlile Campbell, the daughter of Carlile and his second partner, Eliza Sharples. Theophila was writing at the end of the Victorian era and understandably her aim was to make her parents look as respectable as possible, as a result of which there are some gaps and ambiguities in her version of events. According to her account, the couple had long wished to be separated, and had in fact agreed in principle to part in 1819. There is no evidence at all for this idea; in fact in 1819 they were grieving the death of their baby son and Jane was pregnant. What seems much more likely is that the relationship was effectively at an end by the time Carlile was released in 1826, but that the absence of divorce and the expense of a separation kept the couple together. Theophila also suggested that Jane and Carlile formally separated in 1830, when in fact the break did not happen until 1832, after Eliza Sharples' arrival in London from her home town of Bolton.

In that year a supporter left the Carliles an annuity of £50 a year; this was made over to Jane and she moved out with her sons into a new shop in Bride Lane around the corner from Fleet Street. In June 1832 she advertised an extensive range of cut-price radical books and prints for sale.[30] Carlile was by this stage again in prison, and Theophila Carlile Campbell wrote that her father had said that:

'Mrs. Carlile was allowed to take everything in the way of furniture that she desired, and £100 worth of books from the stock which was at her mercy when she left. She did take every article of furniture, every bed, table, and chair in the house, even the chairs which had been purchased for the lecture room. She left me nothing but the business, its stock and debts, and she took the nearest shop she could wherein to oppose and injure me. At that time I had not seen her for a year, though I was in prison; nor would she send me so much as a Sunday dinner. We had separated from all pretences of being man and wife for nearly two years before that. She was only fit for what she now possesses, viz., single retirement with a competency to secure her from the cares and turmoils of life.'[31]

Carlile clearly felt Jane's acquisition of much of the business that she had single-handedly kept afloat on more than one occasion was unreasonable. He also engaged in a systematic character assassination that left a particularly nasty taste in the mouth. He accused her of having an unreliable temper, which:

> 'was often both terrible and dangerous. I have known her to exhibit for days together such appearances than which none could be more amiable or agreeable, more generous or more affable, and then on the most frivolous grounds—for merely *imagined* wrongs—become tempestuous to delirium and hysterics. . . . Her violence generally fell on my immediate friends, man or woman, and a mere act of kindness shown to my mother or sisters has endangered my life as far as threats and preparations were appearances of danger. I never considered my life safe, and lived for years in almost daily apprehension of some terrible domestic tragedy. The wonder is that I ever accomplished anything under such a state of feeling, and I confess, what I have often told her, that to me imprisonment was a great relief; and this is part of the secret why I bore it so well. During the whole of my married life I felt the annoying condition of being without a home to which I could proceed in peace, and introduce a friend with the ordinary rites of hospitality and required civility from the mistress of the house. This necessarily drove me from home and caused me to form associations that I otherwise would not have done.'[32]

Given that throughout the early 1820s he had been lavish in his praise of Jane, and never given any hint of fear of her, there is some ground for doubting the truth of these allegations, particularly when it is remembered that by the time he was making them he was living with Eliza Sharples, a woman nearly twenty years Jane's junior. It would be astonishing if Jane's temper had not been sorely tried by the vicissitudes of her life, but it seems highly unlikely that he had actually ever been in the kind of danger he describes. Moreover, in the last sentence there seems to be a hint that he may not always have been quite the faithful husband he liked to portray himself as. Overall, the separation was an unpleasant affair, but by any standard it is hard not to feel that Jane had more than earned her £50 a year and her security 'from the cares and turmoils of life'.[33]

In the long procession of people who accepted prosecution and imprisonment for the cause of free thought, one more woman stands out. Susannah Wright was a remarkable individual who fought the battle for its own sake, neither gave nor expected quarter and became, for a brief period, one of the most notorious women in England.

Chapter 9

The She-Champion
of Impiety

Susannah Wright was born in Nottingham, probably in 1792.[1] Nothing is known of her early years other than that she was a lace mender and embroiderer in a city with a history of working-class radical and reformist activism. As a girl she would have been aware of various exciting and sometimes alarming events around her. She would have begun work very young; children's sharp eyesight and nimble fingers were of value in an industry that depended on fine and delicate work. She must have witnessed – or at least heard all about – the Nottingham food riots of 1800, when high prices and food shortages drove women to break into granaries and carry corn away in their aprons, gathering in large crowds to hiss menacingly at the troops brought in to disperse them. Perhaps her own mother or aunts had been amongst these women; certainly Susannah had ample opportunity from her earliest youth to see and experience for herself how close even the most skilled of people were to poverty and starvation. In 1811 the lacemakers organized themselves into a trade union, and struck for higher wages. It seems probable that Susannah was involved in this if at that point she was still in Nottingham. She was later described as small and rather delicate, and Richard Carlile, who greatly admired her, also said she was 'a little mild and particularly civil woman, unless insulted'.[2] In 1812, there were food riots in Nottingham as in Lancashire; the women stuck: 'a half penny loaf on the top of a fishing rod, streaked it with red ochre, and tied around it a shred of black crape, emblematic . . . of "bleeding famine decked in Sackcloth".'[3] From a distance the loaf must have borne more than a passing resemblance to a severed head stuck on a revolutionary pike. Perhaps it was after the turmoil of these events that Susannah left her home town. She was well-remembered in Nottingham some years later, and she always recognized the part the town had played in her development, writing in 1822 that it was to 'the distinguished spirit which the inhabitants of Nottingham have uniformly exhibited in the cause of Reform that I owe the formation of my present principles'.[4]

By 1815 she was certainly in London, probably living in the old radical stronghold of Stoke Newington. It is possible that she met William Wright there, but it is more likely that the couple both came from Nottingham and migrated to London at the same time. In 1825, Susannah wrote a letter to Richard Carlile that clearly indicates that William had been involved in an organization in Nottingham called the Odd Fellows, so it seems likely that he had at least lived there for a time.[5] However, if they did go to London together they did not do so as husband and wife, for they were married on Christmas Day 1815 at St Mary's Church, Newington. Susannah, who had probably been taught to write as a child, signed her name in a neat, firm, flowing script in the register, whilst William made his mark. William was by trade a dyer, and Susannah's own craft was, as she later told the court, always in demand and therefore she could earn good money with her needle. They soon settled down to married life in the semi-rural village of Lambeth, and in 1819 their first surviving child, William Henry, was born. Soon after that they moved to Tower Street in Southwark, somewhere near the present site of City Hall.

Over the years there has been some mystery about William Wright. He has always been assumed to have been a bookseller, largely because the court indictment of 18 July 1822 described Susannah as 'the Wife of William Wright, late of London, Bookseller'. Confusingly, there was indeed a bookseller of that name who had a shop in Fleet Street and whose wife was called Susan, but in fact they were not the same couple. Apart from anything else, the Wrights of Fleet Street had a new daughter, Mary Elizabeth, in February 1822, just two months before Susannah gave birth to Thomas Paine Carlile Wright in April. William Wright of Southwark described himself as a 'dyer', and gave his address as Tower Street when Thomas was baptized at St. George the Martyr Church on 15 September. The address given for Susannah at her trial was 11 Tower Street. The description 'Bookseller' in the indictment must therefore actually refer to Susannah herself and not, as has previously been presumed, her husband.

Once settled in Southwark, Susannah and William found like-minded friends, and at some point before 1821 they met the Carliles' friend Benjamin Jones, who held regular Sunday evening gatherings at his house for like-minded working people. Here they discussed the radical publications of the day, but they also had religion in their sights, and Jones described the friends he invited as 'Atheistical'.[6] Susannah had been baptized and presumably brought up as an Anglican, but at some point she had lost any faith she might have had; by the time of her blasphemy trial she was describing herself as a 'deist' and an 'infidel'.

When Jane Carlile was arrested, Susannah was both appalled and fascinated. 'Every day for more than a week', she said later 'I silently and privately followed the footsteps of Mrs. Carlile into the Court of King's Bench to watch the conduct of her inhuman Judges, and her fate'. So upset was she by it that 'fired with resentment at the result, I offered myself to Mr. Carlile as a willing sacrifice to Corruption's shrine'.[7] She therefore had no illusions about what would happen to her if she herself were to be charged, and yet when Mary-Ann Carlile was finally dispatched to Dorchester, Susannah had no hesitation in offering to run the Carliles' shop *'at whatever risk'*.[8] This account almost gives the impression that her decision was made on the spur of the moment out of friendship to Jones, but in reality she may well have known Carlile and his family for some time. William Holmes, one of the prosecuted shopmen, was later rather critical of Susannah, and writing to him to refute this Carlile said: 'I by no means coincide with what you say of Mrs. Wright, there is scarcely another woman in England who would have done for me what that woman has done, and from my knowledge of her in 1817–18 and 1819, I know that a love of principle has been her ruling motive.'[9]

After Mary-Ann had been sentenced, Susannah began to work in Carlile's Fleet Street shop. She was not paid much in the way of wages, although he did cover her expenses including, as she later told the jury at her trial, the cost of a childminder for little William Henry. Her days were now full, not just with the selling of books, but also with the receipt of donations to Carlile's relief fund, which was run from the shop. She said at her trial that she lived 'on terms of affection and conjugal fidelity with my husband, whose earnings are regular and fully competent to make us comfortable', and that she had undertaken her active support of Carlile with William's consent. Nevertheless, it must have been an anxious time for both of them, particularly since by the autumn of 1821 Susannah was again in the early stages of pregnancy.

In December she sold two twopenny pamphlets by Richard Carlile to a man from the Vice Society. She was duly arrested and charged with blasphemy, but because she was pregnant she was released on bail to await trial after the birth. The defiantly-named Thomas Paine Carlile Wright was born in April, though not baptized until September, a circumstance which has sometimes led to confusion with the birth to Jane Carlile of baby Hypatia in Dorchester Gaol in June, in turn leading to a belief that Susannah gave birth in the notorious Newgate Prison. In fact the baby was born in Southwark, and after some delays his mother was finally brought back to court for trial in July 1822.

In the meantime, the trials of other shopmen went on apace, and in February 1822 Susannah was called as a witness at that of William Holmes. Perhaps it was her conduct then at the Old Bailey that annoyed him; knowing that, because of her pregnancy, she was unlikely to be committed to prison for contempt, she was a difficult and obstructive witness who probably did not help Holmes's case. When asked if she had had the 'misfortune' to be charged with blasphemy herself, she replied that she had, 'if you call it misfortune', and refused to be drawn about what she believed about God. 'I shall not answer that', she replied to the prosecutor's question. 'When I am brought to trial, perhaps I may give my opinion.'[10] This should have given the court a pretty good idea of what to expect, and for her it was invaluable experience.

Knowing what treatment she was likely to face in court, Susannah prepared carefully. She probably knew that this was the one chance she, as a working-class woman with no political or civil power, would get to make the case for what she believed. Carlile advised her from Dorchester on what to include in her defence, but much as she respected him she knew exactly what she wanted to say and intended to say it in her own voice. Because they knew that the Chief Justice would make every effort to distract and undermine her, and that she would need all her wits about her, Benjamin Jones accompanied her to act as her junior, keeping track of her place in her notes, reminding her of essentials and helping with the baby. She processed into court surrounded by friends and supporters, including women who had come simply to be there to encourage her. One, known only as 'F', had travelled down from Manchester, and later wrote to Carlile that 'never will the impression be effaced from my memory; the firmness she evinced, and her resolution not to be silenced by the repeated interruption of the judge, and the unwarranted interference of the jury, betrayed a consciousness of integrity, and a stability of principle . . .'[11]

The *New Times*, a publication noted for its detestation of radical, political women as well as its hard-line loyalist opinions, was scathing in its reporting of the case, and, in particular, of the women who accompanied Susannah in court. The editor fulminated that:

'This is the first time . . . that a body of women has defied all shame, and trampled upon all decency, in so profligate and daring a manner—in a manner at which the lowest prostitutes would shudder . . . It is manifest that these female brutes came prepared, not only to applaud what the She-Champion of Impiety had already done; but to hear her load with fresh insults the law of her country and the law of her GOD.'[12]

The trial began with the reading of the charge, which alleged that Susannah: 'being an evil disposed and wicked person and disregarding the Laws and Religion of this Realm, . . . unlawfully, and wickedly, did sell, utter, and publish, and caused to be sold, uttered, and published, a certain scandalous, impious, blasphemous and profane Libel, of and concerning the Christian Religion . . .'[13] The prosecution presented its case, which was simple, and more of an attack on Richard Carlile, who had written the material Susannah had sold, than on Susannah herself. The same man who had been discredited by Henry Cooper during Mary-Ann's trial was produced to testify that he had indeed been sold the pamphlets in question by Susannah, but when she questioned him about this the judge was more than a little annoyed. It was, he said, for the jury to decide whether or not the witness was telling the truth. 'I did not expect to see this man here', said Susannah, 'I do not deny that I have sold the publications before the Court, but not to this man'.

Next the prosecutor read out at length the passages in the pamphlets that were deemed to be blasphemous, but then the packed court was able to settle down to enjoy itself as Susannah, with Benjamin Jones beside her in the dock, began to defend herself in her own words. Her long speech was both shocking and to the point, and whilst some of the arguments were drawn-out, much of it was shot through with an engaging wit and an absolute refusal to say anything other than what she believed in. When the judge, horrified at some of her assertions, tried to intervene, she simply ignored him and swept on, much to the audience's amusement.

After a time the baby began to cry, and Susannah asked for an adjournment so that she could feed him. Probably with some relief, the Chief Justice agreed and, accompanied by her support group, and to much waving and cheering from the spectators assembled both inside and outside the building, Susannah carried her hungry offspring out of the court and across the road to the Castle Coffee House. There she fed and changed him, and after less than thirty minutes returned to court to more cheering. Completely unruffled, she picked up her speech where she had left it and continued triumphantly on to the end.

Although she had pleaded 'not guilty', Susannah made no attempt to challenge the facts of the prosecution's case. Far from it, she was happy to agree that she had indeed sold deist and infidel pamphlets. Her aim, however, was not to disprove the charge, but to state her case against Christianity and the Christian establishment. By not contesting the facts, she was able to focus on what she thought was important. She began by explaining to the court who she was. 'I am', she said:

'a married woman and a mother. . . . I have myself been bred to a genteel employ, as a lace mender, and an embroiderer, at which I could earn double the wages that I have received from Mr. Carlile. . . . I have stood forward in this righteous cause, by and with the consent and advice of my husband. I am not related to Mr. Carlile in the most distant degree. I am scarcely known to him farther than as a customer who has regularly called for his publications.'[14]

She was firm in her opinions and unafraid of the consequences. 'I know my own heart', she remarked at the beginning of her speech, 'and I know that a dungeon cannot damp it'.[15] She explained that:

'. . . I have no desire either to bring the religion or the laws of this country into contempt, although I am a believer in no kind of religion what ever, nor do I like the laws under which I live; but all I wish for on the score of religion is, that it be brought to the touchstone of free discussion, and that there shall be no persecution for matters of opinion.'[16]

She did not like the laws because: 'they are not made by the consent of the people, through their representatives; from whence, in my opinion, all laws should emanate to be just and impartial.' But she also maintained that she actually could not have broken any law, since the laws they were citing against her did not exist. 'Scandalous, impious, blasphemous, and profane, are adjectives that mean nothing at all, in a legal point of view; ... Is it true or false, ought to be the questions for your consideration, for this alone can be the criterion to decide upon matters of opinion.' Next she went on to examine in detail the material she had sold, at which point the Chief Justice tried to stop her. She pretended not to have heard him and carried on regardless whilst Jones kept her papers in order, handed her her notes and kept an eye on the time. Some of her peroration had clearly had input from Carlile and others in terms of the breadth of reading it displayed and the allusions it made, and these do tend to be the more dull parts of the speech. Much of it, however, is very clearly in her voice, the same one that can be heard through her letters (which were published in *The Republican*) and in accounts of her from others. It is a very different tone from that of the speech Carlile had written for Jane, and even from the unfinished speech made by Mary-Ann. Susannah had had time to work on her defence and she had used that time well. The spectators crowded into the galleries were both entertained and informed, which was what most of them had come for. The interruptions and her studied defiance of them were all part of the theatre of the day.

When she moved on to attack the clergy the Chief Justice again tried to silence her, and was again ignored. Sweeping through, amongst other fields, history, comparative religion, the benefits of representative government and freedom of thought and expression, she took apart the prosecution's case. She did not use as many classical allusions as Carlile had done, but concentrated on Christianity, religion generally, and the place they should or should not have in civil law. When she began to criticize the judge who had presided over Mary-Ann Carlile's trial, however, the Chief Justice could tolerate no more. 'I cannot suffer you to proceed upon such a subject', he said 'uneasily', to which Susannah replied as Mary-Ann had done before her: 'This is my defence, and I have no other.' The Chief Justice then ordered her to strike out 'as much as refers to the learned Judge'. Susannah replied: 'I shall strike out nothing', and began the sentence again, to the 'merriment of a crowded Court'.[17] She continued to dissect the judgement in Mary-Ann's case, the Chief Justice continued to try to interrupt her and she continued to ignore him. She attacked the inconsistent implementation of the Sunday Observance laws, which disproportionately penalized the labouring classes, and she resolutely defended Carlile and deism. She attacked the Vice Society and its members head on, and told the jurymen that they did not have to believe or accept everything the judges said. 'Be firm, and do your duty', she told them, finally, 'and believe me . . . that I scorn mercy and demand justice'.

For anyone, let alone a working-class woman with limited formal education and no legal training, this was an extraordinary performance. However, it was all to no avail, since it took the jury precisely two minutes to come to a 'Guilty' verdict. By then Susannah was no longer in the court, having left during the judge's summing up in order to avoid an immediate committal to gaol. After some delays she was back in court in November for sentencing. This time she knew that she was likely to end the day in prison, but she still came prepared with a new speech in which she minutely dissected the nature of blasphemy, repeatedly inquired whom she had injured by the action of selling two pamphlets to a paid agent, and defended her own character and opinions. Despite what she was facing, she refused to be afraid. 'I come', she said:

> 'not to plead for a mitigated sentence, or a lessening of any given punishment assigned by law, I know there is no such law; . . . I come not with a plea of feigned humility and false penitence, but with a mind elated with pride, from the assurance that the cause which has brought me here has been a common good, and not an evil to the community . . . I shall plead for myself; in so doing, I shall do justice to myself, if I miss it every where else . . .'[18]

As before, she was subjected to frequent interruptions as she queried the validity of her conviction, the legality of the charges against her and the integrity of the court that had tried her. At one point, as the judge protested that he could hear no more of this, Susannah fixed him with a steely eye and said: 'You, sir, are paid to hear me.'[19] About halfway through, however, she launched an attack on the Thirty-nine Articles of Religion, the central statement of Anglican faith to which both clergy and laity were required to subscribe. Outraged, and determined to teach her a lesson, the judge cut her short and sentenced her to ten weeks in Newgate Prison for contempt. Carrying seven-month-old Thomas, she was immediately removed and taken away to the most notorious prison in the country.

Once again, both the case itself and Susannah's demeanour during it attracted much attention from supporters and detractors alike. Funds were set up to help with the costs of her defence and her time in gaol, where prisoners effectively had to pay for their own incarceration – Carlile, for instance, reported that he was paying 'two guineas and a half per week . . . for three meals per day, as plain as they are served up in London in a common coffee-shop and eating house for sixpence and one shilling a meal'.[20]

The editor of the *New Times* was very pleased to see Susannah consigned to Newgate and thought it no more than she deserved. He was also sanctimoniously horrified at the nature of her offence.

'. . . here is not only one abandoned creature who has cast off all the distinctive shame and fear and decency of her sex, but her horrid mind has depraved the minds of others who are perhaps already the mothers of families, or to whom the temporal and eternal happiness of a future offspring may be committed . . .'[21]

For Susannah and little Thomas, however, her committal was the beginning of a nightmare from which she – in physical terms at least – never entirely recovered. For her first night she was put into a cell with five other women, two of whom were awaiting execution. Female prisoners in Newgate slept on the stone floor with 'no other bed than a door mat with an old blanket and rug to cover us with, as filthy as the streets and full of holes'.[22] Susannah was so appalled that she complained to the gaoler and demanded that she be moved to better accommodation, or at least to have a bed brought in. However:

'they told me that it was no use for me to make any noise about not having a bed, that I should be treated with the same leniency as the other prisoners, for more I was not to look. I told him I was not a felon, and that I would not be treated as one. His answer was, that there were many women in Newgate who had been well off, and who were obliged to sleep on the floor: there have been two hundred at once sleeping on those mats. Two hundred did you say? Yes. Then more shame for you. Had I been one of them I would have excited a rebellion against you . . .'

Following this she was offered an alternative that was even worse, so she returned to the first floor and slept as well as she could. In the morning she was taken to be measured and was asked how she had slept. 'I asked him how he would have slept if he had been there with an infant seven months old.' Later that day she was able to complain to the Sherriff when he visited the prison and was soon moved into the infirmary, provided that she promised not to talk to other prisoners about religion. After that she was better housed, but 'both me and the child got a severe cold by having to sleep in such a horrid manner the first night'.

Despite the change in sleeping arrangements, the conditions were still dreadful. The building was unheated in winter, and exercise had to be taken in an icy yard in all weathers. Food had to be paid for and was in any case almost inedible, and Benjamin Jones was only able to bring her one hot meal a week. It was impossible to keep the baby clean or safe from the diseases that raged from time to time. Newgate was full of misery and despair. Although the interventions of Elizabeth Fry's Quaker reformers had begun to secure some improvements, such as the segregation of men and women at night, the regime was punishing, the building unhealthy and damp, and the gaolers fully aware of the money-making possibilities offered by the prisoners at their mercy. However brave her spirit, Susannah must have been constantly afraid, and the conditions soon began to tell on her. Typically, however, she refused to give in. She regarded herself as a political prisoner and kept up a constant stream of demands to be better treated, in some of which she was successful. With the Quaker ladies, however, she would have no truck – 'I know you would help me to laugh at them if you were here', she wrote to Jane Carlile, 'They want no pupils but those who are more ignorant than themselves . . .'.[23] In the same paragraph she expressed the (rather unrealistic) hope that Jane and Richard Carlile would be back in London in time for her next court appearance. 'I expect to see the old women on the Bench go into hysterics', she said, 'as I shall prepare for them'. She had taken the precaution of sending copies of the full text of her defence to the judges in advance so that they could see exactly what they had missed by stopping her from speaking.

Her treatment in Newgate made her so ill that her first sentencing date had to be rescheduled, but on 7 February she was back before the bench, still frail but essentially unbowed. Again she had a speech ready, but she was only allowed to read the first page before the judge intervened and sentenced her to eighteen-months imprisonment in Coldbath Fields Gaol, a fine of £100 and a further £200 to be paid as security for future behaviour. Reporting this, Carlile observed that: 'We cannot conceive that this fine can be legal, being a married woman she possesses no property of her own.'[24]

Coldbath Fields[25] was on the whole an improvement on Newgate. She was able to have female visitors and was, by prison standards, reasonably well housed. However, conditions overall remained poor and disease rife. Typically, she immediately started to look at how prisons were organized, and where the power in them lay. Writing to supporters in Birmingham she complained about the way in which magistrates were able to interfere in the running of prisons: 'At first, the allowance of food was delivered to me; now it has been taken off without any intimation, or ceremony, or reason assigned. But this is no great loss, as it required a stronger stomach than mine to consume it, whilst I could get any thing else.'[26] In Coldbath Fields she was further away from friends and relatives and therefore less likely to get food delivered.

Little Thomas's first birthday came and went in April. Susannah had been put into the part of the building known as the school; not much education was done there, but it was better than much of the rest of the building. However:

> 'The children of vagrants and other disorderly persons who are committed here for short periods, are put into my ward. They are unhappy beings wretchedly filthy and diseased, and I say it with horror, that I have not been able, with all my care to keep myself and infant free from that disease which is attendant upon a want of cleanliness and bad living, or a connection with persons in that state.'[27]

By the spring of 1824 it was clear that Susannah's health had been seriously compromised, and that there was a real danger of her dying and becoming the infidel movement's first martyr. Mary-Ann Carlile had been released on similar grounds the previous November, and Peel and the Lord Chancellor, Lord Eldon, knew when they were beaten. Accordingly, and much to her surprise, Susannah found herself released a month early, the government having paid her financial penalties. As Carlile jubilantly reported:

'This heroine in the cause of free discussion, was informed on Thursday, . . . that she was no longer a prisoner, . . . It has been a lingering struggle on the part of *(the government)* to yield even this; and nothing but the fear of Mrs. Wright's dying in prison has made them yield. . . . Throughout the struggle in which Mrs. Wright has engaged, and she was engaged in the hottest part of all, her enthusiasm, her perseverance, her undauntedness, her coolness, were alike conspicuous and excellent.'[28]

Despite her courage, however, Susannah paid dearly for her principles. Through some unspecified illness she had lost the sight of one eye and was suffering from various ailments. In April 1824 she wrote to supporters in Nottingham:

'As to my health, it was too much impaired by the treatment I received in Newgate to be recovered whilst I am a prisoner. I suffer much from fits and a variety of other complaints. My spirits are as good as ever: in truth, I am all spirits and no matter; for I am a mere shadow, a real disembodied spirit.'[29]

Miraculously, little Thomas Paine Carlile Wright survived, and at the age of twenty-seven months was released with his mother. Reunited with William and five-year-old William Henry, Susannah was able to recuperate more or less in peace. But she could not travel to Dorchester to visit Carlile until the following year, when he again wrote in her praise:

'With all her sufferings, her spirits are not broken; but she is as firm as ever, and would enter my shop again with pleasure and alacrity, if there were a renewal of prosecutions . . . I look upon her as by far the most interesting woman in the country, and one who has done more public good than any other one: done it too in the face of sufferings such as but few women would face . . .'[30]

Early in 1826, Susannah's husband William died at the age of thirty-nine, and she was left with two small children and no immediate prospect of employment. Carlile by this point had been released from Dorchester and was back in Fleet Street, but the Vice Society was in financial difficulties and the routine prosecutions had ceased. The old bonds that had held the little group of republicans and infidels together were beginning to fracture, and Susannah felt that she needed both the emotional and practical support of her family in Nottingham. In the spring of 1826 she and her two boys moved back there to live with her mother, but instead of opting for a quiet and retired life, or taking up her needle again to earn her living, she plunged immediately into more controversy.

As a widow with children to feed, she needed to earn some money, and she decided to do this by running a Freethought bookshop. She took premises in Goosegate near the market, ordered in some stock and opened for trade. She ran into trouble almost immediately, explaining in *The Republican* that 'when my sign came home, the man that I had taken the shop of declared that I should not hang out the sign: I declared that I would'. The landlord went to see the mayor and the magistrates, who told him that they could not intervene unless there was a riot. As the evening wore on a large crowd gathered outside the shop, and although they were not directly threatening, it was clear that trouble was coming. Eventually, someone thew a stone through a window breaking both the glass and the shutter, and the landlord, who just happened to be outside, told Susannah's aunt that he wished they had broken all the windows, for then he could have got the magistrates to act. Susannah boldly went out and:

'collared the landlord and marched him into the house; "now, Sir," said I, "are you not ashamed of your self, do not you see that you are a party in this disgraceful, this infamous act? Come, Sir, answer me, and for once try to let it be an honest answer: am I not an ill used woman?" To this he made no reply—I still kept my hold—and repeated the question, indeed I demanded it: at last, as if moved from his astonishment at my spirits, he replied, "Mrs. Wright, you are an ill used woman;" but, with some hesitation, said, "I did not think you was so near going to bed, and thought *you were alone*," . . .'[31]

If the landlord thought that Susannah might take fright he had much mistaken this woman, and over succeeding nights the freethinkers and republicans of Nottingham faced increasingly large crowds of outraged citizens at the shop. A supporter called Luris Smith wrote to *The Republican* that:

'The town of Nottingham is in an uproar, the Saints are in a sweat, and all the bigots and blackguards are in a ferment—and for what? Because a woman is exposing Paine's "Age of Reason" . . . for public sale. . . . The interest which is excited is immense; at night crowds are collected round the door and window, to see this novel show. . . . Every blockhead is condemning books he never read— every bigot feels himself scandalized by the show—every fanatic is enraged at the exhibition—every blackguard is prating about public tranquillity—and every monster of iniquity is prosing upon the demoralizing effects of infidelity.'[32]

Susannah was threatened with prosecution, but this was hardly something to frighten a woman who had slept on the cold, stony floor of Newgate. The local newspapers attacked her, but this merely gave her more publicity for the shop. Grimly, and with the same doggedness with which she had faced down the Chief Justice in his own court, she stood her ground. Repeated attempts were made to break into the shop and drag her out into the angry crowd, where she would certainly have been seriously injured if not killed, but she and her supporters still refused to concede. She kept a loaded pistol on the counter, threatening two youths with it when they came in and started shouting abuse at her. 'Though I am getting rather worse from wear after all this ill-treatment', she reported, 'my spirit is as good as ever. I never saw anything like it in London. – The scenes here are not be described . . .'[33] However, the magistrates seemed to be even more afraid of disorder than they were of freethought, and had been very helpful to her. Nottingham had a history of riots, and men who owned property were not keen to see another one start now.

Following Carlile's example, Susannah had people lined up to take over the shop should she be arrested, and she made sure that the local magistrates and members of the Vice Society were fully aware of this. Faced with a series of expensive prosecutions, as well as with the prospect of gaoling a woman who was unafraid of them and who had already emerged once triumphant from the worst the prison system could offer, the Society backed off and the demonstrations outside the shop began to die down. Two weeks later Susannah was able to report to *The Republican* that:

> 'I have the pleasure to inform you, that the Victory is ours, and that we have succeeded in establishing free discussion in the most fanatical and bigoted town in England. Yes, we are conquerors. . . . When I first came to Goose gate, Nottingham, I was dared to go out by the fanatics. I defied their threats. I have gone out when there has been more than two hundred throwing their curses and prayers alternately at me; but I was well convinced, if I stayed within, it would be much worse. . . . . I have removed a few doors higher up in the same street to a more commodious house, where I hope to continue to vend useful publications without interruption. I have no doubt, but I shall yet do well. . . .'[34]

Susannah Wright was a woman driven by a profound belief in her right to make her own mind up about everything, including religion. As much as Carlile himself, she had an adamantine conviction of the justness of her cause, and she was prepared to go to considerable lengths and endure very considerable hardships in order to maintain what she thought was right. She was by no means alone in this. The large numbers of women who supported her, funded her, wrote to her whilst she was in prison and expressed agreement with her views, demonstrates that even in an increasingly conformist society, women were prepared to think for themselves and to arrive at their own conclusions. Her achievement was recognized by men and women around the country. In Bolton in January 1826, for instance, the republicans and infidels gathered together for their annual dinner to commemorate Tom Paine, drank many toasts, but well up the list came one to 'Mrs. Carlile, Mrs. Wright, and Miss Mary Ann Carlile, may they live to see their Christian Judges brought to trial before a Jury of their own Sex'.[35] The radical poet, Allen Davenport, dedicated a panegyric to her, the last verse of which read:

> 'For not in history's pages
> Shall be found more fair and bright,
> Which may descend to future ages
> Than the name of Susan Wright.'[36]

Whether or not Susannah's shop did indeed do well is unknown, since she disappears from the records after September 1826, and her name has become as obscure as those of so many other working-class women. There seems to be no further record of her in Nottingham, nor is it possible to trace either of her sons. It is difficult to believe that from being a vocal controversialist she would have become silent, but that appears to be what happened. When Carlile visited Nottingham on a lecture tour in 1828 he made no mention of her; it seems highly unlikely that, had she been there, he would have failed to meet up with the woman he had described as 'that pink of female sufferers (I may say the males too: and they must not be angry)'.[37] Susannah's brother, John, also disappeared at the same time, and it is entirely possible that brother, sister and children, like so many radicals and free thinkers before them, emigrated to America. But without records, it is impossible to know.

PART FOUR

Women Without Masters

With the majority of the reform movement's leadership either in prison or becoming less active, the early 1820s saw a lull in mass radical and reformist activity. This is not to say that there was none – the battle for freedom of the press and free thought continued, as we have seen, and both men and women carried on organizing for parliamentary reform, but there were changes in the wind that would lead both to new opportunities and new configurations in the latter part of the decade.

As the Peterloo leaders went on trial in York in early 1820, public attention was considerably distracted by events surrounding Queen Caroline. Now that her estranged husband, the former Prince Regent, had succeeded to the throne, Caroline intended to claim her rights as Queen. On the other hand, George IV, as he now was, wanted a divorce, whilst the government just wanted her to disappear. She had been abroad for nearly six years, and every effort was made to get her to remain there, but she was determined to have what she saw as her due, and arrived in England on 5 June. Radicals and women had always identified with her cause; now there was a huge upsurge of support for her. The details of her time abroad were not widely known, and she was therefore generally regarded as a wronged and innocent wife. However, George had been gathering evidence of her rackety life in Italy, and he was adamant that she should not be crowned and that he would have his divorce. His own life was, and had almost always been, notoriously immoral, and he was detested by many people, but he had the law on his side and he was determined to use it. In July a Bill of Pains and Penalties was introduced into the House of Lords, and the Queen was effectively put on trial for adultery.

Throughout the proceedings she continued to enjoy considerable popularity, and there were hundreds of petitions in her favour from all around the country, particularly from women. From his cell in Dorchester, Carlile thundered continuous support for her, inviting government ministers to: 'Mark the contrast between your puppet of a King and the people's Queen . . .'[1] He also thought that 'the persecution of the Queen has been of great assistance to the cause of reform; it has united all classes of reformers, and in the person of the Queen, our liberties seem to be for the moment centered'.[2] Caroline remained popular throughout the trial, but nevertheless the Bill scraped through the House of Lords by a thin majority. The evidence against her was significant, but so was public disquiet, and there had been riots and mutinies, as well as more peaceful expressions of support. The prospect of getting the Bill through the House of Commons was minimal; most Whigs were firmly opposed to it and the King faced humiliation if he lost. Wisely, the government withdrew it in November and began to negotiate with Caroline over what her future living arrangements were going to be. The settlement they reached severely dented her public support. In July 1821 she tried to attend George's Coronation and famously – and mortifyingly – found the doors of Westminster Abbey slammed in her face. She was probably already ill at this stage; she collapsed that evening and died in early August. Despite everything she remained to the end considerably more popular than her husband.

One of the side effects of this series of events was that the Whigs in Parliament now began to look with new eyes on the radicals. As a result, a degree of rapprochement began that horrified Henry Hunt, who, still in his prison at Ilchester, knew all too well that the Whigs would never have working-class interests at heart. The Whigs, however, began to talk about reform in a more friendly manner, and to exploit the cracks opening up in radical circles. Hunt insisted on sticking to the traditional demands of universal suffrage, annual parliaments and secret ballots, whilst the journalist and author William Cobbett, newly returned from America, was more interested in financial policy and regarded himself as the voice of the agricultural poor.

Meanwhile, Carlile continued to promote the ideas of Tom Paine, of whose legacy he considered himself the guardian, though he was increasingly inclined to accept a gradualist approach to reform. Prompted by Francis Place, he also developed an interest in the ideas of Thomas Malthus and was persuaded to support contentious and unpopular ideas about birth control.

Malthus had been born into the Enlightenment, but he did not share its view about the ultimate perfectibility of humanity and therefore of society. He thought that poverty was a self-inflicted evil that inhibited progress but which could be defeated if procreation was controlled. When, in 1798, he published *An Essay on the Principle of Population, as it Affects the Future Improvement of Society* it caused great controversy, particularly amongst the working class. He suggested that social and economic policy should be managed so as to control the birth rate, and his dictum that 'a man has no right to exist, if another man cannot or will not employ him', was horrifying to many people. They thought they knew exactly where such thinking might lead if it was allowed to become part of government policy, and Malthus was seen as cold-blooded and almost inhuman. Men such as Francis Place did not follow this particular aspect of Malthusian thought, nor was Malthus himself in favour of contraception, preferring the 'moral restraint' involved in late marriage and sexual abstinence. However, both Place and Carlile believed that sexual abstinence was not only impossible but also undesirable and unhealthy, and therefore advocated birth control instead. They proposed cheap and simple mechanisms – such a sponge soaked in vinegar – which was available even to the poor, but they were seen as promoting sexual licence, and the hostility they encountered did much to undermine any effectiveness they might otherwise have had.

For many radical working-class women, attempts to limit their fertility were perceived as attacks on both their social and their political identity. They had positioned themselves as reforming wives and mothers, and indeed, in the eyes of many people, these were the only roles that could give them legitimacy in the public space. They believed that the answer to chronic poverty was not to limit the population, but to change the balance of power, both politically and economically, and to ensure that all children who were born could be properly fed, clothed and educated. Many radical women were also religious, and saw birth control as morally wrong in principle. At almost no stage in the 1820s did any but a very few women see contraception as having the potential to liberate them, and the vast majority of its proponents were men. When, in 1823, Francis Place sent a parcel of handbills on the subject to Mary Fildes in Manchester and asked her to circulate them, she was furious, forwarding them to the attorney general and demanding that he prosecute. By 1825, Carlile was claiming that Mary had become a convert to the utility of birth control; she angrily denied having done any such thing, but he never withdrew the suggestion.

Meanwhile, other ideas about how society should be organized were beginning to emerge. Where Tom Paine and Mary Wollstonecraft had had little experience of industrialization and thought of the redistribution of wealth largely in terms of land ownership, people in the post-war years were beginning to consider new ideas about social and economic systems. One of these was Robert Owen, who brought personal experience of industry and the factory system to the problem of social and economic structures and how they might be changed for the greater good. Against the pre-eminence of the individual he set the possibilities of the collective. He thought that 'if there be one closet doctrine more contrary to truth than another, it is the notion that individual interest, as that term is now understood, is a more advantageous principle on which to found the social system, for the benefit of all, or of any, than the principle of union and mutual co-operation'.[3] This thinking was not necessarily new in itself, but it did open up new perspectives once it was applied to a recently industrialized society.

Owen was significant because he was one of the first people to emerge from an industrial background with new ideas about society that were influenced by practical experience of money and capital as well as land, and who produced – and tried to implement – concepts that went well beyond simply changing parliament and the electoral system. He was a self-made man who used his considerable wealth to develop his thinking about how industrial communities, in particular, could be organized. He shared Richard Carlile's scepticism of religion, and like both him and Hunt was very sure of his own powers, believing in himself to an unusually high degree. Owen's major contribution was his insight that labour had inherent value and was in itself a form of wealth. This proposition, made in 1821, was not original, but Owen's framing and interpretation of it was a revelation, and laid the foundation, not just of what came to be called Owenite socialism, but also of much of socialist thought later in the century. Friedrich Engels was first introduced to socialist ideas in the 1840s at Owenite lectures in Manchester, and although many Marxists disliked the strain of utopian and millenarian thinking that some aspects of Owenite cooperation involved, they also recognized Owen's place in early socialist thought.

Robert Owen made his fortune in the cotton industry, and moved through philanthropy and enlightened employment practices to a conviction that a system that depended on competitive capitalism could never meet the utilitarian aim of producing the greatest good and happiness of all citizens. Given that he combined this with, at the very least, a sceptical approach to religion and a tendency to view parliamentary reform as not necessarily being the sole key to resolving the country's economic problems, he soon found himself at odds with almost everyone. He came from a respectable, working-class background, but at the age of ten he left home to make his fortune. At eighteen he achieved it when he sold his first company in Manchester. At this stage he was focused on both making money and improving the machinery with which that could be done; only gradually did he begin to consider the lives of those who worked the machinery, and even then predominantly in terms of how they could be made more productive. In 1799 he married Ann Caroline Dale and, together with partners, bought a mill at New Lanark, near Glasgow, from his father-in-law. Here he created his famous experiment in benign capitalism, combining good working conditions with profitable output, and attracting thousands of people to come and see how it was done. From there he moved on to trying to resolve wider problems. He supported attempts to get industrial legislation limiting working hours through parliament, and when this failed he began to lose faith in industrialization itself. Moreover, his attempts to regulate work brought him into direct conflict with many radicals, who believed that poverty was caused by excessive taxation and that Owen was opposed, either actively or passively, to parliamentary reform. Against widespread belief in the individual and free trade, Owen set ideas about collectivism and regulation, as well as proposals for the 'moral' regeneration of the nation, which extended far beyond traditional religious or social thought. He believed that the generally accepted 'boom and bust' model of capitalism was not set in stone, that permanent full employment was possible, that poverty could be conquered and that endless mechanization was neither inevitable nor desirable. Many of these ideas he set out most clearly in his 1821 *Report to the County of Lanark*. Noting that the traditional view of how society should be structured was that 'man can provide better for himself, and more advantageously for the public, when left to his own individual exertions, opposed to, and in competition with his fellows', he suggested that this model was actually counter-productive and actively opposed to the public good. In his view, if people gave his cooperative ideas a chance they would soon see that the competitive (or capitalist) system was:

'the most anti-social, impolitic, and irrational, that can be devised; that under its influence, all the superior and valuable qualities of human nature are repressed from infancy, and that the most unnatural means are used to bring out the most injurious propensities; ... From this principle of individual interest have arisen all the divisions of mankind, the endless errors and mischiefs of class, sect, party, and of national antipathies, creating the angry and malevolent passions, and all the crimes and misery with which the human race have been hitherto afflicted.'[4]

Ideas of this kind were bound to put him into conflict with the political and economic mainstream as well as artisan radicals, such as Francis Place, who described working people as being:

'misled and bewildered by the misty doctrine of Robert Owen and others who taught, to them, the agreeable doctrine that whatever was made by or was the consequence of any actions of any man belonged to that man, or that the *whole* produce of every community should be equally divided among such of the members of the community as were willing to perform equal shares of labour, and these notions made them look upon all who were not of their own class as their deliberate and determined enemies.'[5]

Richard Carlile, for whom the concept of the liberty of the individual was a driving force for which he had sacrificed years of his life, was also deeply sceptical, but for many people, particularly the younger, post-revolutionary and post-war generation, Owenite socialism presented exciting possibilities, especially when it came to the organization of society and personal relationships. Owen came to the conclusion, for instance, that traditional forms of marriage were part of the wider problem, since they were essentially about property. If one human being could not, and should not, be the property of another, it followed that women could not and should not be the property of men. This notion had direct implications for the way in which relations between the sexes should be organized, and made socialism particularly attractive to some women, but deeply repellent to others, for whom it became inextricably linked with wickedness and sexual licence.

For one young woman trapped in the backwater of a decaying Irish estate, many of Owen's ideas were compelling, and would help to propel her to the heart of radical and socialist society in London and Paris. From unpromising beginnings, she would become one of the few female political philosophers of the age, ironically describing herself as 'a woman and without a master; two causes of disgrace in England'.[6] Her name was Anna Doyle Wheeler.

Chapter 10
Very Clever, Awfully Revolutionary

In 1800, at the age of fifteen, Anna Doyle married a man of her own choice. There was nothing very unusual in this; girls often got married at fifteen, and, despite Anna's mother's reservations about him, Francis Massy Wheeler looked like a good prospect. At nineteen he had a good income, land, a manor house and a stable full of horses. Anna would have status and should be able to live the kind of life for which her upbringing had prepared her. Bright, pretty and headstrong, she had been determined to get away from home and be her own mistress. Marriage was the only way in which she could do this, and she seized the first available opportunity. It was a disaster.

Over the next twelve years, Anna and her husband were locked in a miserable relationship that made neither of them happy. As the years went on, Wheeler developed a drink problem, and became increasingly brutal. Anna was pregnant for much of the time, giving birth to six living children of whom only two girls survived infancy. Wheeler was desperate for a son and heir, and their daughter Rosina later remembered the fury with which he greeted a new daughter. The one son Anna bore died before he was a year old. Whilst Wheeler led the life of an Irish country gentleman, Anna was largely confined to the house; by the end she felt herself almost a prisoner. Her husband spent his time out riding by day and drinking in the evening, and around him the house fell into decay. The roof leaked but went unrepaired, the drive and paths became overgrown and the walls slowly crumbled. There were a few redeeming features. Wheeler allowed Anna to read, and to order books from

London. Her mind was bright and sharp and her father (who had died before Anna was two years old) had been well connected; her godfather was the Irish politician Henry Grattan and her uncles were military men from whom she had been able to pick up a sketchy knowledge of history and geography.

Now, isolated in her husband's house, she read everything she could find, not just poetry, novels and works of religion, but also history, social commentary and philosophy. Rosina, whose later relationship with her mother was fraught, remembered her Aunt Bessie lying on one sofa reading romantic novels whilst Anna stretched out on another opposite:

> 'deep in perusal of some French or German philosophical work that had reached her translated via London and unfortunately deeply imbued with the pernicious fallacies of the French Revolution, which had then more or less seared their traces through Europe, and *(she)* was besides strongly tainted by the corresponding poison of Mrs Wollstonecraft's book.'[1]

Rosina thought that her mother preferred both her books and her older daughter, Henrietta, to her, remarking later: 'I soon became that most miserable of created beings, the neglected sister of a favoured and favourite child.'[2] Years afterwards, Rosina's estranged husband accused her of indifference to her own daughter, Emily, and an unsympathetic biographer observed that: 'This conduct in Rosina was the very fault from which she had suffered with her own mother, and showed itself in the same manner.'[3] The contrast between the ideas about liberty and equality in books, and the reality of her daily life, cannot have been lost on Anna, and the strain must have been intense. Most women in her position would have seen no option but to remain where they were, continuing to bear one child after another until the longed-for son, the menopause or death intervened. But Anna was not most women, and by 1812 she had had enough.

It is not known what finally made her decide that she had to escape, and she seems not to have been inclined to discuss it. It was by no means uncommon for couples to separate, and often some kind of arrangement was worked out between them as divorce was out of the question. However, it was much less usual – and also illegal – for a departing woman to take her children with her without the consent of their father, to whom they legally belonged. When Mary Wollstonecraft's sister Eliza left her husband she had to leave her baby behind. When Percy Bysshe Shelley abandoned his first wife, Harriet, he was outraged when her family took him to court to contest his custody rights.[4] But Anna had other ideas. Helped by her sister Bessie and brother John, and taking both her little girls with her, she ran away. Some forethought and planning must have been involved because her uncle, Sir John Doyle, Governor of the Channel Island of Guernsey, had sent his own yacht to collect her. Together with Bessie, John and the children, Anna sailed south to freedom.

Once arrived in Guernsey, she could relax a little. Her husband showed no sign of wishing to retrieve either his wife or the children, so that although he also declined to pay her any maintenance, she was relatively safe from him as long as he remained of that mind. Although the appalling events of her marriage must have had their effect, she had not been crushed by them, and she was fortunate in having family willing to help her. Had she had surviving sons, Wheeler would almost certainly have compelled their return, but there were only the despised daughters whom he did not want. Anna could take some time to consider what to do next, and soon she took on the task of acting as hostess for her uncle's social events. Here, amongst others, she met French émigrés with whom she practised and developed her language skills. As they improved, she was also able to begin earning her own money – or at least, money which her husband, to whom it legally belonged, allowed her to keep – by translating works for publication.

In 1816 debt forced Sir John to give up the governorship of Guernsey. Anna paid quick visits to Dublin and London before moving to France and settling in the Norman city of Caen, where living expenses were relatively low and there was interesting company, including a small, but flourishing, socialist community. She soon set up her own political salon, becoming, according to her unsympathetic grandson, the '*bel esprit* of a little group of socialists and freethinkers, to the support of whose doctrines she devoted both her purse and her pen'.[5] She also became known as the 'Goddess of Reason', and 'the most gifted woman of the age', in both of which titles she must have felt a certain amount of pride, given how hard her learning had been to acquire.

In 1820 Francis Wheeler died, leaving Anna a penniless widow with two teenage daughters. However, she could now return to London safely, and this she did for three years, before going back to France, this time to Paris. During her years in London she met radical thinkers and philosophers, including Jeremy Bentham. Bentham, by then in his seventies, was the father of utilitarianism, which, broadly speaking, suggested that the best way to determine whether or not an act was morally or ethically right was to identify the good it produced. In political terms, this meant that a good government would be that which produced the greatest good (or happiness) for the greatest number of people. Utilitarianism was immensely influential, not only on radicals, but also on early socialists, who developed ideas about community and cooperation that went beyond the simpler radical ideas about access to power, and began to identify ways of redistributing it that involved dismantling many of the existing social and economic structures.

Anna had read works by both Bentham and Owen whilst she was still in Ireland, and in France she had moved in socialist circles in Caen and Paris. There, socialist thinking was mainly represented by the ideas of Henri de Saint-Simon, a man later referred to by Friedrich Engels as a 'son of the great French Revolution',[6] but who was also influenced by the American War of Independence, in which, as a very young man, he had fought on the colonists' side. Saint-Simon came to the conclusion that there were two basic groups in society, the workers and the idlers, and that, to date, the balance between them had been wrong. He identified the workers as a wide range of people, not just those who would now be defined as working class, but also merchants, scientists and even businessmen. The idlers lived off the labour of others and were effectively those whom Tom Paine had called the 'parasite class'. Over the years Anna came to regard herself as a bridge between the different emerging strands of thought, and believed that socialism as a whole would be stronger if it could also be international.

Despite her wide acquaintance amongst utilitarians and socialists, it was probably not until 1822, when he came to London, that she encountered William Thompson, who would become both one of the great theoreticians of early socialism and Anna's literary collaborator, friend and, in some senses, life partner. Thompson was staying at the time with Jeremy Bentham, who kept open house for a variety of interesting thinkers and writers, including Anna and women such as the socialist lecturer and abolitionist Frances Wright. Here, at some point between October 1822 and February 1823, Anna and Thompson met, and began an intellectual and personal friendship that lasted for the rest of his life. Quite what that relationship was has never been clear. Certainly there was never a breath of scandal about either of them, but both had ideological objections to marriage, and, in Anna's case, probably a determination never to allow herself to be the property of another human being again. Years later, when the philosopher and politician John Stuart Mill married the philosopher and author Harriet Taylor in 1851, he made a declaration that concluded: 'I absolutely disclaim and repudiate all pretence to have acquired any rights whatever by virtue of such marriage.' Perhaps Anna and William Thompson considered something similar, but they would have known that it could only have been a private agreement between them, and could therefore only have held good for so long as Thompson wanted it to. All the power in the marriage would have remained vested in him, and she would always have felt vulnerable. Whatever their private arrangements were, they remained unmarried, and together they wrote one of the most comprehensive and least-known feminist books of the nineteenth century.

William Thompson was, like Anna, the product of Irish Ascendancy landed gentry and had been radicalized by his reading as well as travels in France and the Netherlands. In 1822 he was in his late forties, an intelligent, thoughtful man who had, unlike many Irish landlords, tried successfully to improve the lot of his tenants in Cork, and to put into practice some of the new ideas he was encountering. He was in many ways a typical eccentric freethinker in a time of much conformity; he was a vegetarian, non-drinking, non-smoker who thought marriage was structurally oppressive of women. When he met Anna he was working on his study of the distribution of wealth, which would become a seminal text in early socialist thought, but they must also have discovered a mutual interest in women's rights, particularly since they were both furious with another utilitarian thinker, James Mill, over a remark about women and the franchise made in his *Essay on Government*, published in 1821.

In the *Vindication of the Rights of Woman*, Mary Wollstonecraft had made only a passing reference to the possibility of women voting, glossing over it with a rueful acknowledgement that most people would find the prospect ridiculous. 'I may excite laughter', she admitted, 'by dropping an hint, which I mean to pursue, some future time, for I really think that women ought to have representatives, instead of being arbitrarily governed without having any direct share allowed them in the deliberations of government'. However, she made it abundantly clear, firstly, that only women 'of a superiour *(sic)* cast' should be included in this, and, secondly, that it was not a priority in the wider scheme of things since:

> '. . . as the whole system of representation is now, in this country, only a convenient handle for despotism, *(women)* need not complain, for they are as well represented as a numerous class of hard working mechanics, who pay for the support of royalty when they can scarcely stop their children's mouths with bread.'[7]

In fact, the idea that women should have equal political rights had already been raised before Mary wrote the *Vindication*. Jeremy Bentham had suggested in 1789 that there could be no justification for women's legal and political disabilities, and he himself was following in a tradition of occasional objections to women's exclusion going back into the seventeenth century. Bentham has often been described as an early feminist, although, as we shall see, he was much more keen on the theory of women's equality than the practice. Radicals such as Richard Carlile also supported women's rights, at least in principle, and his was one of the few voices raised on their behalf during the 1832 Reform Act crisis. But for most people the idea of women voting or, worse, taking an active part in politics or government, continued to be either ludicrous or immoral or both.

James Mill (father of the now more famous John Stuart Mill) was a Scottish philosopher and historian who was an able propagandist in the utilitarian cause. Unlike Bentham, Mill was a practical man with real administrative experience, and his *Essay on Government* examined the propositions that good government should be so structured as to benefit the greatest number of people, that representative democracy was the best way of achieving this, that elections should be frequent and terms of office short, and that the vote should be given to as many people as possible. In considering who should form the body politic he wrote a paragraph so casual in its assumptions that it still has the power to shock two centuries later. 'One thing is pretty clear', he said:

'that all those individuals whose interests are indisputably included in those of other individuals, may be struck off without inconvenience. In this light may be viewed all children, up to a certain age, whose interests are involved in those of their parents. In this light, also, women may be regarded, the interest of almost all of whom is involved either in that of their fathers or in that of their husbands.'[8]

The phrase 'may be struck off without inconvenience' suggested that, even in a representative democracy, a whole section of the community could be summarily removed without either discussion or consideration. Many people, including Bentham and Mill's own teenage son, John, immediately disagreed with him, but he stuck to his guns, and when the *Essay* was reprinted a few years later he left the statement in unchanged. He had the law and commonly accepted public opinion on his side, and he viewed the whole question as a diversion from his central arguments. He saw no need to alter something that he thought was self-evident to any reasonable person.

Anna Doyle Wheeler was incensed. She knew only too well that her interests had been anything but involved with those of her husband, except insofar as it suited him, and she had not had a father since she was two years old. To care so little about half of the adult population seemed outrageous, but she did not know what to do about it. At the point at which the *Essay* was published, in 1820, she had not yet met William Thompson, but she certainly knew Bentham and Mill, and must have raised it with them. However, Bentham, although on the face of it an ally for women's rights, was in fact unreliable when it came to the practice. In 1817, in his *Plan of Parliamentary* Reform, he had concluded that there was no reason why women should not be enfranchised on the same basis as men. However, a decade later, in 1827, he published the first volume of his great work, the *Constitutional Code*, in which he designed a blueprint for representative democracy 'for the use of All Nations and Governments professing liberal opinions'. In this he again included consideration of women's political rights, but although he said that he was broadly in favour of them, he also did not see how they could be implemented in practice. 'Why', he asked, 'exclude the whole female sex from all participation in the constitutive power?'. His answer, sadly, was one which became all too familiar to suffrage campaigners and their successors: 'Because the prepossession against their admission is at present too general, and too intense, to afford any chance in favour of a proposal for their admission.'[9] Worse followed. In considering – and deciding against – allowing women to become MPs or government ministers, he said that: 'The reciprocal seduction that would ensue in the case of a mixture of sexes in the composition of a legislative or executive body, seems a conclusive reason against admitting the weaker sex into a share in those branches of power: it would lead to nothing but confusion and ridicule.'[10] Women should even be banned from observing debates in the House of Commons lest they should distract men's attention. In other words, whilst women certainly had political rights, Bentham could see no circumstances in which they could be allowed to use them. The purpose of government was to produce the greatest possible happiness of all human beings, in practice providing that those humans were male.

Eventually, so many people, including, at least on the face of it, Jeremy Bentham, disagreed with Mill's view that both Anna and William Thompson separately assumed that someone must be writing a rebuttal. However, months passed and none came. Anna herself was earning a living by translating from French and writing occasional articles of her own, but this was a very different matter from producing a full-scale examination of the position of women in society and the necessity for them to have full and equal political rights. Like some other autodidacts she may have felt apprehensive that she would be judged against standards of writing that she had never had the opportunity to acquire, whilst the men all around her had had a 'proper' academic education. Nothing in her life suggests that she lacked confidence, either in her opinions or her ability to express them, but perhaps that assurance faltered when it came to the written page. She had an excellent brain, and although her handwriting was execrable and her spelling poor, these were both defects that publishers often had to deal with, and could easily have overcome.

Like many other women, not to mention working-class men such as Richard Carlile, Anna had read herself into the ideas she now espoused. She had thought about them, and could more than hold her own in conversation, but she had not had the advantage of being taught how to organize and direct information and ideas so as to produce something of the standard she wanted. The speeches and articles Carlile wrote were certainly impassioned and contained a great deal of material, but they had little sense of discrimination in them and tended simply to pile one fact or idea on top of another. Even Mary Wollstonecraft, whose work Anna had read whilst immured in Ireland, had struggled with this. Anna was mixing with some of the best minds of the age, and both James Mill and Bentham were towering intellects who had been educated at good universities. They took for granted skills that most people had never had the opportunity to acquire.

William Thompson had not had a university education, either, but he had had the training appropriate for the sons of well-to-do gentry and had mixed in intellectual circles that had been inaccessible to Anna in her youth. He was very widely read and very clever, but he also had a practical turn and an interest in implementation as well as theory. His book on education reflected his views that the purpose of it should be to 'make useful citizens for active life, to make intelligent and respectable and benevolent tradesmen and merchants and country gentlemen, and to make their wives and daughters equally intelligent, respectable and useful'.[11] Long before he met Anna, he had also read Mary Wollstonecraft, as well as the French revolutionary thinker Nicolas de Condorcet, whose 1790 pamphlet *Sur l'admission des femmes au droit de Cité (On the Admission of Women to the Rights of Citizenship)* had argued that:

'The rights of men stem exclusively from the fact that they are sentient beings, capable of acquiring moral ideas and of reasoning upon them. Since women have the same qualities, they necessarily also have the same rights. . . . Why should people who experience pregnancies and monthly indispositions be unable to exercise rights we would never refuse to men who have gout every winter or who catch cold easily? People argue that, differences in education apart, men are still naturally more intelligent than women; but this is far from being proven, and would have to be before women could justly be deprived of a natural right.'[12]

Attacking the idea that women were unsuited by their nature and lack of education to public life and the vote, he went on to say that:

'If we accept such arguments against women, we would also have to deny citizenship rights to anyone who was obliged to work constantly and could therefore neither become enlightened nor exercise his reason. Before long, citizenship would be open only to men who had completed a course of public law. The necessary consequences of accepting these arguments is the renunciation of a free constitution.'[13]

Thus in 1822, when Anna Doyle Wheeler and William Thompson met, they already shared a great deal of common ground. Unlike many other men who thought of themselves as supporters of women, Thompson appears to have recognized that his role was that of an ally rather than a leader, and that his opinions were no substitute for Anna's lived experience. In his letter to her dedicating the book they produced together, he said that:

'not having been in the situation you have been, to suffer from the inequalities of sexual laws, I cannot join with a sensibility equal to yours, in your lofty indignation and contempt of the puerilities and hypocrisy with which men seek to cover or to palliate their life-consuming and mind- and joy-eradicating oppressions, . . . though I do not *feel* like you – thanks to the chance of having been born a man . . . yet can I not be inaccessible to the plain facts and reason of the case.'[14]

Even today, women are familiar with men who describe themselves as feminist, but who are unable to avoid thinking that a woman's viewpoint sounds better in a man's voice. Thompson was not one of these, and he seems to have been acutely aware of the fact that the book they wrote should have been Anna's. He had been, he said, anxious that she:

'should take up the cause of your proscribed sex, and state to the world in writing in your own name, what you have so often and so well stated in conversation . . . I long hesitated to arrange our common ideas . . . Were courage the quality wanting, you would have shown, what everyday experience proves, that women have more fortitude in endurance than men.'[15]

The book they wrote together, *Appeal of One Half of the Human Race, Women, against the Pretensions of the Other Half, Men* (the *Appeal*) was published in 1825 and covered a huge amount of ground. It was, however, published in Thompson's name only. In addition to any reservations Anna may have had about her ability to produce a major philosophical work single-handed, there was the question of reputation to consider. Given that the content of the book included observations on sex, power and politics, as well as an all-out assault upon marriage as an institution, the omission of her name may have been wise. The idea of a woman collaborating with a man to whom she was not married to produce a book about such subjects was shocking enough; to have her name on the title page would undoubtedly have caused a scandal. Nevertheless, Anna is constantly present, particularly in descriptions, such as that of a marriage in which 'a woman superior in talents, in virtue, or in both, is bound down in hated obedience to a fool or a vicious wretch, who exercises his power with the more brutality, from the suspicion of his inferiority, from the dread of being looked down upon by the male brutes, his brethren, around him . . .'.[16] Over the years there have been various attempts to determine which parts were written by Thompson and which by Anna alone, and there are clearly two distinct voices at work in the text. Thompson himself said in the introduction that the ideas had been much discussed between them and that many had come originally from her. Assuming that this was true, Anna Doyle Wheeler emerges as one of the most radical women of the nineteenth century, applying an Owenite socialist eye to the question of her oppression and gazing unblinkingly at the challenges that confront women.

Although the *Appeal* covered a variety of subjects and a great deal of ground, its main thrust was that women:

'having been reduced, by the want of political rights, to a state of helplessness, slavery, and of consequent unequal enjoyments, pains and privations, they are *more in need* of political rights than any other portion of human beings, to gain some chance of emerging from this state.'[17]

Political rights were necessary to women:

'as a check on the almost inveterate habits of exclusion of men. It is in vain to sanction by law a civil right, or to remove an exclusion, if the law affords no means to those whom it designs to benefit of causing the right or permission to be enforced. . . . the law may protect [women] when married from personal violence or constraint of any kind of their husbands, as fully as it protects husbands against them; but if none but men are to be the electors, if none but men are to be jurors or judges when women complain against men of partiality and injustice, is it in human nature that a sympathy from old habit . . . from love of domination, should not have a tendency to make men swerve from the line of justice and strict impartiality, should not make them underrate the pretensions of women and be lenient to the errors of men?'[18]

Moreover, the kinds of oppression that happened in domestic settings were private and even secret, so that it was doubly hard for women to enforce their rights, even when they had them. Political rights would resolve this, or at least make access to justice fairer. Political rights would also lead to women being better educated, with a wider perspective on the world. Owenite socialism envisaged a society in which women were nobody's property but their own, and in which they would be able to make choices about how and with whom they lived and slept in the same way that men did. Moreover, Owenites had also developed a distaste for the traditional family, which they believed taught children 'selfishness and hypocrisy', and to 'consider their own individual family their own world and . . . to do whatever they can to promote the advantages of all the legitimate members of it . . . No arrangement could be better calculated to produce division and disunion in society'.[19] The same, argued Anna and William Thompson, could be said of women, who were actively encouraged to look no further than their own front door, and to pretend ignorance of the wider world. This was not good for women, but it was also bad for men and for the community as a whole.

Like Mary Wollstonecraft before her, Anna Doyle Wheeler frequently found women's passivity in the face of their oppression depressing, and sometimes doubted whether they would ever be able to free themselves of it. Both she and Thompson correctly thought that women would have to organize and fight to get their rights, but that the prospect of their actually doing so seemed remote.[20] However, they also understood the gulf between aspiration and achievement that women faced. In a passage that Anna almost certainly wrote they said:

'the *power of imprisonment* which man in marriage holds, cuts off his household slave from all sympathy but with himself, his children, and cats or other household animals. To some lighter public or private amusements where these associated pleasures may be enjoyed, husbands occasionally *permit* their wives, as they do children, to have access; but from all scenes, assemblies, and incidents, that could really enlarge their minds or sympathies, they are, partly by positive law, partly by man's public opinion, backed by persecution, effectually excluded.'[21]

Women were considered unfit for public duties because they were not educated; the answer, said Thompson and Anna, was not to exclude them, but to educate them, and to allow them the access to colleges and universities that was now denied them. Whilst it was true that this would only benefit a limited number of women, nevertheless 'the very eligibility would be an incentive to knowledge and exertion amongst women; it would raise them in their own opinion'. Women would be able to see what was possible and aim for it. So long as they were excluded and subjected to unequal restraints 'the brand of inferiority, of degradation is impressed upon them'.[22] Kindness and good intentions alone would not be sufficient to remove this; only equal civil and criminal laws could achieve it.

Unusually, perhaps, both for their time and for now, they did not hold up the male as the standard to aim for and the female as inferior. If anything, they thought that the political equality of men and women would lead to something new. Despite much pessimism about both male and female behaviour, they retained a hopeful outlook as to what the result of including women in the legislature and the government might be. Although they perceptively thought it very probable that 'partly from want of inclination, partly from motives of convenience, numbers of women qualified would not offer themselves for offices, and would not exercise their political rights', they also rather optimistically considered that the mere knowledge of women's political power would 'cause [men] so to regulate their conduct' that it would be unnecessary for women to act against them. Even if only a few women were elected:

'their influence would cause such men to be elected as would enact equal laws between the two great portions of the race, or would cause such men as showed an inclination to revive the old reign of brutality and injustice to be replaced by other men or by women. Now is it possible to conceive that any set of legislators, male or female, particularly men, would not be more inclined to make and preserve laws of entire reciprocity and equal justice between women and men, when they knew that their constituents were equally balanced, and that injustice on their part would necessarily enlist a few of either party amongst the injured half, and thus create a majority of constituents against them?'[23]

Two centuries later this aspiration seems almost naïve, yet Anna Doyle Wheeler and William Thompson were amongst the first people to seriously consider what a democracy in which both sexes had equal rights and equal power might look like. However, their socialism and their attacks upon the institution of marriage, both of which were unpalatable to most women (and even to some feminists), combined with uncertainty about authorship, led to their achievement being largely disregarded. This happened despite Anna repeatedly making it clear that:

'I have no antipathy to men but only to institutions; no leaning to the interests of one sex above the other; my object is to deprecate that narrow, stupid policy which divides their interests, and in so doing, makes a pandemonium of our earth, by forcing its inhabitants to be in constant opposition to each other!'[24]

The *Appeal* was so controversial in both its content and its conclusions that the mainstream press could not bring itself to review it, though socialist, co-operative and radical groups received it with enthusiasm. Despite its flaws, it remains one of the great declarations of female social, political and economic rights to be published before the twentieth century, but it was buried by both women and men because its analysis of the relations between the sexes was seen to be so extreme that it could not be countenanced in respectable circles. By the time the feminist movement of the later nineteenth century began to develop, it had more or less been forgotten. Moreover, the great scandal of the breakdown of Anna's daughter's marriage also blurred Anna's own reputation. In 1827, Rosina Wheeler married Edward Bulwer Lytton, an eligible young man whose mother objected to the match on the grounds of Anna's notoriety. Sadly, the marriage was an even greater disaster than Anna's had been. Within a few years the couple were separated. Rosina was not allowed to see or have contact with her children, and her husband embarked on a systematic destruction of her character. At one point he even managed to have her briefly committed to an asylum for the insane.[25] Inevitably, Anna's reputation was attacked together with Rosina's, and later generations of feminists, many of whom wanted to be seen as respectable rather than threatening, chose not to include Anna in their history.

Nevertheless, Anna Doyle Wheeler remained a feminist and a socialist for the rest of her life, though increasing illness limited her work. In 1833, in the wake of the Reform Act crisis, the future Prime Minister Benjamin Disraeli met her at dinner at Rosina's house and described her as 'not so pleasant, something between Jeremy Bentham and Meg Merrilees,[26] very clever, but awfully revolutionary. She poured forth all her systems upon my novitiate ear and while she advocated the rights of woman Bulwer abused system-mongers and the sex and Rosina played with her dog'.[27] Like a great many of his contemporaries, Disraeli found an articulate female unnerving. Anna's voice was (and perhaps still is) unsettling to a great many people, but she remains a notable pioneer of both feminism and socialism, a woman for whom all things might be possible, if only women were free.

Chapter 11
Petticoat Government

In May 1832, the Parliament at Westminster passed a piece of legislation that came to be known as the Great Reform Act. Having resisted any such move for decades, it now granted representation to the industrial areas outside the South of England, created sixty-seven new constituencies and abolished fifty-six. Many constituencies found that in future they would be represented by only one Member of Parliament, where previously they had had two. The hotchpotch of franchises, which had meant that voting qualifications were different in different towns and counties, was swept away. Across the board, any man owning, leasing or renting land or property with a rental value of £10 or more was to be entitled to vote. For the first time there was to be a national system of voter registration, with provisions for detecting fraud and challenging both the exclusion and inclusion of individuals. At a stroke, large parts of the middle classes were enfranchised, increasing the electorate by about sixty per cent, and giving votes to some eighteen per cent of the total male population. For the first time, and almost unnoticed by most people, women were now specifically excluded from the franchise. The Act was finally passed only after a major constitutional crisis that terminated the political career of the Duke of Wellington, caused riots in many parts of the country and, for the first time, saw militant political and economic action on the part of the growing middle classes. It seemed to be in every respect a triumph.

It might have been expected that Henry Hunt, who had given his life to the cause of political reform, would be elated by all this, but, in fact, he was angry and depressed. In his view it constituted a great betrayal of the working class he saw himself as representing, and he understood all too well how the middle-class activists had used the working-class movement to achieve their own ends. None of the reform agitation's long-standing demands – universal suffrage, annual parliaments and secret ballots – had been achieved. Working people living in the insecure and badly constructed houses and tenements of towns such as Manchester and Leeds would never be able to afford to pay £10 in rent; for many people it was a huge sum representing several weeks' wages. Hunt, who by 1832 was himself an MP, knew that the chance to achieve the objectives demanded by the demonstrators on the field of Peterloo a mere thirteen years before had gone by. Political reform was now considered by the governing classes to be off the table for at least a couple of decades, and hopefully longer.

Despite continuously warning about the consequences of the Act, Hunt and his northern supporters were disregarded in the sea of enthusiasm for it that engulfed much of the country. Its passing seemed almost miraculous given the government's crushing of the reform movement after Peterloo and the relative weakness of radical political activity during the 1820s. But in the event the catalyst for change was not the reform movement itself but the old question of the repeal of the Test and Corporation Acts. In 1790, Anna Laetitia Barbauld had been enraged by Parliament's failure to repeal them and grant full civil and political rights to middle-class non-conformists. However, since then there had been a noticeable shift in public opinion, and by the late 1820s the idea of repealing the Acts was much less contentious. In practice, they had more or less fallen by the wayside anyway, as every year Parliament passed an Act of Indemnity that waived the requirement for Anglican conformity so far as Protestant sects were concerned. The new Sacramental Test Bill, which abolished the conformity requirement altogether, successfully passed through both Houses of Parliament and became law in early 1828. Anna Laetitia Barbauld had died in 1825 and so did not live to see the day, but no doubt she would have approved.

However, waiting in the wings was an even more contentious issue than the Test Acts, and one on which radicals were not necessarily so united. The question of Catholic emancipation was seen as tending to the nature, not only of the British state, but of Britishness itself, and the battle over it was fought with unusual ferocity. Behind that again lurked wider parliamentary reform, the cause to which so many radicals had given their entire adult lives, and which had seemed almost to be lost.

Catholic emancipation would require extensive reform in Ireland, since it would change both the size and the nature of the electorate. Once one part of the representational structures had been modernized, might others not inevitably have to follow?

The campaign for Catholic emancipation was led by Daniel O'Connell, an inspired and inspiring Irish nationalist leader who became known as 'the Liberator', and after whom O'Connell Street in Dublin is named. He had fiercely opposed the 1801 Act of Union between Ireland and Great Britain, and throughout the first three decades of the nineteenth century he doggedly pursued an all-or-nothing strategy of refusing concessions designed to minimize Catholic demands. He developed a forthright and brilliant oratorical style that made him at least the equal of Henry Hunt at his best, and he harried the British government at every turn, building widespread support in Ireland and increasing his fame in England. When, in 1825, Sir Francis Burdett's bill for Catholic emancipation failed in the House of Lords, it was evident to many people that the setback was likely to be temporary, and that change was only a matter of time.

In 1828, O'Connell won a sensational by-election victory in County Clare, defeating the incoming Tory government's nominee for President of the Board of Trade. As a Catholic he could not take his seat, but his election added even further to his prestige and increased the pressure on the government. In 1829 it published its own Catholic Emancipation Bill. Henry Hunt knew that what happened in Ireland could easily set a precedent for Britain, and he was therefore appalled to find that it was proposed to raise the Irish property threshold for the vote from forty shillings (£2) to £10. He had assumed that O'Connell, who had always presented himself as a radical reformer, would vigorously oppose this, but despite having previously given assurances that he would, O'Connell actually did no such thing. O'Connell's absolute priority was Catholic emancipation, whilst Hunt's lifelong obsession was parliamentary reform, and neither of them could quite grasp that the other was always bound to put his own mission first. Once the Emancipation Act was passed, however, the old cause came to the surface again, and in the general election caused by the death of George IV in 1830 there was, for the first time, cross-party support for some kind of parliamentary reform.

There was now increased public excitement and expectation, especially in the industrial centres, where what had once been a working-class campaign was now in the hands of middle-class agitators. The Birmingham Political Union (BPU) was established in January 1830 and the London Metropolitan Political Union (MPU), a radical counterpoint to the group in Birmingham, two months later. Soon after that the National Union of the Working Classes (NUWC) was formed in London by an assortment of radicals, including Richard Carlile, to 'obtain for every working man, unrestricted by unjust and partial laws, the full value of his labour, and the free disposal of the produce of his labour', as well as to secure the rights of man, which they set out in a Declaration. Article IX of this document said that: 'Every adult member of society, has an equal right to nominate those who legislate for the community; thereby concurring through his representatives in the enactment of the laws.' This may or may not have been construed as including women; if it did, it meant that the NUWC was one of the very few places where there was any consideration of women's political rights at all throughout the whole reform crisis.

Over the next couple of years the situation became increasingly unstable. In 1830, radical leaders were accused of fomenting the Swing Riots in rural areas of the South and East of England. In the summer of 1832, uprisings in France[1] and Belgium intensified the sense of unease and expectation, and once more raised the spectre of revolution. However, Hunt and his allies were becoming increasingly alarmed at the middle-class takeover of the reform movement, correctly fearing that this would lead to the disappointment of working-class hopes. In December there was a by-election in Preston and, to his astonishment and elation, Hunt was elected. He was at last a Member of Parliament, and since Preston was one of the few constituencies with a large electorate, he had not had to buy a rotten borough to do it. He was now in a position to have his say on reform both inside and outside the House of Commons, and he entered it pledged to work tirelessly 'in behalf of the poor, the honest, and the industrious who live by the sweat of their brow'.[2]

By 1831, the Duke of Wellington's Tory government had fallen and the Whigs were in power under the leadership of Earl Grey, who had a long history of being in favour of reform. The Bill his government published at the beginning of March seemed to promise everything. It abolished the rotten boroughs, thereby also abolishing the detested boroughmongers. It gave representation to the industrial towns and broadened the franchise so as to increase the middle-class vote. To people who had been waiting all their lives for any movement at all from government, this looked like an incredible success. Radicals of all kinds rowed in behind it, including even Richard Carlile, who by this time was back in prison but who hailed it from his cell as 'My Triumph', and predicted that it would go down in history as one of the great turning points like the Reformation and the Glorious Revolution. In fact, he was right about this; the Act that eventually emerged in 1832 is still, despite all its failings, referred to as the Great Reform Act. People who had campaigned for decades for universal suffrage now accepted that achieving it would have to be done gradually, and that the Whig Bill was a good start. Still deeply hostile to Hunt, Carlile was wary of organized political action and collectivism, and had also come to the conclusion that only gradual reform would work. A man of extremes himself, he possibly did not recognize the irony in his referring to Hunt's newly-established Radical Reform Association (RRA) as being driven by 'radical mania'. He attacked Hunt on the grounds that his refusal to compromise actually impeded reform; 'I think it better', he said, 'to reform practically and effectually the smallest twig of the tree, than to talk, and do nothing but talk, about reforming down to the root'.[3] He retained – for the time being – his belief in infidelism and his adherence to the doctrines of Tom Paine, with which he had first fallen in love nearly two decades earlier and for whose sake he and his family had endured so much. 'Thomas Paine has drawn up a political alphabet for them', he said, referring to the reformers, 'but they are either too corrupt to look at it, or too dull to learn it'.[4] The split with Hunt, begun in the aftermath of Peterloo, was irrevocable, and would never be healed.

Carlile's fortunes had not gone well since his release from Dorchester Gaol in 1826. *The Republican* had finally failed at the end of that year, and none of its replacements ever enjoyed the same circulation. New movements were catching radical interest, and there was an increasing tendency for people to set up membership organizations that were becoming more attractive than the loose associations of infidelism and even the old reform movement. For a time he toured the Midlands and the North lecturing, but then when he returned to London, he and his partner, Robert Taylor, a Christian clergyman turned infidel who rejoiced in the nickname of the 'Devil's Chaplain', bought and refurbished the Blackfriars Rotunda to serve as a temple of radical and infidel preaching.

In 1831, however, both he and Taylor found themselves in gaol with convictions for sedition and blasphemy respectively, and the Rotunda began to run into difficulties. It was temporarily rescued by the appearance of Eliza Sharples, a young woman from Bolton who, in the character of Isis, began to lecture there on political and religious subjects and to draw large audiences. Eliza was the daughter of a Lancashire counterpane manufacturer, and had had a relatively orthodox upbringing and education. In her late twenties she had been converted to infidelism and, having met Carlile when he was touring the country, had followed him to London. Their sexual relationship seems to have begun in prison before his separation from Jane, and soon she was using his name and referring to herself as his wife. Together they set up a paper called *The Isis*, which Eliza edited, and she enjoyed a brief period of fame before the arrival of children led inexorably to her withdrawal from public life.

Unlike Carlile, Henry Hunt was able to sit through the debates on the Reform Bill, and he soon realized that there was a significant difference between what the radicals and their supporters were thinking and what the Whigs themselves intended. The Bill was supposed to be a final settlement, at least for a generation. It was designed to remove the possibility of universal suffrage, not make it more accessible. The £10 franchise qualification would, as it had done in Ireland, deprive existing electors in some parts of the country of their votes. Hunt argued unsuccessfully for the threshold to be reduced to £3, which would have enfranchised many working-class men, and proposed that the vote should be the right of everyone who paid taxes. Though he voted for the Bill because it got rid of the rotten boroughs, he did so with a heavy heart. To the end he remained wedded to the same demands that he had always espoused, and both inside and outside Parliament he became increasingly critical. However, only a tiny number of radical papers agreed with him. The vast majority were for 'the bill, the whole bill, and nothing but the bill'. Hunt himself recognized the role that newspapers were having in whipping up support for the Bill in all classes, later noting that:

> 'The lying press had deceived them, or they would know that . . . the ministry, had never pretended that this bill was to give any substantial benefits to the working classes; they had all along declared that they had proposed it as a means of cementing the tottering institutions of

the country, by giving to a large portion of the middle class the right of exercising the elective franchise. It was their agents and the public press out of doors that had said otherwise, and endeavoured to make the nation believe that it would benefit the mass of the people . . .'[5]

Occasionally, a northern paper might express reservations; *The Leeds Patriot* observed that:

'Of course, we do not mean to insinuate that the labouring classes can receive any positive injury from the measure, further than the delay of their just and proper demands. Whether with a Parliament elected under the new bill, without the Ballot, they would have any surer prospect of obtaining their rights, experience alone can determine. . . . with all sincerity we would caution our readers amongst the labouring class against too sanguine expectations of its results.'[6]

Hunt went off on a tour of the North, where he tried to whip up opposition to the Reform Bill on the grounds that, if nothing else, it would hand political power to the employers and mill owners who would use it to oppress the labouring classes. When he returned to Parliament he told MPs that people had told him that 'they would much rather see their Representatives chosen by the gentry and the higher classes of society than by that class which was immediately above themselves'.[7] By this time, however, the Bill was in any case in deep legislative trouble, and when the government started to lose procedural motions in the Commons, Grey opted to go to the country for the second general election in a year. In 1830 the electorate had returned a hung Parliament; they did not make the same mistake again. Grey's Whigs were returned with a landslide victory and a clear mandate for reform.

This did not mean, however, that the next – the Second – Reform Bill would have a clear run. For one thing, the forces of reaction massed in the House of Lords could still at least delay the legislation and quite possibly halt it altogether, whilst, at the other extreme, radical opposition had been growing in the North. In London and the South, however, support for the Whig proposals remained strong, and Hunt was attacked and driven off platforms. From his prison cell, Carlile continued the old feud, and his deputies at the Rotunda criticized Hunt freely. Northern radicals visiting the capital were dismayed by the disunity and in-fighting they found there, and soon realized that they would get no support from the NUWC, which, apart from being focused on London, was all too predictably riven with factionalism. In any case, it had a much less complimentary view of Henry Hunt than the Lancashire weavers did, and, together with Hunt, they now found themselves isolated.

In July, the Second Reform Bill was brought back to the House of Commons where, despite getting stuck in the committee stage for several weeks, it was passed with a healthy majority. However, although many peers absented themselves or abstained, the Bill was defeated in the House of Lords. This was the cue for outbreaks of rioting in pro-Bill parts of the country. In Nottingham the disorder was severe and the castle was burned down. Grey was still determined to get reform of some kind through but was not prepared to risk another election. The House of Commons passed a motion of confidence in the government, but because the Bill could not be re-introduced into the same parliamentary session, Grey persuaded the King, William IV, to prorogue Parliament. As soon as the new session convened in December, he introduced the Third Reform Bill.

He did so in a febrile and uncertain political atmosphere, in which the riots of the summer stood as a stark warning as to what might happen if reform did not get through. Hunt, as always, had been appalled by the violence, particularly since it was abundantly clear that middle-class organizations, such as the BPU, were more or less encouraging the working class to take to the streets for an objective from which they themselves could not possibly benefit, and which might actually be to their detriment. He was particularly critical of radicals who now lined up behind Grey and the Whigs. Of Francis Place and Sir Francis Burdett, for instance, he observed that they should 'look sharp about them, or these working classes will *make use of them*, instead of their *making use* of the working classes'.[8] (*Hunt's italics.*) Carlile, who had always thought Hunt wrong not to allow people to come armed to the field of Peterloo, published Colonel Francis Macerone's *Defensive Instructions for the People*. This was an insurgent's guide to street fighting against both infantry and cavalry. Macerone was in favour of the idea that 'the people should form armed associations for the preservation of the peace, and for resistance to illegal and arbitrary measures' adding 'if, "by arming the people," it is meant, as I hope it is, to include the men who work, as well as those who employ them'.[9]

This kind of talk was anathema to Hunt, but he understood all too well what was happening. Everywhere, radical voices were raised to support a partial measure that they would never have countenanced before, and, as tension mounted, the prospect of real social and economic disaster loomed. The new middle-class reform associations may not overtly have encouraged or endorsed riots themselves, but they certainly did stand by and wring their hands helplessly when only fifteen years previously they would have been sending for troops. As the Bill progressed through Parliament, the crisis became even more intense. In March 1832 it again got through the House of Commons, but as soon as it arrived in the House of Lords it hit resistance. This time, however, instead of rejecting it outright, the Lords tried to amend and delay it. Determined to win, Grey recommended to the King – William IV – that he ennoble a large number of new peers to create a majority who would pass the Bill. Furiously, the King refused, and Grey resigned.

In the riots and demonstrations that now broke out again, the target of popular rage was not the King, but the Queen, Adelaide of Saxe-Meiningen. She was widely believed to have influenced her husband in his refusal, and this brought to the fore all the inconsistencies in accepted views of women's role in politics and society. Women were not supposed to participate directly in politics, but could use their feminine influence to refine their men's coarser instincts. One speaker supporting reform in 1831 had said that he hoped that the wives of newly-enfranchised voters would have over their husbands 'that influence which ladies generally exercised over their lords; and sure he was, that if ladies had been sent to Parliament for the last 40 years, the country would not have been in the state in which it was at present'.[10] Queen Adelaide's influence, however, was a different matter. Properly exercised it might be benign, but she had persuaded her husband to a course of action that was directly contrary to the people's interests, and she had done it in league with reactionary politicians, including the Duke of Wellington. In the demonstrations that followed, hostility to the Queen was manifest, amongst women as well as men.

In the pages of her paper, *The Isis,* Eliza Sharples addressed Queen Adelaide directly in a series of letters, in which she reflected on many subjects, from the Reform Bill itself to religion and the role of women and queens. She was one of the very few commentators to consider that the reform crisis had any specific implications for women, though even then she did not advocate the immediate enfranchisement of women, nor did she spot that women were, in fact, about to be specifically excluded from voting for the first time in history. She did, however, think that the Bill mattered to women at least as much as to men, telling Adelaide that:

'The reform which is so much talked of and so much needed, is of more importance to the women than to the men of the country. The women are subject to more abuses than the men, and have more need of a public reformation of affairs. The men do work out a rough kind of liberty for themselves; but in addition to the public burthens, which are felt as much by women as by men, the cares of a family fall more on the woman; the prospects of her children are more vividly painted on the mind of the mother than on that of the father; the woman is more trammelled by the customs of the country, and tenfold more a slave than the man. Her prospects of better condition under a reformation are many fold more than those of the man: it will be the first step toward her proper equality in society and toward her share in the election of representatives. Therefore, to see a woman opposed to the spirit of reformation is strange and pitiable; it is lamentable, and argues a mistake of the principle, an ignorance of the effect.'[11]

These letters – twelve in all – vary in both tone and content, sometimes expressing sympathy for Adelaide and sometimes roundly castigating her. Throughout, Eliza spoke to the Queen as to an equal, advising, educating and instructing as she thought necessary. In all probability, Adelaide never read them, but they stand as the product of a rare political voice who, at that moment, considered herself at least the equal of any other woman in the kingdom. The last letter, published on 19 May when the fury over the intransigence of the King and the House of Lords was at its height, was merciless in its hostility. 'You have fallen into the pit which you were seeking to dig for the re- formers of this country . . .' said Eliza, 'Your Majesty's name is lisped with execration from one end of this metropolis to the other. You are classed . . . as an intruder and a nuisance in the country, exercising the influence of your station as an enemy to the country's welfare'. The monarchy was being undermined by its own behaviour, and this would continue until there was much more far-reaching change. 'Nothing is yet settled; nothing will be settled, until we come to a republic; for it is not in the nature of things that the royalty of this country can survive its present disgrace and weakness.' In her final sentence, Eliza dismissed the Queen and wished that she and her family might end their days in some peaceful retirement, and 'beware how they commit themselves in opposing the wishes of a nation struggling to be free . . .' Despite everything, she told Adelaide she would still have 'wished you wiser, and . . . would have saved you from that contempt and execration, by which you are now overwhelmed'.[12]

Eliza Sharples wrote to Adelaide with sorrow as well as anger, but the anonymous M.A.B.'s Address to the Women of England in the *Poor Man's Guardian* was more forthright:

'Women, in former times, were celebrated for courage, and the performance of heroic deeds—and shall it be recorded, for future ages to learn, that, in the nineteenth century, when tyranny reared its fiend-like head, . . . English women, belonging to by far the most useful part of the community, stood unmoved, . . . No! let not succeeding generations have to brand our memories with such charge; nor shall the Amazons in high life, those hell-kite politicians of the present day, sneer at our ignorance and want of information; we will convince them, though we form part of the rabble, the mob, and the populace, we have heads as wise as theirs, and hearts infinitely better.'[13]

At meetings and demonstrations up and down the country there were protests against 'petticoat government'. In the early eighteenth century this term had been an ambiguous one, used in different ways in different circumstances. Sometimes, as with regnant queens, or dutiful wives, petticoat government could be a good thing, but at other times it could be pernicious. In the case of the Reform Bill, the foreign wife of an otherwise popular King was believed to be conspiring with the enemies of the people to confound a measure that was in the nation's interests. As *The Morning Chronicle* put it:

'How is it that the King gives his confidence to Earl Grey, who entered office on the understanding that he should propose Reform . . . and yet, after allowing his Lordship to proceed with the measure for a year and a half . . . now determines that all that has been done shall go for nothing? . . . It does not follow that, because in this country women do not appear publicly to meddle with State affairs, that they are without influence. The Queen and the Princesses have, in fact, never ceased tormenting his Majesty with all manner of sinister reports and forebodings as to the evils which will result from Reform. . . . the Queen has done more injury to the cause of Reform than any person living.'[14]

There was much more in this vein, and the Queen, a woman of upright and religious personal rectitude, was subjected to a great deal of abuse, including insinuations about her relationship with her Lord Chamberlain, Lord Howe, who was also known to be highly reactionary. At public meetings she was much reviled and on occasion burned in effigy. Some of the meetings were very large; the one held at the Cloth Hall in Leeds on 14 May, for instance, was estimated to have attracted more than 40,000 people. A mere thirteen years previously, mill owners had been locking their employees in to prevent them going to mass reform meetings, but now they were letting them off work early and paying them to attend. An engraving of the event shows a platform of male speakers addressing a crowd composed mainly of men. Gone are the placards with slogans such as 'Hunt and Liberty', which used to be carried at such events. Now the flags say: 'The Bill, the whole Bill and nothing but the Bill!' and 'Earl Grey and the People'. One proclaims, 'No Petticoat government', whilst above the speakers' heads float signs that proclaim 'We will pay no more taxes' and 'Three groans for the Queen'. One of the few female figures in the picture is in fact a man clad in a black dress and veil who carries an axe, as if to remind Adelaide of what the fate of bad queens might be. At the front of the crowd a man holds up a female effigy on a stick. There are no organized groups of women visible, nor are any mentioned in contemporary reports of the day. Though only a little over a decade separates them, this reform meeting is a far cry from Peterloo, and the Bill for which they were agitating would exclude almost all of the working men who attended the mass gatherings of either time.

Despite the impression given by this particular picture, however, women were both active and visible on both sides of the reform question. The vast majority unsurprisingly took the same side as their husbands, fathers or brothers, although disagreement was by no means unknown, either between women or between women and men. The Reverend Patrick Brontë, for instance, described himself to a female parishioner as 'an advocate of the Bill', but his sixteen-year-old daughter, Charlotte, was of the reverse opinion, writing to her brother Branwell in May 1832 that she felt 'extreme pleasure . . . at the news of the Reform Bill's being thrown out . . . and of the expulsion or resignation of Earl Grey . . .' adding with youthful nonchalance 'I have not yet lost *all* my penchant for politics'.[15] Evidently in the Brontë family, the Bill did not cause serious trouble, but the whole question could be intensely divisive. The actress Fanny Kemble observed that: 'old friendships are broken up and old intimacies cease; . . . houses are divided, and the dearest relations disturbed, if not destroyed, Society is become a sort of battlefield, for every man (and woman too) is nothing if not political.'[16]

During the 'Days of May', as the period immediately after Grey's resignation was called, many people feared that the country was on the brink of revolution, and there was a great deal of anxiety on all sides as to what might happen next. Increasing numbers of radicals were coming to oppose the Bill, influenced either by Hunt's steady criticisms of it or by the constant meetings, speeches and pamphlets with which they were bombarded. In Manchester and the surrounding towns, where radical anti-Bill feelings ran high, workers were imprisoned in the mills so that they could not attend meetings; when, in order to get round this, the meetings were scheduled for Sundays, they were declared illegal. Rumours of arms caches and night drilling were rife. There were savage sentences for rioters, particularly in Nottingham, and the organizers of a Sunday meeting in Manchester were imprisoned for a year for unlawful assembly. Part of the trouble was that there was no coherent radical opposition, and no viable alternative Bill that would stand any chance in Parliament. Rage though they might, neither Hunt nor the radicals could persuade the bulk of the working class that the Whigs' Bill was not in their interest. Middle-class pro-Bill reform leaders went out of their way to court working-class support, and, even in some parts of Lancashire, where Hunt was still revered, they found it easy to whip up enthusiasm. They also realized almost for the first time that, in a country increasingly dependent upon trade and finance, they had new collective powers. The Duke of Wellington, brought back by the King to try to lead what would turn out to be his last government, was faced with a run on the Bank of England, tax strikes – or at least the threat of them – mass demonstrations and sustained and vociferous demands for Grey's return. Some people hoped that the crisis would result in an improved Bill that would extend the franchise, and thousands of people, women as well as men, signed petitions to Parliament to stop payment of the civil list to the King, or to halt payment of funding for the military. There was much feeling against the aristocracy, and even some republicanism. On the same page as one of her letters to Queen Adelaide, Eliza Sharples published the full text of the 1648 Acts abolishing the House of Lords and establishing a republican Commonwealth after the Civil War; the strapline above it said ominously: 'What has been done once may be done again.' Constitutional debate was the order of the day, but so too was an air of deep apprehension and uncertainty.

Despite doing his best to be conciliatory, the Duke of Wellington was unable to form a government, let alone get anything through Parliament. *The Times*, almost sympathizing with Wellington's predicament, did not envy him his task of putting together a Cabinet 'of which the first condition is that every man who enters it must leave his good name behind him'.[17] Britain was effectively without a government for several days, and more than £1.6 million was withdrawn from the Bank of England. There were rumours that the army was to be ordered to attack reformers in Birmingham. Inevitably, Grey and his ministers had to be returned to office. Still faced with resistance from the Lords, he made it clear to the King that, without the agreement to create extra peers if necessary he and his Cabinet would not return. The King had no option but to concede, regardless of Adelaide's view. The Reform Bill passed its third reading on 4 June and received the reluctant royal assent three days later. In the end, the extra peers had not been needed.

At the end of the year there was a general election on the new constituency boundaries and with a new electorate. It very soon became obvious, even to the most casual observer, that not everything had changed. For one thing, the idea that all the rotten boroughs had disappeared turned out to be an illusion. Certainly, the grossest abuses had been done away with, but many others remained, and determined landlords could still find ways round the new rules. In the Yorkshire town of Ripon, for instance, there was much interest in the forthcoming election. For more than a century, a small number of electors had sent two MPs to the House of Commons, but, as *The Times* had observed in 1828:

'. . . the elective franchise in the borough of Ripon is limited to the occupiers of burgage tenures, the whole number of which does not exceed 146, of which Mrs Lawrence of Studley Royal, the patroness and most liberal benefactress of the borough, possesses a decided majority, and of course really returns the members sent from this borough to Parliament.'[18]

Sophia Elizabeth Lawrence (who never married, despite being conventionally referred to as Mrs) controlled the majority of the qualifying properties in Ripon and had effectively owned the constituency since 1808, when she inherited it from her aunt. Her reach in all political matters was extensive. She supported many public and charitable projects in Ripon, and effectively decided who the mayor should be and who should sit on the council. Her political influence also extended far beyond Yorkshire. In 1823, the Tory Prime Minister offered the post of Chancellor of the Exchequer to the Ripon MP Frederick Robinson. Robinson said that he would be happy to accept but that he would be grateful 'if I may communicate with Miss Lawrence, who of course will be interested in what concerns my seat at Ripon, but I have no doubt that she will make no difficulty'.[19]

Sophia Elizabeth and her predecessors had been able to avoid an actual election for decades by the simple mechanism of making sure that there was never any viable challenge to their nominees. This was done by ensuring that only their own candidates got through the hustings stage of the election, which was the most important part of the process and preceded the poll itself. The hustings were also the stage at which non-voters could have a direct and influential effect. Candidates were required to present themselves at a meeting that was open to everyone, regardless of whether or not they could vote. Each candidate would be formally nominated and seconded before making a speech to the assembled townspeople. A show of voters' hands was taken, and if the candidate won at this stage there would not be a ballot. If he lost, or if there was not a clear result, or if one of the other candidates felt he had sufficient support to demand it, then there would be a full election. Hustings were as much entertainment as politics, and were usually attended by large numbers of people. Like football crowds, they could create atmosphere and influence the small number of voters, sometimes by intimidation, but often simply by noise and enthusiasm.

Obviously, it was in the interest of candidates and their backers to ensure that matters were settled at the hustings without the expense and inconvenience of a poll, and in pocket boroughs such as Ripon this had previously been relatively straightforward to achieve. Sophia Elizabeth had been able to impose two Tory candidates at successive elections without too much trouble, but elsewhere, Whig and Tory grandees often split the two-seat constituencies between them so as to avoid a vote and keep everyone happy. The consequence of so much negotiating, manoeuvring and downright bribery was that in any election before 1832, only a minority of seats were ever contested past the hustings stage. In 1812, for instance, only 25 per cent of constituencies actually went to the polls.

In 1832, that level of control would be impossible, but it remained to be seen whether, now that the electorate in Ripon had increased from 146 to 341, Sophia Elizabeth Lawrence would be able to continue to maintain discipline. She was less than pleased to find herself faced with a determined opposition able to force a full election. The campaign was bitterly contested, with the Whig candidates directly attacking Sophia Elizabeth. In a campaign speech one of them announced:

'. . . I now stand before you (ladies, I am sorry to say it) to do away with petticoat influence. Men could no longer bear it, that one immense blue petticoat should cover the whole town of Ripon and exclude from its inhabitants those bright rays of light and liberty which are now shining forth in all their glory from one end of the borough to another.'[20]

Many of the electors turned out to agree with him; 330 of them voted and a narrow majority of them chose the Whig candidates. Sophia Elizabeth Lawrence tried to get the result overturned but failed, so instead she evicted any of her tenants who had voted against her. Since there was little, if any, legal protection for them, they had no means of redress, and the courts were beyond their means. Next, Sophia

Elizabeth set about creating new electors by the simple mechanism of splitting some of her £10 plots of land in two and letting both parts for £10 a year each. Doing this was technically illegal, but neither Miss Lawrence nor any other landowner who did it was prosecuted or deterred. The next general election was in 1835, by which time there were 383 voters who dutifully elected the two Conservative candidates with a resounding majority. The next contested election in Ripon was not until 1852, a few years after Sophia Elizabeth's death. The Reform Act had extended the electorate, and it had provided representation for the new industrial areas, but in some older seats things went on very much as before. Nor was Sophia Elizabeth Lawrence alone in her dubious electoral practices. Up and down the country the old order strove to maintain its grip and was partially successful for decades to come.

In Preston, Henry Hunt lost his seat after an unpleasant election campaign during which the Riot Act had to be read twice, and he himself had to leave town because of fears for his safety. In an emotional farewell address he observed that: 'Money, bribery, treating, intimidation, and hired bludgeon-men have prevailed, and the working-classes of Preston must remain in the power of the Whig and Tory factions, till they have the protection of the ballot.'[21] Examples such as that of Sophia Elizabeth Lawrence in Ripon suggested that this was, indeed, true. The next major extension of the franchise did not come until 1867, and the secret ballot would not be introduced until 1872. Adult male suffrage had to wait until 1918, and universal suffrage until 1928. Within months of the passage of the Reform Act, people began to realize that Hunt had been right about it, and that it was not going to deliver what they had hoped for, but by then it was too late.

Epilogue: An Ignorant Woman

In the last days of the unreformed Parliament, Henry Hunt presented a petition to the House of Commons. It was from a woman called – or calling herself – Mary Smith, who was asking for the vote for women and for the right to sit on juries. The few MPs present were highly amused. The MP for Cambridge, Sir Frederick Trench, remarked that: 'it would be rather awkward if a jury half males and half females were locked up together for a night, as now often happened with juries. This might lead to rather queer predicaments.' Hunt replied that: 'he well knew that the hon. and gallant Member was frequently in the company of ladies for whole nights, but he did not know that any mischief resulted from that circumstance', to which Trench responded that he was not locked up with them.[1] The whole exchange was conducted with much laughter by the MPs present, and no mention of the vote was made by anyone.

There was, for various reasons, much hostile comment in the newspapers, but there was also what may be one of the first pieces in the British press defending women from Parliamentary abuse. The radical *Examiner* printed a long attack on the 'licentiousness of the legislature', in the form of a letter over the signature of 'Junius Redivivus'. This was the pen name for William Bridges Adams, a railway engineer turned radical author whose identity was obscure, though his pseudonym was famous. On this occasion, he was clearly infuriated by the lack of respect shown to women by MPs. He noted:

'how coolly and complacently a deliberative body took it for granted, as a thing beyond dispute that women, in the abstract, were a species of animal, the very mention of whose mental capacities was only fitted to call up a jest – utterly unworthy of serious deliberation. This gear must be much amended, ere any largely beneficial changes can take place.'

Accusing them of using 'language which would have disgraced a brothel', he rounded, not only on the men who had taken part in the exchange, but also on those who had not intervened or objected.

'Base and brutal were the actors in it, but baser were the spectators – the listeners to the oratory of the stews – amongst whom not one was found possessed of courage, or eloquence, or moral feeling, to enable him to wither up the reptiles, whose atrocious baseness makes us doubt whether they be born of women.'

The way the men had spoken and behaved had given 'convincing proof of their utter unfitness for the objects of legislation'. They were 'deficient in the attribute of humanity', because they had: 'stated in their legislative capacity, or they have heard stated, and have not contradicted . . . that women are only fit to be regarded as the objects of sensuality, as the necessary furniture of a harem, beyond whose precincts they should not be permitted to stray . . .'[2] Such men should not be re-elected in the forthcoming general election:

'Then let it not be said that the most degraded men in the British empire shall be again chosen for its legislators! Let the voices of the electors avenge the insult offered to public morality, and show that no station however high, can be beyond the reach of responsibility.'

Junius Redivivus did not suggest that women should be allowed to vote, and – other than to refer to Mary Smith as 'an ignorant woman' – he carefully did not make any comment on the content of the petition, but his letter still stands as an unusually impassioned plea for women to be treated as 'reasoning beings' in the public space. Mary Smith's petition itself disappeared, and the question of women's votes was seldom mentioned again in the House until John Stuart Mill (son of the

James Mill who had so infuriated Anna Doyle Wheeler) presented the first mass suffrage petition in 1866.

However, before Mary Smith's 1832 petition sank into obscurity, it was reported on by the press, mainly because Mary Smith herself sent it to some of the London papers with a request that they print it. This a few, including the *London Evening Standard* did, together with a report on the debate. The next day they apologized for having done so, explaining that they had not read it. *The Times*, in whose offices somebody obviously did read it, was so alarmed by the content that on 8 August they effectively printed a retraction of an item they had not published. This is worth quoting in full.

> 'Some portions of the petition of "Mary Smith, of Stanmore, Yorkshire," to the House of Commons, contain allusions so revolting, that it is impossible even to allude to the nature of them. To accede to her request and publish the petition is of course, out of the question. By the way, if the petition she has sent us be the same that was laid on the table of the House of Commons on Friday, and which it was proposed should be printed by the House, we are quite sure that it could not have been read. We would recommend some hon. member to take the trouble of perusing it *note*, and whoever does so will, we have no doubt, get it burned, and look more sharply after the petitions of this unfortunate person for the future. Had the house been aware of the contents of this petition (supposing it to be the same that "Mary Smith" has sent to us), they certainly would not have received it, nor would the passages of it to which we allude have been listened to without the strongest expressions of disgust and indignation.'

When Henry Hunt was asked why he had presented such a petition, he admitted that he had not read it properly either. He had been very busy, and there had not been time. This raises the question of why he presented it at all, unless he simply glanced at the first few sentences, took them at face value and decided that it would fill a few minutes without too much controversy. In this he was correct; as we have seen, the MPs present enjoyed a ribald couple of jokes at the expense of the petitioner and her sex and then moved on to something else. Clearly they did not read the full text either. After the furore in the press, nobody was particularly keen to discuss Mary Smith, her demand for the vote or the sting in the tail of her request any further. The petition sank into the deep pre-history of the suffrage movement from which it surfaces only to be referred to as the lone cry of a 'lady of rank and fortune' before her time. Now, as then, very few people read the petition, and when they do, they find some parts of it so obscure that it is hard not to conclude that Mary Smith must have been slightly unhinged. Parts of the text exude an indignant fury that tends to suggest some ghastly, unresolved but now unknowable personal experience.

Why, then, was Mary Smith so angry that she took the unusual step of sending a petition to Parliament, and why was it so incendiary that *The Times* felt it necessary to apologize for it when they had not printed it in the first place?

The trigger for Mary Smith's petition seems to have been something she read in William Cobbett's *Weekly Political Register*, a popular and widely read paper that reported political news as well as serving as a vehicle for its editor. Cobbett was one of the best-known men in England, a great speaker, a champion of the poor and oppressed, and a man with a voice that was able to speak directly to millions. In the middle of July, Cobbett had sent Daniel O'Connell, the Irish radical MP, a petition of his own on the subject of the Reform Act and, as was his habit with such things, he published the text of it in his *Weekly Register*. The gist of Cobbett's petition was that since the Reform Act was going to be very complicated to implement, it would be much easier, and more just, simply to extend the franchise to 'every man arrived at the state of manhood, being of sane mind, and untarnished by indelible crime . . .'[3] This wording does not occur in the Act itself, but only in Cobbett's petition; it is repeated, word for word, and italicized, in Mary's. Moreover, as we shall see, there are other indications that Cobbett was the source of her indignation.

The petition opened with the usual form of words, in which the petitioner described herself as 'Mary Smith, Stanmore, in the county of York'. When Hunt introduced it in Parliament he described Mary Smith as a 'lady of rank and fortune', but, in fact, the petition as reproduced by the *London Evening Standard* on 8 August 1832 does not describe her in this way. Despite sporadic efforts over the decades, it has never been possible to identify who Mary Smith might have been, and this is largely because at the time everyone involved, including Mary herself, took care to make sure that the waters of her identity were thoroughly muddied. Researchers have also not been helped by the fact that Mary Smith is such a common name, or that there is no obvious place that can be identified as 'Stanmore, in the county of York'. It is often assumed that she was a single woman, but, in fact, she did not say whether she was married or not. It is entirely possible that Mary Smith was a pseudonym; the author of a document that contained material which was both potentially libellous and unsuitable for discussion by a respectable lady might very reasonably not want her identity to be known. She may have known the Cobbett family, or her claims may have been based purely on what she read in the newspapers. Probably Hunt himself did not know who she was; thousands of people sent him petitions, and he had a habit of just grabbing a handful from the top of the pile of unanswered correspondence. Certainly if he only read the first few paragraphs he would not have seen anything problematic; it seemed if anything rather dull.

Having complied at the beginning with the legal formalities, Mary Smith went on to observe: 'That to raise the female sex from the degradation to which it was depressed by the ancient heathens . . . being one of the manifest purposes for which Divine Providence was pleased to bless the world with the light of revelation, it is the sacred duty of every Christian legislature to direct its proceedings in conformity therewith.'[4] It followed, therefore, that 'the said purpose cannot be *fully* effected otherwise than by admitting both sexes to equal, or very nearly equal, enjoyment of social rights and privileges'. However, 'by laws or usages, originating in times of gross barbarism, one entire half the inhabitants of this realm, that is to say, all the women thereof, are deprived of the elective franchise, one of their clear and most valuable rights'. The petitioner therefore prayed 'that an end may be now put to that monstrous and cruel injustice'.

In the next section, Mary Smith pointed out that there were many women of sense and ability who not only inherited money but also made it by their own efforts, and that however gained it was all taxed by the state. Moreover, women were 'not only liable to every punishment (that of death not excepted) appointed by the law for the transgression thereof, but are tried for the same by judges and jurors, all whom are of the other sex'. The next section dealt with the nub of the problem, as she saw it.

'That not to allow to women any voice in the election of any member of the legislature, that make the laws that dispose of their lives, liberties, and properties, and are administered exclusively by the other sex, is not only a most flagrant tyranny and cruel oppression, but in a country wherein women not only inherit, devise, purchase, and sell estates real and personal, possess extensive manorial rights, and present clergymen to ecclesiastical benefices, but are qualified by law to fill the very highest and most important of all offices, the regal office, and thereby constitute one of the three estates the legislature, is also a monstrous absurdity. That your petitioner is well aware that there are men who maintain that no woman, single or married, be her wealth, station, and character, moral and intellectual, what they may, ought to have any voice in the election of any member of the legislature that makes the laws disposing her liberty, property, and life; and that the elective franchise ought to be kept exclusively *"in the hands of men arrived at the state of manhood, being of sane mind, and untarnished by indelible crime"* but your petitioner submits that, for the following among other sound reasons, your honourable house ought not to be influenced by men who maintain the said opinions.'

Women might be the weaker sex, said Mary, but that was all the more reason why they should be able to claim the franchise. She was particularly exercised by the idea of an 'indelible crime', and it is here that the petition clearly veers into the personal.

'. . . although there are crimes of a nature so horrid as, when committed by married men, to drive their wives to cut their own throats; and although indelible infamy attaches to the man convicted of the said crimes, or tacitly admitting himself to be guilty thereof by not instituting any legal process, criminal or civil, against persons whom he knows publicly charge him therewith, nevertheless the expression *indelible crime* is downright nonsense; and accordingly your petitioner is well advised that although legislators and lawyers have divided crimes into many classes, and distinguished them by names more or less appropriate, no legislator or lawyer has ever attempted to define such thing as an indelible crime.'

But, even if such a crime could be identified and defined, it would mean that, when excluded, women were 'degraded, not only below the condition of all idle, ignorant, and drunken male mendicants, but down to the condition of wretches guilty of indelible crimes'. Opponents of enfranchising women said that they did not need the vote because they were protected by their husbands, but Mary pointed out that many women were spinsters or widows, and that 'of many married women, the husbands, as the courts of law abundantly testify, so far from being protectors, are the only persons against whom their wives have occasion to sue for protection'.

Finally, Mary Smith asserted that:

'the men who maintain opinions of such monstrous absurdity and cruel injustice are the notorious and avowed worshippers of the bones and doctrines of Thomas Paine, of reputation nearly as infamous as their own, and are consequently peculiarly prone to those execrable propensities which are cursed with a malignant hostility to the female, and which are of a nature so horrible that the indulgence of them, when detected, drives their wives to cut their own throats.'

Had Hunt, or the *Evening* Standard, or any of the other newspapers that printed the petition in full actually read the paragraphs relating to 'indelible crimes', they would have quietly put it aside, and it is no wonder that the *Evening Standard*, otherwise inexplicably, apologized for having published it. Its immediate significance is lost to later eyes, but to people in political circles at the time it would have been all too clear. Mary Smith was accusing William Cobbett, one of the most famous men of the age, of homosexuality, and using another famous politician, known to be hostile to him, to do it under the cover of parliamentary privilege. When *The Examiner* referred to her as 'an ignorant woman', it must have known only too well that the problem was not that she was ignorant at all, but that she may have known far too much.

William Cobbett was identifiable as the subject of her incendiary document at least in part because of his fame as the person who had brought Tom Paine's bones back from America. But Mary Smith was also resurrecting a scandal from five years previously, when Cobbett's wife, Nancy, had attempted suicide, allegedly because she had found Cobbett in compromising circumstances with his male secretary. Sodomy was a criminal offence that could attract the death penalty, whilst attempted suicide carried a prison sentence. Any suggestion of either of them, whether true or not, was highly damaging. Henry Hunt would have known at least some of the details of the episode, particularly since in August 1829 Cobbett's three sons had been convicted of assaulting a barrister called Daniel French who had repeated the allegations. The case had had widespread coverage in the press, and the Cobbett brothers had been fined rather than gaoled, on the grounds, according to the reports, that the provocation had been considerable. Exactly what that provocation was, was not spelled out, though some papers included coded references to it. The Cobbett family as a whole had always drawn, and continued to draw, a determined veil over the whole affair, though William Cobbett and his wife had certainly lived apart after 1827.

Viewed in the light of this episode, the angrier parts of the petition become more explicable, though the homophobia they reveal is repugnant. There seems to be no evidence to substantiate the allegations about Cobbett, but of course that does not necessarily prove that they were not true. What really happened will probably never be known, but Mary Smith, whoever she was, evidently thought she knew the whole story. It may be a long and rather curious step from her claims about Cobbett to a demand for votes for women and places on juries, but clearly she thought that political and civil powers of her own might have made a difference to Nancy Cobbett's fate.

Needless to say, her petition was unsuccessful. It was ruthlessly buried by everyone who knew anything about it, and the question of votes for women went with it. In the *Monthly Repository*, the journalist W J Fox, in an article that was cautiously supportive of women's political rights, spoke for most people then and since when he said: 'Who or what Mary Smith is, we neither know nor care', and although he also said of the debate in the House that he 'would not insult the poor by calling [it] pot-house ribaldry',[5] it was clear that he did not consider the issue as a whole as being of more than passing interest.

There is one small addendum to this story that suggests that someone may have known exactly who Mary Smith was. On 11 August, a week after Hunt had presented the petition, the *Westmorland Gazette* published the text in full, and added a note at the end that said: 'Mrs. Smith informs us that the concluding observations have reference exclusively to some arguments adduced by Mr. Cobbett against the rights for which Mrs. Smith contends. We are, however, very sorry to be obliged, for once, to agree with Mr. Cobbett.' This note does not appear in other papers, and it seems odd that the editor of a small regional newspaper should know someone whose identity mystified everyone else. However, he may have had local knowledge they did not; the village of Stainmore, which lies in Westmoreland on its border with Yorkshire and County Durham, had in previous times been known as Stanmore. This little circumstance is in itself proof of nothing, but it does suggest a direction for future research if Mary Smith is finally to be found.

The last sentence of the petition requested that Parliament 'make a law giving the elective franchise to every unmarried woman having that pecuniary qualification whereby the other sex [is] entitled [to] the said franchise'. This was almost precisely the demand that suffrage campaigners would begin to make in the middle of the nineteenth century, and the question of whether or not married women should be allowed to vote would still be a matter for discussion well into the twentieth.[6] Women were going to have to fight very hard indeed to achieve even basic political rights in future.

Other kinds of rights, however, were a slightly different matter, though the first small crack in the overwhelming supremacy of state patriarchal power was not made by organized women, or even radical women, but by a lone Tory woman, Caroline Norton, whose rage and grief at being deprived of her children by her estranged husband drove her to try to change the law in order to get access to them. Her social connections meant that she was eventually, after a long campaign, able to get male legislators to help her, and the result was the 1839 Custody of Infants Act. Her continued campaigning on divorce led to the 1857 Matrimonial Causes Act, but married women had to wait until 1870 to get even limited property rights. The battle for the vote, the start of which is usually dated to the 1860s, arose as part of a wider fight for education, property and legal access to children, many of which continued well into the twentieth century.

Meanwhile, working-class women, who saw very clearly that they had an identity of interest with their men, continued to support male claims for political power. But they also fought for their own interests when they thought they were threatened. The 1834 New Poor Law, for instance, which came as a crushing disappointment to so many people who had thought that the reformed Parliament would act in the better interests of working-class communities, directly penalized women in ways that the old Poor Laws had not. The underlying assumption that there was always work enough for those who wanted it, and that the unemployed were therefore 'indolent' and 'undeserving', was now the main driver of the welfare system. Everyone who needed help was deemed to be at fault in some way, and treated accordingly. The Poor Law was particularly unpopular in Northern England, where women were heavily involved in the struggle against it. By the end of the decade, a combination of renewed attacks on the working classes, the effects of the Poor Law and the failure to enact factory legislation, had given rise to the Chartist movement.

In all this, Mary Smith's petition was easily forgotten and her voice suppressed by a combination of people who did not want to hear it, and those who had never listened in the first place. In her case, she actively colluded in maintaining the mystery around her identity, but this was not so with others. Anna Laetitia Barbauld, for instance, was turned by the Victorians into a rather saintly children's writer who would certainly not have done anything so unladylike as express a political opinion. Mary Wollstonecraft was buried by the scandals of her life, and Helen Maria Williams by her life and her revolutionary opinions. Jane and Mary-Ann Carlile were working-class women without voices, and Jane's reputation was destroyed by her own husband. The women of the Female Reform Societies of 1819 are often mildly patronized because they were the wives of male reformers, and even their writings – some of the first political statements by working-class women – are usually attributed to men. Despite his best efforts, the feminist ally William Thompson is better remembered than the feminist Anna Doyle Wheeler. Susannah Wright, who once told a judge that he was paid to listen to her and that she would not be quiet, simply vanished into silence.

Our understanding of our history is poorer because, with the exception of Mary Wollstonecraft, these women and many others are usually absent from it. Women have always been political in ways that had nothing to do with the vote or, indeed, with women's rights *per se*, and they have always been driven by passions and obsessions other than – or in addition to – feminism. Behind the story of women's fight for the franchise lie many others, all of which are deserving of recognition, and many of which are hidden or have been deliberately concealed. From philosophers and writers to the uncontrollable woman on the night of Peterloo, radical women were contributing to the development of British politics and democracy long before they were agitating for the vote. With Helen Maria Williams they could all say that they had not been indifferent spectators of events, but could proudly 'claim a share of merit from the friends of liberty, for having so long defended its cause'.

Notes

Abbreviations

MO	The Manchester Observer
PMG	Poor Man's Guardian
Rep	The Republican
TNA	The National Archives

Introduction

1 *Wheeler's Manchester Chronicle,* 21 August 1819.

2 *The Times*, 22 November 1822.

3 *Bath Chronicle & Weekly Gazette,* 12 August 1819.

4 *London Evening Standard*, 8 August 1832.

5 James Mill, *The Article, Government*, 1821, p 20–1.

6 *Gentleman's Magazine,* December 1795, in Kenneth R Johnston, *Unusual Suspects*, p 131.

7 Antje Blank & Janet Todd (Eds), Charlotte Smith *Desmond,* (1792) p 45.

8 Condorcet, Nicolas de, *Political Writings*, Steven Lukes & Nadia Urbinati (Eds), 2012, Cambridge University Press p 157.

9 Karl Marx himself was born in Trier in modern-day Germany in 1818 and would not reach British shores until after the revolutionary year of 1848.

10 Iain McCalman, *Radical Underworld: Prophets, Revolutionaries and Pornographers,* p 135.

Part One: Frantic 'Midst the Democratic Storm

1 The Seal of the United States Senate still includes a red Cap of Liberty, as does that of the US Department of the Army, and it appears on the flags of several states, including New York, New Jersey and West Virginia.

2 This law was abolished by Napoleon in 1804.

3 The last vestiges of these Acts were repealed by the 1998 Crime & Disorder Act.

4 Anna Clark, *The Struggle for the Breeches*, pp 146–7.

5 Ibid., p 145.

6 Ibid., p 146.

7 Edmund Burke to Mrs Crewe, 1795, in Deborah Kennedy, *Benevolent Historian* in Adriana Cracium & Kari E Lokke (Eds), *Rebellious Hearts: British Women Writers and the French Revolution*, p 326.

Chapter 1 The Furies of Hell

1 Mary Wollstonecraft, *Thoughts on the Education of Daughters,* p 56.

2 Ibid., p 69.

3 Helen Maria Williams, *Letters From France*, 1.1.66 in Kennedy, *Benevolent Historian* in Cracium & Lokke, p 318.

4 Laetitia-Matilda Hawkins, *Letters on the Female Mind,* Vol 1 p 5–6.

5 William Roberts, *Memoires of the Life & Correspondence of Mrs Hannah More*, 1834, p 431

6 This *Declaration* still forms part of the modern French Constitution. Despite difficulties, Lafayette remained committed to democracy and later refused either office or honours from Napoleon. During the French Revolution of 1830 he declined a request to become Dictator of France. When he died in 1834 there was public mourning for him on both sides of the Atlantic.

7 The women clearly had a dim view of the City Council; some were seen 'forcing the downstairs doors and others snatching papers in the offices, saying that that was all the city council had done since the revolution began and that they would burn them'.

8 Stanislaus Maillard Describes the Women's March, in World History Commons, https://www.worldhistorycommons.org/stanislaus-maillard-describes-women%E2%80%99s-march [accessed 3 May 2020].

9 *The New Annual Register, 1789,* p 56.

10 Edmund Burke, *Letter to a Noble Lord*, in *Writings and Speeches,* 1796, Vol 5 p 187.

11 *The Times*, 15 October 1789.

12 A year later, shortly before his death, Richard Price was speculating about forms of communism, an unusual line of thought even for radicals.

13 Richard Price, *A Discourse on the Love of our Country*, p 38.

14 Ibid., p 45.

15 Ibid., pp 54–5.

16 Ibid., p 56.

17 This address later helped to inspire the creation of Jacobin Clubs in France, which in turn contributed to the establishment of artisan organizations, such as the London Corresponding Society in 1792.

18 Mary Wollstonecraft, *Vindication of the Rights of Man*, pp 22–5.

19 Ibid., pp 63–4.

20 Ibid., pp 105–6.

21 Ibid., pp 140–1.

22 Ibid., p 6.

23 Charles-Maurice de Talleyrand was a French priest and diplomat who managed to survive and serve six different regimes during the Revolutionary, Napoleonic and Bourbon periods.

24 Mary Wollstonecraft, *Vindication of the Rights of Woman*, p 11.

25 *Letters from the Mountains,* p 210, Letter LXXXIX, Anne MacVicar Grant to Miss O., 2 January 1794.

26 Hannah More to Horace Walpole, 18 August 1792, in William Roberts, *Memoires of the Life & Correspondence of Mrs Hannah More*, 1834 Vol. II p 371.

27 Horace Walpole to Hannah More, 26 January 1795, *Letters of Horace Walpole,* (1905) p 337, in Claire Tomalin, *The Life and Death of Mary Wollstonecraft.*

28 Letter to William Roscoe, 12 November 1792 in Tomalin, *Mary Wollstonecraft*, p 156.

Chapter 2 Wicked Little Democrats

1 Helen Maria Williams, Letters Vol I, 1790 p 2.

2 Kenneth R Johnston, *Unusual Suspects*, p 121.

3 Williams, *Letter from France,* Vol 1, 1790, p 14.

4 Williams, *Letters*, Vol. II, p 204.

5 Helen Maria Williams, *Letters Containing a Sketch of the Politics of France*, Vol I p 102.

6 In its internationalist phase, during the Girondin period, the Convention had a number of foreign members. Paine was imprisoned for a year after being ejected from it in late 1793.

7 Williams, *Letters,* Vol I p 86.

8 Mary Wollstonecraft to Everina Wollstonecraft, in *Tomalin*, p 164–5.

9 Mary Wollstonecraft to Roscoe, 12 November 1792, in Barbara Taylor, *Mary Wollstonecraft and the Feminist Imagination* p 205.

10 *Posthumous Works,* pp 94–5, vol. IV, in Tomalin, *Mary Wollstonecraft*, p 160.

11 Williams, *Letters Containing a Sketch*, Vol I, p 5.

12 Ibid., p 10.

13 Ibid., p 12.

14 Ibid., pp 15–16.

15 Olympe de Gouges was a playwright and author who was particularly interested in women's rights and campaigned for the abolition of slavery. In 1791 she published her Declaration of the Rights of Woman and of the Female Citizen, which was modelled on the Declaration of the Rights of Man.

16 Robespierre and Napoleon between them abolished most of the gains women made during the Revolution, and French women did not gain the vote until 1945.

17 Williams, *Letters Containing a Sketch*, Vol I, p 88.

18 William Godwin, *Memoirs of the Author of a Vindication of the Rights of Woman*, Chapter VII.

19 Mary Godwin grew up to become the author of *Frankenstein*, to marry the poet Percy Bysshe Shelley and to live as his widow well into the Victorian era. Her son, Percy, was a Victorian gentleman who, together with his wife Jane, tried to 'sanitize' his grandmother's story and papers. Fanny Wollstonecraft Imlay, child of the Revolution, committed suicide in 1816 at the age of 22.

20 Johnston, *Unusual Suspects,* p 136.

21 Ibid., p 133.

22 Ibid., p 137.

23 Boswell, *Life of Johnson,* ed. R W Chapman, OUP, 2008, p 1,283, n 2. Helen Maria Williams's account of events at the Tuileries in August 1792 occurs in her *Souvenirs de la revolution française,* pp 31–4; this was published in 1827 in French, only in Paris. Boswell also removed the word 'amiable' from the description of Helen Maria in his account of Johnson's meeting with her.

24 *British Critic,* June 1801.

25 Ibid.

26 Helen Maria Williams, *Sketches of the State of Manners and Opinions in the French Republic* (1801), p 6.

27 Johnston, *Unusual Suspects*, p 117.

28 Williams, *Souvenirs de la Revolution Française,* pp 199–201. Translation my own.

Chapter 3 Such Mighty Rage

1 William McCarthy, *Anna Barbauld: Voice of the Enlightenment,* p 280. The Alexander Pope quotation is from Canto I of his *Rape of the Lock.*

2 Warrington became part of Cheshire in the local government boundary review in 1974.

3 McCarthy, *Anna Laetitia Barbauld,* p 110.

4 D O Thomas (Ed), *Richard Price: Political Writings*, (1991), p 161.

5 T C Hansard, *The Parliamentary History of England, Vol. 28, Columns 370–1,* in McCarthy, *Barbauld,* p 274

6 Ibid., Vol. 28, Col 439, 2 March 1790.

7 This and all succeeding quotations are taken from the text of the *Address to the Opponents* reproduced in *The Works of Anna Laetitia Barbauld, with a Memoir by Lucy Aikin*, pp 239–55, published in 1826. Lucy Aikin was Mrs Barbauld' s niece and early biographer.

8 Horace Walpole to Hannah More, 29 September 1791, quoted in Betsy Rodgers, *Mrs Barbauld and her Family*, p 112.

9 Quoted in Betsey Rodgers, *Mrs Barbauld and her Family*, pp 112–13.

10 This and all succeeding quotations are taken from the text of *Sins of the Government, Sins of the Nation, or a Discourse for the Fast, appointed on 19 April 1793* reproduced in *The Works of Anna Laetitia Barbauld, with a Memoir by Lucy Aikin*, pp 256–79, published in 1826.

11 Anna Laetitia Barbauld, *Civic Sermons to the People*, 1792, p 5.

12 McCarthy, *Anna Barbauld,* p 340.

13 Betsy Rodgers, *Georgian Chronicle: Mrs Barbauld and her Family,* p 141.

14 McCarthy, *Anna Barbauld,* p 478.

15 Ibid., p xvii.

Part Two: More Turbulent than the Men

1 PMG, 10 October 1835.
2 The Riot Act remained on the statute books until 1973, by which time it had fallen largely into disuse. It remains in force in a handful of former colonies and dominions, including Canada, where the prescribed form of words for reading it is almost the same as that laid down in 1714.
3 TNA, HO 42/168/176, Elizabeth Mitchell to John Mitchell, July 1817, in Katrina Navickas, *'Reformer's Wife ought to be a Heroine': Gender, Family and English Radicals Imprisoned under the suspension of Habeas Corpus Act of 1817*, in *History*, Vol 101 (345): 246–64, April 2016, p 259.
4 HO 42/172/585, Charlotte Johnston to John Johnston, 30 December 1817, http://protesthistory.org.uk/the-story-1789-1848/primary-sources/state-prisoner-letters#172 accessed May 2020.
5 *Leeds Mercury*, 22 August 1812.
6 *Humble Petition of the Poor Spinners,* in Sheila Lewenhak, *Women and Trade Unions*, pp 16–17.
7 *The Times,* 25 June 1808.
8 *The Times*, 11 February 1828.

Chapter 4 Determined Enemies to Good Order

1 Malcolm I Thomis & Jennifer Grimmett, *Women in Protest* 1800–1850, pp 47–8 and Note.
2 *Annual Register 1812*, p 61.
3 *A Correct Report of the Proceedings on the Trial of Thirty-eight Men . . . on Thursday, 27th August 1812*, p v.
4 If this is indeed the case, Perceval would have appointed the judges only a few days before he was assassinated.
5 Proverbs 24:21.
6 *Lancaster Gazette,* 30 May 1812.
7 The development of online genealogy resources has been invaluable in tracing details about individuals concerning whom next to nothing was known previously. However, this resource is not infallible, and sometimes, as here, guesses or assumptions based on the available documents have to be made.

8   Westhoughton Mill was rebuilt after the fire but not used for the production of cotton again until 1840. It was finally demolished in 1912.

9   Tatton, Pauline, *Local population statistics 1801–1986, Bolton Libraries.*

10 Samuel Bamford, *Passages in the Life of a Radical*, Vol. I, p 302.

11 Ibid., pp 304–5.

12 This was probably William Ewart, the father of the MP of the same name who later conducted a long campaign against capital punishment. He was the godfather of Liberal Prime Minister William Ewart Gladstone and the grandfather of the educationalist Mary Anne Ewart.

13 HO, 42, 124, 2 June in JL Hammond & Barbara Hammond, *The Skilled Labourer,* p 294.

14 Newspaper reports are rather confused, and there may have been two Ann Butterworths of the same age (19) charged with the same offence.

15 Mrs Goodair's letter published in *The Times*, 17 April 1812.

16 This was Charlotte Brontë's second novel and was published in 1849.

17 *Leeds Mercury,* Saturday, 13 June 1812.

18 *Leeds Mercury,* 13 August 1812.

19 *Cobbett's Political Register*, 25 April 1812.

20 *Leeds Intelligencer*, 24 August 1812.

21 Robert Poole, *Peterloo*, p 68.

22 *Lancaster Gazette,* 6 June 1812.

23 Thommis & Grimmett p 34.

24 This picture is reproduced in Robert Poole's *Peterloo*.

25 When, in 1834, six farm labourers from the village of Tolpuddle in Dorset were sentenced to seven years' transportation to Australia, it was for the swearing of oaths rather than, as is generally believed, the forming of a trade union.

26 *A Correct Report of the Proceedings on the Trial of Thirty-eight Men,* p viii.

27 Ibid., p viii.

28 This was a popular venue for radical meetings and stood on the corner of the Strand and Arundel Street, opposite St Clement Danes Church. Its main meeting room could accommodate 2,500 people. It was destroyed by fire in 1854.

29 TNA, HO 42/168/41 Elizabeth Knight to John Knight, 9 July 1817 http://protesthistory.org.uk/the-story-1789-1848/primary-sources/state-prisoner-letters#168 accessed May 2020.

30 Ibid.

31 TNA, HO 42/172/435 Wolstenholme to Wolstenholme, 6 December 1817 http://protesthistory.org.uk/the-story-1789-1848/primary-sources/state-prisoner-letters#172 accessed May 2020.

Chapter 5 The Most Abandoned of their Sex

1 Samuel Bamford, *Passages in the Life of a Radical*, Vol I, p 165.

2 *MO,* 10 July 1819.

3 Hobhouse to Norris, 18 June 1819, HO 79/3, quoted Poole, *Peterloo*, p 247.

4 In 1649, Elizabeth Lilburne was one of the leaders of a group of women in London who organized all-female petitions to the House of Commons to try to secure the release of Leveller leaders and to establish the right of women to petition Parliament.

5 Boroughmongering was the term used to describe the trade in parliamentary seats, which were regarded as a commercial asset and which could have considerable value. Boroughmongers were the owners, buyers and sellers of those seats.

6 This and subsequent quotations from the Address are reproduced from *The Manchester Observer* of 10 July 1819, unless indicated otherwise.

7 The explosion of the volcano at Mount Tambora in the Dutch East Indies in April 1815 had a serious effect on European and American climate conditions and harvests; 1816 was known as the 'year without summer'.

8 *MO,* 31 July 1819.

9 Ibid.

10 HO 43/90 fol.164, Charlotte Johnston to John Johnston, 19 July 1819, quoted in Poole, *Peterloo*, p 240.

11 *The Morning Post*, 19 July 1819.

12 Ibid., 20 July 1819.

13 *MO,* 17 July 1819.

14 Quoted in Poole, *Peterloo,* p 286.

15 Ibid., p 244.

16 Ibid.

17 As late as the 1840s, older working-class women still referred to 'my master' rather than 'my husband'. See, for instance, Elizabeth Gaskell's *Mary Barton*, (1848) for examples of this usage. Mrs. Gaskell's novel was both praised and attacked for its realistic portrayal of working-class life.

18 *The Times,* 13 July 1819.

19 *Bath Chronicle & Weekly Gazette,* 12 August 1819.

20 *Yorkshire Gazette,* 7 August 1819.

21 *The Manchester Chronicle*, 14 August 1819, quoted in Malcolm I Thomis & Jennifer Grimmett, *Women in Protest, 1800–1850*, p 97.

22 *The Morning Post*, 14 August 1819.

23 *Black Dwarf,* 9 September 1818.

24 *MO,* 17 July 1819.

25 Ibid.

Chapter 6 Persistent Amazons

1 HO 79/3, Hobhouse to Byng, 4 August 1819, quoted in Poole, *Peterloo,* p 256.

2 *MO*, 17 July 1819.

3 Samuel Bamford, *Passages in the Life of a Radical*, Vol I pp 191–2.

4 George Swift, MSC 920, Manchester Central Library.

5 Jemima Bamford in Samuel Bamford, *Passages in the Life of a Radical*, Vol. I, p 220.

6 Archibald Prentice, *Historical Sketches and Personal Recollections of Manchester,* 1851, p 159, quoted in Read, p 131.

7 Quoted in Poole, *Peterloo,* p 286.

8 Ibid.

9 *Sherwin's Political Register*, 21 August 1819.

10 *Wheelers' Manchester Chronicle,* 21 August 1819.

11 *The Times*, 19 August 1819.

12 Jemima Bamford in Bamford, *Passages*, Vol. I, p 220.

13 For the size of the crowd see Michael Bush, *The Casualties of Peterloo*, p 13.

14 *Rep*, 1 March 1822.

15 William Joliffe in *Three Accounts of Peterloo by Eyewitnesses* c 1844 quoted in Donald Read, *Peterloo*, p 129 & 131n.

16 *Annual Register* 1819, General History pp 106–17.

17 *Rep*, 1 March 1822.

18 Petition 1821 quoted in Poole, *Peterloo*, p 306.

19 *MO*, 21 August 1819.

20 *Liverpool Mercury*, 20 August 1819.

21 *Leeds Mercury,* 21 August 1819.

22 This and other descriptions of injuries that follow are quoted in Michael Bush, *The Casualties of Peterloo,* unless indicated otherwise.

23 *Rep.*, 21 August 1819.

24 Quoted in Poole, *Peterloo,* p 312.

25 Judith Kilner's baby, a daughter, was born early in 1820 and was named Martha, possibly after Martha Partington, but also after Judith's mother and another daughter who had died in 1818. Judith continued to have several more children, her last being born in 1832, when Judith was forty-six years old. Judith herself died in 1854.

26 Jemima Bamford in Samuel Bamford, *Passages in the Life of a Radical*, Vol. I, p 223.

27 Bamford, *Passages*, Vol. I, p 210.

28 *Wheelers' Manchester Chronicle,* 21 August 1819.

29 *The Times*, 19 August 1819.

30 *Wheelers' Manchester Chronicle,* 21 August 1819.

31 Poole, *Peterloo,* p 354.

32 Quoted in Graham Pythian, *Peterloo: Voices, Sabres and Silence*, pp 215–6.

33 Mary Ward spent some time in a lunatic asylum and may have been the woman of that name who died in May 1843 in the Manchester Workhouse.

34 *The Manchester Gazette,* 21 August 1819.

35 Poole, *Peterloo,* p 352.

36 *The Morning Post*, 19 August 1819.

37 *The Morning Chronicle*, 15 September 1819.

38 Henry Hunt, *Memoirs,* Vol. III, p 611.

Part Three: Monsters in Female Form

1 *Sherwin's Political Register*, 21 August 1819.

2 The term 'infidel' was used, both by Carlile and his opponents, to describe those who, like deists and atheists, put themselves outside the Christian religion in any of its forms or sects.

3 The Act was repealed in Scotland in 2010.

4 In the event, five of the conspirators, including Arthur Thistlewood, were executed on 1 May and five more transported.

5 *Rep*, 20 September 1820.

6 Barbauld, *Sins of the Nation, Sins of the Government, A Discourse for the Fast,* pp 12–13.

7 *An address to the public from the Society for the Suppression of Vice,* (London, 1803), p 4.

8 *Statement of proceedings*, pp 4–9, quoted in MJD Roberts, *The Society for the Suppression of Vice and its Early Critics* in *The Historical Journal*, March 1983, Vol. 26, No. 1 (March 1983) pp 159–76.

9 *Edinburgh Review*, Volume 13, p 342.

10 Ibid., p 338.

11 *New Times*, 16 November 1822.

Chapter 7 Beyond Expression Horrible

1 *The Trials with the Defences at Large of Mrs. Jane Carlile etc.,* 1825, p 31.

2 *A Scourge*, 18 October 1834, quoted in George Holyoake, *The Life and Character of Richard Carlile*, 1849, p 9

3 Ibid.

4 *Rep*, 30 May 1823.

5 Quoted in Iain McCalman, *Popular Radicalism and Freethought in Early Nineteenth Century England: A Study of Richard Carlile and his Followers, 1815–1832,* p iv.

6 *Rep,* 30 May 1823.

7 Four men, including Arthur Thistlewood, were charged with high treason following a riot at a radical meeting at Spa Fields on 2 December 1817. Three years later, Thistlewood was also involved in the Cato Street conspiracy and was convicted and executed.

8 *Rep*, 30 May 1823.

9 House of Commons Debates, 26 March 1823, vol 8 cc709–35.

10 *Rep.* 7 April 1820.

11 William Wilberforce to Thomas Babington, 31 January 1826, in Robert Isaac Wilberforce and Samuel Wilberforce, *The Life of William Wilberforce by His Sons*, (1839), V: pp. 264–5.

12 1 Corinthians 14:34.

13 Mary Wollstonecraft, *Thoughts on the Education of Daughters*, 1787, p 20.

14 *New Times*, 16 November 1822 quoted in McCalman *Females, Feminism and Free Love in an Early Nineteenth Century Radical Movement*, Labour History, May 1980, No. 38 (May, 1980) p 10.

15 Both blasphemy and blasphemous libel were abolished as offences in 2008, although the latter remains an offence in Northern Ireland.

16 *Rep,* 30 May 1823.

17 Ibid.

18 Ibid.

19 Sir John Copley went on to become Lord Chancellor in 1834 and, in the 1850s, a strong supporter of divorce law reform and married women's property rights.

20 Address in *The Trial of Mary Ann Tocker*, c 1818, p 13, quoted in Frow & Frow, *Political Women*, p 2.

21 *Trials with Defences at Large,* p 11.

22 Ibid, p 28.

23 *The Morning Post*, 5 February 1821.

24 *Rep*, 4 January 1822.

25 *The Times*, 24 October 1821.

26 *Trial of Jane Carlile* p 32.

27 *Suppressed Defence of Mary-Ann Carlile*, p 10.

28 *Trials with Defences at Large* p 49.

29 Ibid, p 52.

30 BB Jones in *Reasoner,* 5 June 1859, in Edward Royle, *Infidel Tradition, From Paine to Bradlaugh*, p 25.

31 *The Times*, 16 November 1821.

Chapter 8   This Infatuated Family

1 *Rep*, 4 January 1822.

2 *Rep,* 8 September 1820.

3 Carlile to Henry Hunt, 20 February 1822, in *Rep*, 1 March 1822.

4 *Rep,* 5 December 1823.

5 *Rep*, 8 March 1822.

6 Ibid.

7 *Rep*, 4 May 1822.

8 *Rep*, 22 February 1822.

9   Elizabeth Gaunt to Jane Carlile, 29 April 1822, *Rep*, 10 May 1822.

10 Jane Carlile to Elizabeth Gaunt, 4 May 1822, *Rep,* 10 May 1822.

11 Theophila Carlile Campbell, *The Battle for the Press, As Told in the Story of the Life of Richard Carlile By His Daughter*, 1899.

12 George Holyoake (1817–1906) was a campaigner for secularism, a journalist and co-operator.

13 George Holyoake, *The Life and Character of Richard Carlile*, 1849 p 9–10.

14 Ibid.

15 The Female Republicans of Manchester to Mrs and Mary-Ann Carlile, 30 April 1822, *Rep,* 10 May 1822.

16 *The Times*, 16 November 1821.

17 Jane and Mary-Ann Carlile to the Female Republicans of Manchester, *Rep*, 10 May 1822.

18 Ibid.

19 Carlile to Henry Hunt, 20 February 1822, in *The Republican*, 1 March 1822.

20 *New MO*, 23 March 1822.

21 *Rep*, 20 December 1822.

22 House of Commons Debates, 26 March 1823, vol 8 cc709–35.

23 *New Times*, 27 March 1823, quoted in Parolin p 91.

24 House of Commons Debates, 26 March 1823, vol 8 cc709–35.

25 *Rep,* 4 January 1822, 11 January 1822.

26 House of Commons Debates, 26 March 1823, vol 8 cc709–35.

27 Ibid., p 28.

28 EP Thompson, *The Making of the English Working Class*, p 797.

29 Theophila Carlile Campbell, *The Battle for the Press*, quoting a letter of 7 July 1837: 'My sister's [Mary Ann Carlile] marriage improves on more information. It is a captain in the army, who has served much in India, that has married her, and I am told his income is not less than a thousand pounds a year. It is curious that he is a Methodist or attends the Methodist church.'

30 *PMG*, 9 June 1832.

31 Theophila Carlile Campbell, *Battle for the Press*.

32 Ibid.

33 Jane Carlile is listed in the 1841 Census as living in Water Lane, just off Fleet Street, with her son Alfred, a publisher. She died in March 1843, a month after Richard.

Chapter 9 The She-Champion of Impiety

1 She may actually have been christened Sarah rather than Susannah; it seems likely that she was the Sarah Godber baptized in that year.

2 *Rep.* 18 November 1825.

3 Thompson, *English Working Class,* p 70.

4 Susannah Wright to Alfred Cox, 20 August 1822, *Rep*, 23 August 1822.

5 *Rep.* 25 November 1825.

6 *The Reasoner*, 5 June 1859, in Christina Parolin, *Radical Spaces: Venues of popular politics in London, 1790–c. 1845* p 85.

7 Susannah Wright to Alfred Cox, *Rep*, 23 August 1822.

8 BB Jones, *Reasoner,* 5 June 1859, in Edward Royle, *Infidel Tradition, From Paine to Bradlaugh*, p 25.

9 Theophila Carlile Campbell, *The Battle for the Press*. No date is given for this letter, but it is presumably in the Richard Carlile Papers held by the Huntingdon Library at San Marino, California, to whom Theophila's granddaughter sold them in the 1930s.

10 Parolin, *Radical Spaces*, p 89.

11 *Rep*, 20 September 1822.

12 *New Times*, 16 November 1822.

13 Richard Carlile, *Report of the Trial of Mrs. Susannah Wright*, p 1.

14 Ibid., p 10.

15 Ibid., p 10.

16 Ibid., p 11.

17 Ibid., p 44.

18 Speech of Mrs. Susannah Wright, before the Court of King's Bench, on the 14 November 1822, pp 6–7.

19 *The Times*, 22 November 1822.

20 *Rep,* 4 January 1822.

21 *New Times*, 16 November 1822.

22 This and subsequent quotations about Susannah's first night in Newgate are taken from her letter to Jane Carlile, published in *The Republican*, 13 December 1822.

23 Ibid.

24 *Rep*, 7 February 1823.

25 This prison was closed in 1885 and the Mount Pleasant Sorting Office now stands on the site.

26 Susannah Wright to Thomas Lakins, 20 March 1823, published in *The Republican*, 11 April 1823.

27 Ibid.

28 *Rep*, 16 July 1824.

29 *Rep* 9 April 1824.

30 *Rep,* 24 September 1825.

31 *Rep*, 11 August 1826.

32 *Rep*, 18 August 1826.

33 *Rep,* 1 September 1826.

34 *Rep*, 15 September 1826.

35 *Rep*, 17 February 1826.

36 Allen Davenport, *The Captive,* in *Rep.* 9 April 1824.

37 *Rep* 23 September 1825.

Part Four: Women Without Masters

1 *Rep*, 17 November 1820.

2 *Rep,* 29 November 1820.

3 Robert Owen, *Report to the County of Lanark*, pp 31–2.

4 Ibid.

5 'Papers relating to the National Union of the Working Classes', in *London Radicalism 1830–1843: A Selection of the Papers of Francis Place*, ed. D J Rowe (London, 1970), pp. 134–46. *British History Online* http://www.british-history.ac.uk/london-record-soc/vol5/ pp134–46 [accessed 29 August 2020].

6 Letter to Marc-Antoine Jullien, 15 November 1832, in Dooley, *Equality in Community*, p 356.

Chapter 10 Very Clever, Awfully Revolutionary

1 Louisa Devey, *Life of Rosina, Lady Lytton*, pp 7–8.

2 Ibid., p 10.

3 Mary Waldron, (Ed) *Woman to Woman: Female Negotiations During the Long Eighteenth Century,* p 72.

4 This was a landmark case in which the court removed the children from both parents and sent them to foster parents nominated by Shelley.

5 Edward Robert Bulwer Lytton, *The Life, Letters and Literary Remains of Edward Bulwer, Lord Lytton*, Vol. 2, CUP, 1883, p 34.

6 During the Revolution, Saint-Simon had been involved in various money-making schemes, including one to sell the lead from the roof of Notre-Dame Cathedral; predictably, he was imprisoned during the Reign of Terror.

7 Mary Wollstonecraft, *Vindication of the Rights of Woman*, p 335.

8 James Mill, *The Article, Government*, 1821, pp 20–1.

9 Miriam Williford, *Bentham on the Rights of Women*, *Journal of the History of Ideas,* Vol. 36, No. 1 (Jan–Mar, 1975) p 169.

10 Ibid.

11 Richard Pankhurst's Introduction to William Thompson, *Appeal of One Half of the Human Race*, p iv.

12 Condorcet, Nicolas de, *Political Writings*, Steven Lukes & Nadia Urbinati (Eds), 2012, Cambridge University Press pp 156–7.

13 Ibid., pp 159–60

14 Thompson (& Wheeler), *Appeal,* pp xxi–xxii.

15 Ibid., pp xxii–xxiii.

16 Ibid., p 104.

17 Ibid., p 107.

18 Ibid., p 172.

19 Robert Owen, *Lectures on the Marriages of the Priesthood of the Old Immoral World*, 1835, p 30, in Barbara Taylor, *Eve and the New Jerusalem*, p 40.

20 Anna Doyle Wheeler would have been glad to know that her great-granddaughter, Lady Constance Lytton, became a famous suffragette at the turn of the twentieth century.

21 Thompson (& Wheeler) *Appeal*, p 79.

22 Ibid., p 164.

23 Ibid., pp 173–4.

24 Mrs Wheeler, *Rights of Women*, April 1830, p 13, in Dolores Dooley, *Equality in Community*, p 230.

25 When, in the late 1850s, Charles Dickens was separating from his wife Catherine, he approached Edward Bulwer-Lytton for advice on the possibility of having Catherine, who was not insane, similarly committed to an asylum. However, he did not take it any further.

26 Meg Merrilees was a wild and vocal gypsy queen who appeared as a character in Walter Scott's *Guy Mannering* in 1815 and was the subject of a poem by John Keats in 1816.

27 Disraeli to his sister, 29 January 1833, in *Lord Beaconsfield's Correspondence with His Sister 1832–52,* London: John Murray, 1886, p 15.

Chapter 11 Petticoat Government

1 The Paris Uprising provided much of the setting for Victor Hugo's novel *Les Misérables*.

2 *The Preston Chronicle,* 18 December 1830.

3 *The Lion*, 6 March 1829.

4 Ibid., 23 October 1829.

5 *Poor Man's Guardian*, 3 November 1832.

6 *The Leeds Patriot*, 12 March 1831.

7 John Belchem, *'Orator' Hunt: Henry Hunt and English Working Class Radicalism*, p 175.

8 Ibid., p 187.

9 Francis Macerone, *Defensive Instructions for the People,* p 1.

10 *The Times*, 17 March 1831.

11 *The Isis*, 7 April 1832.

12 *The Isis*, 19 May 1832.

13 *PMG*, 26 May, 1832.

14 *The Morning Chronicle*, 9 May 1832.

15 Kathryn Gleadle, *Borderline Citizens*, pp 178 and 182.

16 Ibid., p 184.

17 *The Times*, 15 May 1832.

18 *The Times*, 11 February 1828.

19 https://www.historyofparliamentonline.org/volume/1820-1832/constituencies/ripon accessed April 2020.

20 Kathryn Gleadle & Sarah Richardson (Eds), *Women in British Politics, 1760–1860,* p 1.

21 *Preston Chronicle*, 22 December 1832.

Epilogue: An Ignorant Woman

1   House of Commons Debates (Hansard) HC Deb 3 August 1832 vol 14 c1086.

2   *The Examiner*, 26 August 1832.

3   *Cobbett's Weekly Political Register*, 21 July 1832.

4   All quotations from the text of the petition are taken from the full version published by the *London Evening Standard* on 8 August 1832.

5   Kathryn Gleadle, *Radical Writing on Women,* p 167.

6   The 1910 Conciliation Bill, for instance, would only have enfranchised unmarried women.

Bibliography

Archival and online sources

British Newspaper Archive
London School of Economics, Digital Library
    Mary Wollstonecraft, *A Vindication of the Rights of Woman*, 1792
    Mary Wollstonecraft, *Thoughts on the Education of Daughters*, 1787
Oxford Dictionary of National Biography
The National Archives
The Times Archive

Newspapers and magazines

Bath Chronicle and Weekly Gazette
Black Dwarf
British Gazette and Manchester Observer
Cobbett's Weekly Political Register
Edinburgh Review
Lancaster Gazette
Leeds Intelligencer
Leeds Mercury
Liverpool Mercury
London Evening Standard
Manchester Comet
Manchester Gazette
New Times
Poor Man's Guardian
Sherwin's Political Register
The Annual Register
The British Critic
The Examiner
The Isis

The Leeds Patriot
The Lion
Wheelers' Manchester Chronicle
The Manchester Observer
The Morning Post
The Preston Chronicle
The Republican
The Times
Westmorland Gazette
Yorkshire Gazette

Printed primary sources

Report of the Trial of Mrs Susannah Wright, 8 July 1822
Speech of Mrs Susannah Wright before the King's Bench, 14 November 1822
Suppressed Defence, The Defence of Mary-Anne Carlile, to the Vice Society's
    Indictment etc., 24 July 1821
Trials with the Defences at Large of Mrs Jane Carlile, 1825
Aikin, Lucy (Ed), The Works of Anna Laetitia Barbauld, with a Memoir, 1826
Bamford, Samuel, Early Days, 1849; Passages in the Life of a Radical, 1844
Burke, Edmund, Reflections on the Revolution in France, 1790
Carlile, Richard, Report of the Trial of Mrs Carlile, 1825
Cobbett, William, Advice to Young Men, 1829
Condorcet, Nicolas de, Political Writings, Steven Lukes & Nadia Urbinati (Eds),
    2012, Cambridge University Press
Godwin, William, Memoirs of the Author of a Vindication of the Rights of
    Woman, 1798
Grant, Anne MacVicar, Letters from the Mountains, 1845, Longman
Holyoake, George, The Life and Character of Richard Carlile (1849)
Macerone, Francis, Defensive Instructions for the People: Containing the New
    and Improved Combination of Arms, Called Foot Lancers, etc., (London,
    1832)
Mill, James, The Article Government, Reprinted from the Supplement to the
    Encyclopædia Britannica, Traveller, (London, 1821)
Owen, Robert, Report to the County of Lanark, 1832
Polwhele, Richard, The Unsex'd Female, 1798
Price, Richard, A Discourse on the Love of Our Country, 1789
Smith, Charlotte, Desmond, 1792
Swift, George, The Swift Narrative, 1820
Thompson, William (& Wheeler, Anna), Appeal of One-Half the Human Race,
    Women, Against the Pretensions of the Other Half, Men, with a New
    Introduction by Richard Pankhurst (London, 1983)

Tocker, Mary Ann, *The Trial of Mary Ann Tocker, for an Alleged Libel, on Mr. R. Gurney*, 1818

Washington, William, *A Correct Report of the Proceedings on the Trial of Thirty-eight Men*, 1812

Williams, Helen Maria, *Letters Written in France*, 1790, 1792

Williams, Helen Maria, *Sketches of the State of Manners and Opinions in the French Republic*, 1801

Williams, Helen Maria, *Souvenirs de la Révolution Française*, 1827

Wollstonecraft, Mary, *Thoughts on the Education of Daughters*, 1787

Wollstonecraft, Mary, *A Vindication of the Rights of Men*, 1790

Wollstonecraft, Mary, *A Vindication of the Rights of Woman*, 1792

Secondary sources

Archer, John E, *Social Unrest and Popular Protest in England, 1780–1840* (Cambridge, 2000)

Barker, Hannah & Chalus, Elaine (Eds), *Women's History: Britain, 1700–1850, An Introduction*, (Abingdon, 2005)

Belchem, John, *'Orator' Hunt: Henry Hunt and English Working Class Radicalism*, (London, 2012)

Belchem, John, *Popular Radicalism in Nineteenth-Century Britain*, (London, 1996)

Bromwich, David, *Wollstonecraft as a Critic of Burke*, in *Political Theory*, Vol 23, No. 4, (Nov 1995), pp 617–34

Bush, Michael, *Richard Carlile and the Female Reformers of Manchester: A Study of Gender in the 1820s viewed through the Radical Filter of Republicanism, Freethought, Feminism and a Philosophy of Sexual Satisfaction, Manchester Region History Review* 16 (2002–3), 2–12

Bush, Michael, *The Casualties of Peterloo*, (Lancaster, 2005)

Bush, Michael Laccohee, *The Friends and Following of Richard Carlile: A Study of Infidel Republicanism in Early Nineteenth-Century Britain*, (London, 2016)

Bush, Michael, *The Women at Peterloo: The Impact of Female Reform on the Manchester Meeting of 16 August 1819*, Historical Association, 2004

Campbell, Theophila Carlile, *The Battle of the Press*, (1899)

Chase, Malcolm, *1820: Disorder and stability in the United Kingdom* (Manchester, 2013)

Clark, Anna, *The Struggle for the Breeches: Gender and the Making of the British Working Class*, (London, 1997)

Colley, Linda, *Britons: Forging the Nation 1707–1837*, (Yale 1992)

Cracium, Adriana & Lokke, Kari E, (Eds), *Rebellious Hearts: British Women Writers and the French Revolution*, (New York, 2001)

Dooley, Dolores, *Equality in Community: Sexual Equality in the Writings of William Thompson and Anna Doyle Wheeler*, (Cork, 1996)

Favret, Mary A, *Spectatrice as Spectacle: Helen Maria Williams At Home in the Revolution*, *Studies in Romanticism*, Vol. 32, No. 2, Romanticism and the Feminine (Summer, 1993), pp. 273–95

Frow, Ruth & Frow, Edmund (Eds), *Political Women 1800–1850*, (London, 1989)

Gleadle, Kathryn, *Borderline Citizens: Women, Gender and Political Culture in Britain, 1815–1867*, (Oxford, 2009)

Gleadle, Kathryn, *British Women in the Nineteenth Century*, (Basingstoke, 2001)

Gleadle, Kathryn (Ed), *Radical Writing on Women, 1800–1850: An Anthology*, (Basingstoke, 2002)

Gleadle, Kathryn & Richardson, Sarah (Eds), *Women in British Politics, 1760–1860: The Power of the Petticoat*, (Basingstoke, 2000)

Hague, William, *William Wilberforce: The Life of the Great Anti-Slave Trade Campaigner* (London, 2008)

Hammond, JL & B, *The Town Labourer*, (London, 1917, 1985)

Hammond, JL & B, *The Skilled Labourer*, (London, 1919, 1995)

James, Felicity & Shuttleworth, Rebecca, *Susanna Watts and Elizabeth Heyrick,: Collaborative Campaigning in the Midlands, 1820–34*, in *Women's Literary Networks and Romanticism: A Tribe of Authoresses*, (Eds) Andrew O Winkles and Angela Rehbin, Liverpool University Press, 2017

Johnson, Claudia L (Ed), *The Cambridge Companion to Mary Wollstonecraft* (Cambridge, 2001)

Johnston, Kenneth R, *Unusual Suspects: Pitt's Reign of Alarm and the Lost Generation of the 1790s*, (Oxford, 2013)

Landes, Joan B, *Women and the Public Sphere in the Age of the French Revolution*, (New York, 1988)

Lewis, Judith S, *Sacred to Female Patriotism: Gender, Class and Politics in Late Georgian Britain*, (New York, 2003)

McCalman, Iain, *Females, Feminism and Free Love in an Early Nineteenth Century Radical Movement*, Labour History, May 1980, No. 38 (May 980) pp 1–25

McCalman, Iain, *Radical Underworld: Prophets, Revolutionaries and Pornographers in London, 1795–1840*, (Oxford, 1993)

McCarthy, William, *Anna Letitia Barbauld: Voice of the Enlightenment*, (Baltimore, 2008)

McFadden, Margaret, *Anna Doyle Wheeler (1785–1848): Philosopher, Socialist, Feminist* in *Hypatia*, Vol 4, No 1, The History of Women in Philosophy (Spring 1989) pp 91–101

Mellor, Anne K, *Mothers of the Nation: Women's Political Writing in England, 1780–1830*, (Indiana, 2002)

Navickas, Katrina, *Protest and the Politics of Space and Place 1789–1848*, (Manchester, 2016)

Navickas, Katrina, *"A Reformer's Wife ought to be a Heroine": Gender, Family and English Radicals Imprisoned under the Suspension of Habeas Corpus Act, 1817*, in *History*, Vol. 101 (345): 246–64, April 2016

Pankhurst, Richard K P, *William Thompson*, (London, 1954)

Parolin, Christina, *Radical Spaces: Venues of popular politics in London, 1790-c. 1845*, (Canberra, 2010)

Pearce, Edward, *Reform!: The Fight for the 1832 Reform Act*, (London, 2003)

Poole, Robert, *Peterloo: The English Uprising*, (Oxford, 2019)

Pythian, Graham, *Peterloo: Voices, Sabres and Silence*, (Stroud, 2018)

Read, Donald, *Peterloo: The 'Massacre' and its Background*, (Manchester, 1958)

Reid, Robert, *Land of Lost Content: The Luddite Revolt 1812* (London, 1986)

Reid, Robert, *The Peterloo Massacre*, (London, 2017)

Rendall, Jane, *Women in an Industrialising Society: England 1750–1880*, (Oxford, 1990)

Richardson, Christopher, *A City of Light: Socialism, Chartism and Co-operation – Nottingham 1844*, (Nottingham, 2013)

Richardson, Sarah, *The Role of Women in Electoral Politics in Yorkshire during the Eighteen-Thirties*, in *Northern History: A Review of the History of the North of England*, Volume 31, 1996.

Riding, Jacqueline, *Peterloo: The Story of the Manchester Massacre*, (London, 2018)

Roberts, MJD, *The Society for the Suppression of Vice and its Early Critics*, in *The Historical Journal*, (March 1983), Vol 26, No 1, pp 159–76

Roberts, William, *Memoires of the Life and Correspondence of Mrs Hannah More*, (London, 1834)

Rodgers, Betsy, *Mrs Barbauld and her Family*, (London, 1958)

Rogers, Helen, *Women and the People: Authority, Authorship and the Radical Tradition in Nineteenth-Century England* (Aldershot, 2000)

Rowbotham, Sheila, *Hidden from History*, (London, 1977)

Royle, Edward, (Ed), *The Infidel Tradition, from Paine to Bradlaugh*, (London, 1976)

Schama, Simon, *Citizens: A Chronicle of the French Revolution*, (London, 1989)

Stafford, William, *English Feminists and Their Opponents in the 1790s: Unsex'd and Proper Females*, (Oxford, 2002)

Stevenson, John, *Popular Disturbances in England, 1700–1832*, (Harlow, 1979, 1992)

Taylor, Barbara, *Eve and the New Jerusalem: Socialism and Feminism in the Nineteenth Century*, (London, 1983, 2012)

Taylor, Barbara, *Mary Wollstonecraft and the Feminist Imagination*, (Cambridge, 2003)

Thomis, Malcolm I & Grimmett, Jennifer, *Women in Protest 1800–1850*, (London, 1982)

Thompson, EP, *The Making of the English Working Class*, (London, 1963, 2013)

Todd, Janet, *Mary Wollstonecraft: A Revolutionary Life*, (London, 2000)

Tomalin, Claire, *The Life and Death of Mary Wollstonecraft*, (London, 2012)

Vickery, Amanda (Ed), *Women, Privilege and Power: British Politics 1750 to The Present*, (Stanford, 2001)

Williams, Carolyn & Escott, Angela & Duckling L (Eds) *Woman to Woman: Female Negotiations During the Long Eighteenth Century*, (Delaware, 2010)

Williford, Miriam, *Bentham on the Rights of Women* in *Journal of the History of Ideas*, Vol. 36, No. 1 (Jan–Mar, 1975), University of Pennsylvania Press

Unpublished theses

McCalman, Iain, *Popular Radicalism and Freethought in Early Nineteenth Century England: A Study of Richard Carlile and his followers 1815–32*, 1970, ANU

Index